Our Country's Story; an Elementary History of the United States

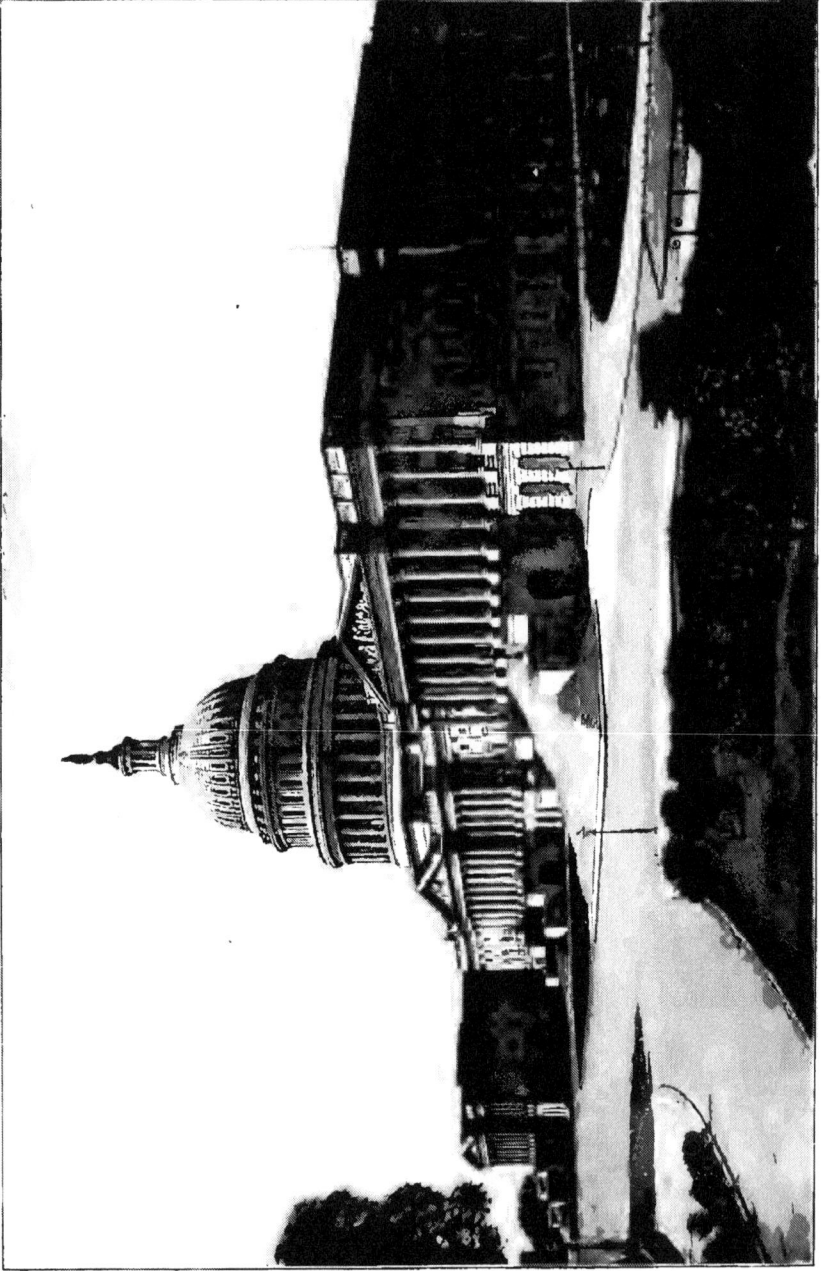

THE CAPITOL, WASHINGTON

OUR COUNTRY'S STORY

AN ELEMENTARY HISTORY OF
THE UNITED STATES

BY

EVA MARCH TAPPAN, Ph. D.

Author of " England's Story," " Old Ballads in Prose,"
" In the Days of Alfred the Great," etc.
Editor of "The Children's Hour."

BOSTON, NEW YORK, AND CHICAGO
HOUGHTON, MIFFLIN AND COMPANY
The Riverside Press, Cambridge

CONTENTS

Acknowledgment is due to General James Grant Wilson, the Lenox Library, Messrs. S. P. Avery, Jr., Walter Bailey Ellis, George A. Clough, Grover Flint, Charles Scribner's Sons, and The Century Co. for permission to reproduce illustrations.

IMPORTANT DATES IN AMERICAN HISTORY

1492 Columbus discovers America.
1497 First voyage of Cabot to America.
1497 Vespucius sails to America.
1513 Ponce de Leon visits Florida.
1522 Magellan's ships sail around the world.
1534 Cartier explores the St. Lawrence.
1542 De Soto discovers the Mississippi.
1565 First town in the United States founded at St. Augustine.
1607 Virginia, the first English colony in America, settled at James-
        town.
1608 Champlain founds Quebec.
1609 Hudson explores the Hudson River.
1614 New York first settled on Manhattan Island.
1617 New Jersey first settled at Bergen.
1619 First legislative assembly in America.
1619 Negro slavery introduced into America.
1620 Massachusetts first settled at Plymouth.
1623 New Hampshire first settled at Dover.
1625 Maine first settled at Pemaquid Point.
1630 Boston founded.
1634 Maryland first settled at St. Mary's.
1636 Rhode Island first settled at Providence.
1636 Connecticut first settled at Hartford.
1638 Pequot War.
1638 Delaware first settled at Wilmington.
1663 North Carolina first settled near Albemarle Sound.
1670 South Carolina first settled near Charleston.
1673 Marquette and Joliet explore the Mississippi.

1675 King Philip's War.

1682 La Salle explores the Mississippi.

1682 Pennsylvania first settled at Philadelphia.

1690 Witchcraft excitement in Massachusetts.

1733 Georgia first settled at Savannah.

1745 Capture of Louisburg.

1759 Capture of Quebec and end of French power in America.

1765 The Stamp Act.

1773 The Boston Tea-party.

1774 First Continental Congress.

1775 April 19. Battle of Lexington and beginning of the Revolution.

1775 June 17. Battle of Bunker Hill.

1776 July 4. Declaration of Independence.

1778 Clark saves the Northwest.

1781 Surrender of Cornwallis and close of the Revolution

1787 Framing of the Constitution.

1789 Washington becomes first president.

1793 Invention of the cotton-gin.

1803 The Louisiana Purchase.

1804 Suppression of the Barbary pirates.

1812–1815 War with England.

1820 Missouri Compromise.

1825 Opening,of the Erie Canal.

1844 Invention of the telegraph.

1846 War with Mexico.

1846 Settlement of the Oregon boundary.

1848 Mexican cession.

1848 Discovery of gold in California.

1850 Compromise of 1850.

1861 Capture of Fort Sumter and beginning of Civil War.

1862 Battle between Monitor and Merrimac.

1863 Emancipation Proclamation.

1863 Battle of Gettysburg.

1865 Surrender of Lee and close of Civil War.

1866 The Atlantic cable laid.

1867 Purchase of Alaska.
1869 Completion of the Union Pacific Railroad
1876 Centennial Exposition.
1893 Columbian Exposition.
1898 War with Spain.
1898 Annexation of the Hawaiian Islands.
1899 Annexation of Porto Rico, Guam, and the Philippines.

PRESIDENTS OF THE UNITED STATES

eorge Washington . .	1789–1797	Franklin Pierce . . .	1853–1857
ohn Adams	1797–1801	James Buchanan . . .	1857–1861
homas Jefferson . .	1801–1809	Abraham Lincoln . . .	1861–1865
ames Madison . . .	1809–1817	Andrew Johnson . . .	1865–1869
ames Monroe . . .	1817–1825	Ulysses S. Grant . . .	1869–1877
ohn Quincy Adams .	1825–1829	Rutherford B. Hayes .	1877–1881
ndrew Jackson . . .	1829–1837	James A. Garfield . .	1881
[artin Van Buren . .	1837–1841	Chester A. Arthur . .	1881–1885
/illiam Henry Harrison	1841	Grover Cleveland . . .	1885–1889
ohn Tyler	1841–1845	Benjamin Harrison . .	1889–1893
ames K. Polk	1845–1849	Grover Cleveland . . .	1893–1897
achary Taylor . . .	1849–1850	William McKinley . .	1897–1901
[illard Fillmore . . .	1850–1853	Theodore Roosevelt . .	1901–

OUR COUNTRY'S STORY

I

COLUMBUS SHOWS THE WAY TO AMERICA

IF a group of schoolboys had been talking about their geo-
raphy lessons four hundred years ago, one would perhaps have
said : —

"Our teacher tells us that the world is flat.   The land is in the Early ideas
ntre, the ocean flows all around, and if any one should sail to of the world
ie edge of the world, he would fall off."

Then another boy would have said : —

"Our teacher told us that many learned men believe the earth
round ; and he says a few of them think that if a ship should

through the Straits
Gibraltar and sail
est across the Atlan-
c Ocean far enough, it
ould come to India."

"But no ship could
ver do that," another
oy would have ob-
cted. "The Atlantic
cean is the Sea of
arkness, and every-

DANGERS OF THE SEA OF DARKNESS
(From a sixteenth century illustration)

ody knows that the farther you go from the land, the darker it The Sea of
comes. There are thick, black fogs. In one place the sun is Darkness
hot that the water boils, and it might be hot enough to burn

A NORWEGIAN SHIP

the ship. The waves are as high as mountains, and there are mermaids and horrible demons. A monstrous bird flies over the water, strong enough to carry off a great ship and all the sailors; and worse than that, Satan sometimes stretches up a great black hand as big as a cliff and draws a ship down under the sea."

These stories of the dangers of the ocean were not fairy-tales told to amuse children; they were what most men really believed. It is no wonder, then, that when the people of Genoa in Italy were asked to furnish funds for sending a ship across the Atlantic to India, they looked upon the plan as a wild and hopeless scheme. It is probable that five hundred years before this time some hardy mariners of Norway and Sweden sailed south from the settlement that they had made in Greenland, and even tried to found a colony in Massachusetts; but there is little reason to think that any one in Italy knew of their voyages.

It was one of the citizens of Genoa who had asked for this money, a man named Christopher Columbus. He was born in Genoa, and all through his boyhood he had seen ships coming into the harbor and unloading rich cargoes of spices, pearls, per-

Trade with Asia

fumes, silks, ivory, and fine Cashmere shawls. These luxuries were brought from eastern Asia, or the Indies, as people then called that country. The journey was long and hard, for the goods had to be taken on the backs of camels across great tracts of land to the eastern shore of the Black Sea. Then they were put on board ships and carried past Constantinople and over the Mediterranean to Genoa

Columbus went to sea when he was fourteen, and three or four ars later there were few rich cargoes from the Indies unloaded the wharves of Genoa. The reason was that the Greeks had t Constantinople to the Turks, and the Turks would not allow

Why this trade failed

Genoese vessels to ss through the Bosorus.

Columbus did not lieve half the ries that were d about the ngers of the a of Darkness, d he reasoned: f the earth is

CARAVAN TRAVEL IN ASIA

und, we can sail across the Atlantic to the very coast of Asia, d that would be a much easier journey than to go by the Black a." He thought that it would be an exceedingly short way,

Columbus's reasoning

for even the learned men who believed that the world was round thought it only half as large as it really is. He had studied and read and thought, and he felt sure that he was right.

Only a rich city or a king could provide money for such an expedition. Genoa had refused, but Portugal had long been interested in finding an easier way to India, and therefore Columbus went to see the king of Portugal. The royal advisers called the plan a foolish notion, but the king was

COLUMBUS'S ARMOR
(Now in Madrid)

half convinced that Columbus was in the right, and he said: "My advisers do not believe that ur plan is possible, but I should like to borrow your maps and ok into the matter for myself."

The maps were lent most willingly, for Columbus thought that

at last he had found a friend. After a while a ship sailed in from the west, and it became known that to make sure of the glory and gain for himself the king had sent out a vessel secretly. It went

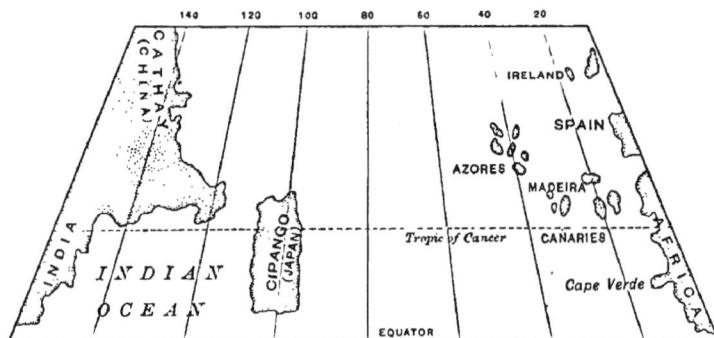

THE MAP COLUMBUS USED

but a little way, however, because the captain was afraid of the high waves of the Atlantic.

Columbus was so angry at this trickery that he took his little

son Diego and went to Spain. King Ferdinand and Queen Isabella were on the Spanish throne, and to them Columbus appealed. Ferdinand called a council of wise men and asked them to decide whether these new ideas were reasonable or not. Now that so much more is known about the earth, some of the arguments brought forward by these learned councilors seem so foolish that it is hard to believe they were really in earnest. One asked: "How can there be people on the other side of the earth? Do they hang on by their feet? Do the trees grow down and does the rain fall up?" Another was willing to admit that the world was round. "But if you should go to the other side," said he, "how could you ever sail up hill and return?"

For several years Columbus waited. Spain was at war, and all the king would say was that he would consider the matter later.

ple laughed at the wild dream of this persistent stranger. Delay and discourage-ment
children in the streets pointed their fingers at him and whis-
ed, "Look! there's the crazy man who thinks he can cross the
of Darkness!" Columbus had some reason to hope for aid
a France, and he had sent his brother to England to ask for
. He determined to leave Spain.

ne morning a man with gray hair and keen blue eyes stood
re the convent of La Rabida near Palos and asked for food Columbus at La Rapida
is little son. The prior of this convent was a learned man who
especially interested in geography. He noticed the stranger
he gate and began to talk with him. When he found what a
derful plan he had in mind — for the stranger was Columbus
self — the prior wrote to Queen Isabella and pleaded for her

He told her what glory such a discovery would bring to
in and how much wealth would pour in from the trade with
Indies. She became greatly interested, but a difficulty arose.

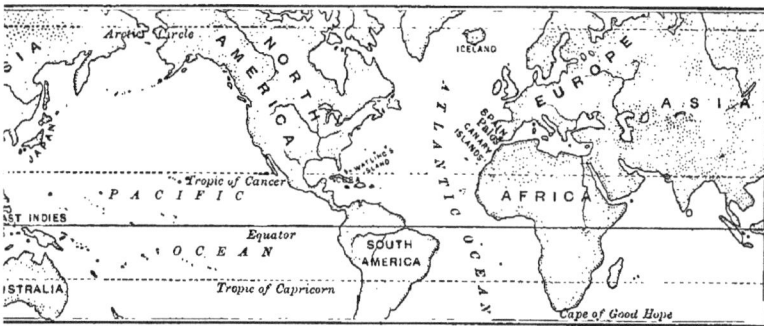

-THE REAL POSITION OF THE CONTINENTS

mbus demanded the title of admiral, the right to rule over
lands that he should discover, and one tenth of all gains that
ht be made.

he Spanish courtiers were jealous that an unknown man, a
igner, should dream of having so much power, and although Jealousy of the courtiers
vas ready to risk his life, one of them said to him sneeringly:

"You have nothing to lose if you fail, and you make sure of yo
title, whether you accomplish anything or not. You're a shrew
man."

Columbus was not selfish, but he felt that he had a right
Isabella aids share in whatever gain might come from his years of study a
Columbus thought. Moreover, he needed a large sum of money to carry o

CONVENT OF LA RABIDA
(The part Columbus knew is to the right)

a plan of his for rescuing from the Turks, who ruled in the Ho
Land, the tomb in which Christ was said to have been buried, a
he declared that he would rather seek for the aid of France th:
yield a single point. The enthusiasm of Queen Isabella w
aroused. "I will undertake the enterprise for my own crown
Castile," she declared, "and I will pledge my jewels to raise t
necessary funds."

Then there was a bustle of preparation. For some misdemean
Preparations the town of Palos had been required to provide two ships, w
for the manned and armed, to serve the king for one year. The ord
voyage was given that these two ships should be at Columbus's dispos
The sailors of the town were terrified at the thought of such

arney. Some hid themselves, and others ran away. At last
o brothers, wealthy shipowners, offered to go on the fearful
yage, and also to furnish one vessel.

After this some sailors volunteered, others were forced to go, **Columbus**
d one morning in August the three small vessels, the Pinta, **sails**
e Niña, and the Santa Maria, set out from Palos to cross the
known ocean. The rudder of the Pinta broke, and a visit had
be made to the Canary Islands to repair it. Then word came

at three Portuguese vessels
d been seen off the coast
aiting to capture Columbus.
hat matter was easily ar-
nged, for he slipped past them
rectly out into the open ocean,
nowing well that no Portu-
ese ships would dare to fol-
w into the Sea of Darkness.
The farther they went, the
ore frightened became the **The fears of**
panish sailors. They wept **the sailors**
d lamented, saying that never
gain should they see their
mes and their friends. Every-
ing alarmed them. The mast
: a vessel floated by, and this
ey took as a sure sign that
ey would be wrecked. They
w a meteor, and they were

QUEEN ISABELLA
(After a picture in Madrid)

ertain that it was a bad omen. The wind blew steadily from the
st, and the discouraged mariners wondered how they could ever
ake their way home. They found themselves in the midst of
e great masses of seaweed that we call the Sargasso Sea, and

then the sailors talked about quicksands and the dangers of running aground. The needle of the compass no longer pointed directly to the north star. That was worst of all, for they thought they had lost their way. They were so angry with the admiral that they even planned to throw him overboard.

Columbus was very patient with them. He sounded many times to convince them that there was plenty of water below the weeds of the Sargasso Sea. He made up the best explanation that he could of the needle's failure to point to the north star, and he told them of the wonderful countries that they would soon see, the home of spices and perfumes, of gold and jewels. He told them how much land they would own and what great lords they would become, and so day after day he led them on.

THE SANTA MARIA
(Columbus's own ship)

Flocks of birds began to fly past, nearly all going to the southwest, and the course of the ships was changed to follow their flight, in the hope that they were going to **Signs of land** the land. Fresh-water weeds were seen and a branch of thorn with berries on it. At last a piece of wood was picked up that some one had carved. Then the sailors were almost as eager as their leader to find the unknown country, and one after another began to declare that he could see land, and to claim the reward promised by Ferdinand and Isabella

AN EARLY COMPASS

to him who should first discover the farther shore. Columbus increased the reward by the offer of a velvet doublet, but there were so many of these false alarms that he declared no man

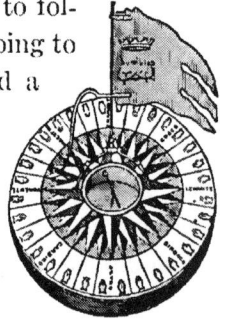

ıo shouted "Land!" should receive the reward unless land was
scovered within three days after the time when it had been
nounced.

It seems only right that the great discovery should have been
ıde by the admiral himself, and so it was, for one evening as he **Land at last**
ıod gazing into the west, he was sure that he saw a light that

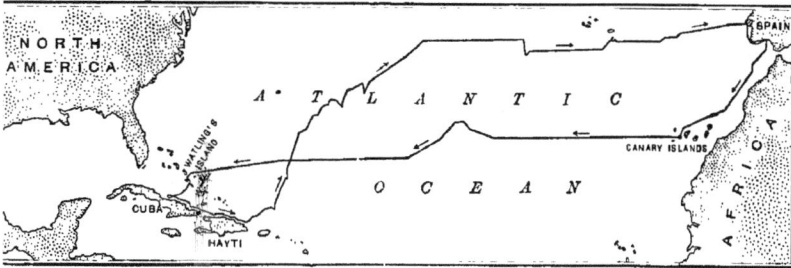

COLUMBUS'S ROUTE
(From Winsor's Columbus)

ıved up and down as if some one was carrying a torch in his
nd. Early the next morning, October 12, 1492, the land was
 full view. Columbus put on his rich scarlet robes, took the
yal banner in his hand, and was rowed to the shore. What a
ore it was! The water was clear as crystal, the sand was
zzlingly white, there were strange trees and fruits, unknown
wers, birds of most brilliant plumage, and, strangest of all,
ıat numbers of copper-colored natives, who at first hid behind
ıes, but soon gathered around the Spaniards, gazing with rev-
ınt curiosity upon their white skins, their steel armor, their
ttering weapons, and especially upon the admiral in his scarlet
ess.

The Spaniards knelt down and kissed the ground. They rose
d chanted the Te Deum. Then Columbus unfurled his banner **Landing of**
d formally claimed the land for Spain. He named the island **Columbus**
n Salvador, or Holy Saviour. It was one of the Bahamas, no
e knows which one, but many think that it was the one now

THE LANDING OF COLUMBUS
(From Vanderlyn's painting in the Capitol at Washington)

known as Watling's Island. The natives he called Indians, because he supposed that he was on the coast of India. He asked the Indians where Cipango, or Japan, was, and they pointed to the south, for they thought that he meant some mountains with nearly the same name. They told him of "great water" to the westward, and he supposed they meant the Indian Ocean.

The Indians had a tradition that some day white men would come down from the skies to visit them. They were overjoyed that the heavenly visitors, whom they thought the Spaniards to be, had come in their time, and when Columbus asked some of **The return to Spain** them to go to Spain with him, they were delighted. Such a reception as the successful voyager had when he returned to Spain! There was a triumphal procession with soldiers and music and banners and gorgeous robes to escort Columbus to the king and

.een. He knelt before them, but Isabella begged him to rise
d seat himself — a rare honor in the Spanish court — and tell
em all about his voyage and his discoveries. What a wonderful
le it must have been!

There is a story that at a dinner in honor of Columbus not long
:er this reception a jealous courtier asked him: —

"If you had not sailed to the Indies, don't you suppose there
e other men in Spain who would have made the voyage?"

Instead of answering, Columbus held up an egg and asked if
y one present could make it stand on end. No one succeeded,
til he took the egg, broke the end slightly, and in that way was
le to make it stand.

"Any one could do that," muttered the envious courtier.

"Yes," said the admiral quietly, "after I have shown the way."

That was the work of Columbus, to "show the way." He made
ree other voyages, visiting more of the Bahama
lands and the West Indies, and sailing along
ntral America, Panama, and the northern coast
South America. He tried to govern a colony
turbulent Spaniards in the New World, but
failed, and his enemies reported such mali-
)us stories of him that a new governor was
pointed for the colony. He put the great admi-
l in chains and sent him back to Spain. The
ptain of the vessel would gladly have removed
e fetters, but Columbus said: "No, the rulers
Spain have put chains upon me, and they alone
all take them off. So long as I live I will keep
ese chains, and they shall be buried with me."

Ferdinand and Isabella were indignant at such
eatment of so great a man, and there was no
lay in striking off the chains. Yet sovereigns

Columbus shows the way

SOUTH AMERICAN
INDIAN, 1497
(From the earliest
picture)

and kingdom were alike disappointed. Columbus had crossed the ocean, but he had discovered no gold; and although he was so sure that the islands were off the coast of India that he called them the Indies, no great oriental cities had been found, and there seemed no reason to expect any great wealth to come from the new lands. He fell into loneliness and suffering. The queen died, and he was friendless. Again the children in the streets pointed their fingers at him, the "admiral of the lands of deceit and disappointment," as they called him. He died neglected and forgotten. Seven years after his death, King Ferdinand built him a handsome tomb, but it would have been better to treat him kindly when he was alive.

COLUMBUS
(From the statue in Fairmount Park, Philadelphia)

Why Columbus was great

Columbus was a great man, neither because he was the first to sail across an unknown sea, nor because he thought the world was round, for a wise man named Aristotle believed that eighteen hundred years before Columbus's time; he was great because he knew what was true, and was ready to risk his life for truth's sake.

SUMMARY.

Four hundred years ago most people thought the Atlantic could not be crossed.

New difficulties in getting goods from the Indies made Europeans wish to find a shorter route to Eastern Asia.

Columbus believed that ships could reach Asia by sailing west.

In vain he appealed for aid to Genoa and to Portugal. Finally, Queen Isabella became interested in his plan, and by the aid of Spain he set out on the voyage.

October 12, 1492, he landed on one of the Bahamas, but because he thought he was off the coast of India, he named the islands the West Indies.

un was disappointed that he found neither gold nor cities. Columbus died not knowing that he had discovered a new continent.

SUGGESTIONS FOR WRITTEN WORK.

scribe Columbus and Diego at the gate of La Rabida.
e the conversation between Columbus and the prior.
at would a frightened sailor have said to Columbus to try to persuade
   him to return ?
at would Columbus have answered ?

II

THE EARLY FOLLOWERS OF COLUMBUS

Now that Columbus had shown the way, others were ready to Voyages of
ow, and within fifty years Italians, Spaniards, Portuguese, the Cabots
glishmen, and Frenchmen visited different
ts of the land across the sea.
An Italian merchant named John
bot was living in England when
lumbus made his first voyage. He
s eager to cross the ocean, for he
ged, as he tells us, "to attempt
ne notable thing." The English
g was much interested, but he
. not care to spend the neces-
y money. Moreover, he was
ing to arrange a marriage
ween his ten-year-old son and
little daughter of Ferdinand
l Isabella, and the Spanish am-
ssador told him there would be

ENGLISH SHIP OF THE SIXTEENTH CENTURY

CABOT DESCRIBING HIS VOYAGE TO THE ENGLISH KING
(From an old engraving)

trouble with Spain if he should send out explorers. After a whil
however, he gave John Cabot the royal permission to cross th
ocean on condition that he received one fifth of the profits of th
enterprise.   In 1497, just before Columbus went on his third voy
North America discovered age, John Cabot set sail.   He is thought to have steered almos
directly west and to have been the first European to have
glimpse of North America, though whether he sighted land first a
Labrador, at Newfoundland, or at Cape Breton, no one can tell.

When he came home he was received in England with as muc
rejoicing as Spain had made over Columbus.   An Italian who wa
living in England wrote to his friends in Italy, "Honors ar
heaped upon Cabot, he is called Grand Admiral, he is dressed i
silk, and the English run after him like mad men."

The next year Cabot and his son made another voyage and
uised along the coast perhaps as far as South Carolina. These
plorations were interesting, but no cities were found and no
w opportunities for trade opened. England was disappointed,
d sent out no more expeditions for nearly eighty years.

The land across the sea was not forgotten, however. Another
alian named Americus Vespucius sailed as a pilot, first in the Why our
rvice of Spain and then in that of Portugal. "What a thing country is
is to seek unknown lands!" he said. He followed down the named America

stern coast of South
merica, and finally
ent a long way east
Cape Horn. When
came home and told
here he had been,
erc was much ex-
ement. More than
teen hundred years
fore this time a Span-
1 geographer had
ught that south of
sia and Africa was a
eat body of land.
ople thought that

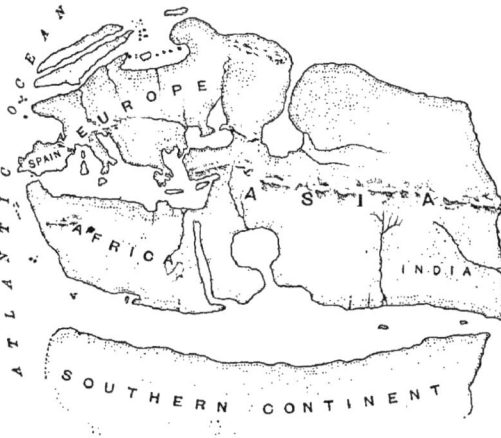

THE IDEA OF A SOUTHERN CONTINENT
BEFORE VESPUCIUS'S TIME

olumbus had found India, and now that Vespucius had discov-
ed a wide extent of country so far south of where Columbus had
en, they thought it must be this southern continent which no one
d visited, though most people believed it existed. In a little
ok on geography written soon after Vespucius's voyage it was
ggested that this land should be named for him. That is why
r country is named America; but Columbus is not forgotten,
r in our songs it is almost always called Columbia.

Twelve years after the voyage of Vespucius, there was another expedition, the story of which seems like a fairy-tale. It was led by a wealthy Spanish nobleman named Ponce de Leon, who had been with Columbus on one of his voyages. His hair was growing white, and he longed to be a young man again. There was an old story that somewhere in Asia was a magical fountain whose waters would make an old man young. So many things were new and strange and mysterious in those days that this seemed no more impossible than anything else; and when De Leon heard

Ponce de Leon seeks the Fountain of Youth

SPANISH HELMET

that the Indians declared there was such a fountain in their land, he could not rest till he had tried to find it.

Discovery of Florida

He had been living in Porto Rico as governor, and therefore the voyage to the mainland was a short one. He landed on the coast of Florida on Easter Sunday, and as the Spanish word for Easter is "Pascua Florida," or Flowery Easter, he gave the name of Florida to the new land. It was a beautiful country, full of bright green trees, and flowers of many colors. There were rivers and lakes and springs. "Surely among all these," thought De Leon "we shall find the Fountain of Youth." However, though he drank the water now of one and now of another, and hoped at each draught that he would feel himself becoming stronger and younger, nowhere did he find the magical fountain. Instead of growing young in Florida, it was there that he met his death, for the Spaniards had treated the Indians so badly that they hated the white people whose coming with Columbus had been so welcome, and on De Leon's

PISTOL OF DE LEON'S TIME

second visit he died by an Indian arrow.

The year 1519 had come. Many different voyagers had sailed to America. They had landed on islands, or had explored the

st for a little way, but few realized that a vast new continent
west of the Atlantic. Most people thought all this expanse of
d was connected with southeastern Asia, and that to the west
it lay the cities with which Europe had traded. They hoped
re was some passage through this land which would give them
1ort route to India. One man who was especially interested
his idea was a Portuguese named Magellan. He was a warm-
rted man, and it is quite possible that one reason why he
hed to cross the seas was because a dear friend of his was in
eastern Indies.

Magellan's idea of a passage to India

'he king of Portugal refused to have anything to do with the
edition. Then Magellan asked, " Have I your
jesty's permission to offer my services to some
er monarch?" The king replied shortly, "Do
you please," and would not allow Magellan to
; his hand at parting.

Iagellan did not wish to give up the
age, and he sailed in the service of
in, though Spain and Portugal were
on the best of terms. He had five
ps, and the brother of his friend was
tain of one of them. He went to the
tern coast of South America, and when
came to the La Plata River, he felt al-
st sure that this was the passage that
ry one was hoping to find. He explored
stream for three hundred miles, but it

MAGELLAN

w narrower and the water grew fresher. There was nothing
lo but to go back to the coast and try to find some other pas-
e. He sailed to the south, keeping near the shore. There
re fearful storms that strained and weakened the ships, no
: knew what dangers were before them, and they were short

He sails in the service of Spain

of food. " Let us go home," pleaded the sailors. "Our ships are weak, and we shall either be wrecked or else die of starvation." "Never," answered the commander, "I will go on if I have to eat the leather from the ship's yards."

On he went. The sailors rebelled. "He is only a foreigner," said they, "and what better service could he render to the king of Portugal than to lead a company of Spaniards to certain death?" They even seized some of the ships, but Magellan found a way to

ROUTE OF MAGELLAN'S SHIPS

He enters the Pacific Ocean

suppress the mutiny, and sailed on until he came to the strait that bears his name. Through the strait he went, and behold, a wide ocean stretched out before him! This ocean seemed so calm and peaceful after all the storms that he had been through that he named it the Pacific. It is said that when he saw the quiet water, he was "so glad thereof that for joy the tears fell from his eyes."

Across the Pacific

The sailors were in despair, but it would do no good to rebel, for they were so far from Spain that there was not nearly enough food to last for a return voyage. The only course was to press on in the hope that aid would be found somewhere in the wide ocean. It was long before the help came, and they suffered so severely from hunger that they actually did eat "the pieces of leather

ich were folded about certain great ropes of the ship." At last
y came to a group of islands where they could indeed buy

ie food, but the natives
ved to be so dishonest that
 Spaniards called them
idrones," or thieves, and
 name has clung to the
ole group of islands.

oon Magellan reached the
lippines, and there he was
ed in a fight with the na-
es, but not before he had
t ships coming from the
st, and knew that his ves-
s could make the rest of the

NATIVES OF MAGELLAN'S STRAITS

First voyage
around the
world

rney home through well-known waters. One of them did
s, and in 1522 the first voyage around the world was com-
ted.

'he name, New World, had often been used, but until this voy-
 of Magellan's was made, few thought that this New World
s a great double continent. Some supposed that what we call
rth America was probably a group of islands, and that some-
ere among these islands there was a passage through which
ps might sail to Japan without going as far south as Magellan
l done. They spoke of this strait which they hoped to find as

The New
World

 " Northwest Passage," and one man after an-
er went out hopefully in search of it. How
couraged these bold navigators would have
n if they had known that no such passage

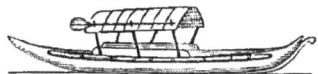

PHILIPPINE CANOE

ild be found until the middle of the nineteenth century, and
t even then it would prove to be so far north as to have little
ctical value!

France is
interested in
the New
World

In all these early voyages whoever landed on an unknown shore unfurled his banner and claimed the land for the sovereign in whose service he had sailed. France began to feel that it was time for her to have a share in these new countries, for even if there were no rich cities with which she could trade, there might be gold mines and precious stones. There is a tradition that the French King said: "Show me Father Adam's will that gives the earth to Spain and Portugal and shuts out France."

Spanish voyagers had gone to South America and Mexico, and from those countries gold was pouring into Spain; but if the Northwest Passage could be discovered, the nation that controlled it need not envy Spain her wealth, for trade with the Indies would be as valuable as a gold mine. In 1534 a Frenchman named Jacques Cartier went in search of the passage. He seems to have thought that there was a better chance of finding it farther north, for he sailed directly west to Newfoundland, which the Cabots had probably first visited. He went into a beautiful bay, but it was so warm that he could think of no better name to give it than Baie des Chaleurs (Chaleur Bay), or the bay of heat. In the usual fashion of the early explorers,

Jacques
Cartier

A MEXICAN INDIAN

aimed the land for his king and set up a great wooden cross. French claim in America established
natives had received him kindly, but when the cross was set
he chief spoke as well as he could by signs and said: "This
ʳ country, not yours. I am its king, not you." This made
fference to Cartier, for it never entered the
s of these voyagers that the Indians had
rights. He did not care to have trouble,
ver, and he thought it was quite unneces-
to tell the truth to an Indian, so he
"That is nothing. The cross is
a beacon to show sailors the way
ur country."
hen once in the Saint Lawrence,
er hoped that he had found the
hwest Passage, but just as it
een with Magellan in the La
t, so it was here, for the stream
narrower and the water fresher
arther they went. At last they
to admit that this was not the
ge so long desired. Cartier went
owever, to an island in the river
e Montreal now stands. Here was

JACQUES CARTIER

le Indian village. Back of it was a high hill, and the view The Saint Lawrence explored
this hill was so beautiful that he named it Mont Réal, or the
mountain. To the river itself he gave the name Saint Law-
ɔ, because he had discovered it on Saint Lawrence's Day.
few years later another great river, the Mississippi, was
ɔd. This discovery was made by De Soto, the Spanish gov- De Soto's expedition
ɔ of Cuba. He set out with a thousand men in nine ships.
arried with him cattle, mules, horses, and also fierce blood-
ds which were sometimes used to hunt the natives. It is

DE SOTO REACHING THE MISSISSIPPI
(From Powell's picture in the Capitol at Washington)

no wonder that the Indians who had welcomed the Spaniards warmly became as savage as the invaders, and tortured eve Spaniard that fell into their hands.

The Mississippi River discovered De Soto had been told that if he went to the westward he wou find a land rich in gold, so to the west he made his way. He can to the Mississippi River in 1541, but he found no gold. The I dians had become bitter enemies, two thirds of his thousand m had died in the wilderness, and he decided to build two boa float down the river to the Gulf of Mexico, and then push on Cuba. Before the boats could be made, De Soto died. He w so hated by the Indians that, for fear they should insult his grav his followers hollowed out the trunk of an oak and buried th dead leader at midnight in the waters of the mighty stream th he had discovered.

Nearly fifty years had passed since the first voyage of Columbus. ain, England, Portugal, and France had all sent out explorers. le general course of the Spaniards and the Portuguese had been lands around the Gulf of Mexico and to the south of it. The iglish had sailed to Newfoundland and Labrador. The French d explored the Saint Lawrence. Both English and French had plored part of the eastern coast of North America.

Explorations of different nations

SUMMARY.

.thin fifty years after the voyage of Columbus : —

[he Cabots visited the mainland of America.

Vespucius coasted along South America.

De Leon went to Florida.

Magellan's ship sailed around the world.

Cartier explored the Saint Lawrence.

De Soto discovered the Mississippi.

ese voyages, together with that of Columbus, gave Spain, France, **and** England claims to land in North America.

.ey proved : —'

[hat the world was round.

[hat it was much larger than had been supposed.

[hat a continent lay between Europe and Asia.

SUGGESTIONS FOR WRITTEN WORK.

:ite a conversation between two persons about the New World.

scribe Cartier's planting the cross at Chaleur Bay.

scribe the burial of De Soto.

III

THE EARLY ATTEMPTS TO MAKE SETTLEMENT

OLD SPANISH GATEWAY AT ST. AUGUSTINE

Claims of France, England, and Spain

As has been said, it wa the custom for each ex plorer to take possessio for his king of whateve land he visited. This i why the French claime the country about th Saint Lawrence, the Eng lish claimed all betwee Maine and Florida, an the Spanish claimed Flo ida, Mexico, the West Ir dies, and South America There were no bounda ries between these terr tories, no one knew ho far west the continent extended, and each sovereign had a vagu idea that he had a right to all the land that was connected wit the place where his explorer was the first to land.

Fifty years after Columbus's death neither Spain, France, no England had settled on the mainland of what is now the Unite States. Different explorers had tried to found colonies, and eve on Columbus's first voyage some of his followers were so d lighted with the new country that they persuaded him to allo them to remain there when he sailed for home. This colony faile

owever, and so did all the others. The chief reason was that the Why the early colonies failed
lonists had no thought of making their homes in the New
orld. What they wanted was to fill their pockets with gold or
earls or diamonds and then go back
Europe to spend their money.

Filled with this idea, they paid little
tention to the character of the region
which they were going. What the
il was, and whether it was a good
ace for a home, made little differ-
ice to them. So much treasure had
een found in America that men were
ady to believe that anything was of
due if it only came from across the
ean. The caterpillars of Florida
ley took for remarkably fine silk-
orms. Quartz crystals from near
uebec they felt sure were diamonds,

SPANISH TREASURE SEEKER
(Showing the soldier's cuirass and halberd)

d when a sea-captain carried home a black stone from the frozen
nds north of North America, he was immediately sent back across
le ocean for a cargo of black stones, for the wise men of Lon-
on declared that the specimen was full of gold. To colonists
with such ideas as these, it seemed absurd to
waste their time planting corn, when by
a little searching they could perhaps discover a gold mine. This
is the chief reason why during the First permanent settlements in the United States
second fifty years after Columbus
discovered America only two permanent settlements were made in

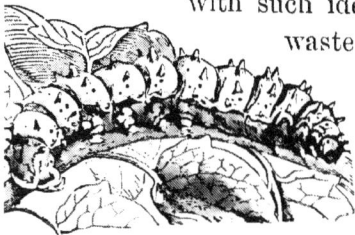

A SILKWORM

hat is now the United States. One was at Saint Augustine, in
lorida, which the Spanish founded in 1565. The other, also
panish, was at Santa Fé in New Mexico.

Of the colonies that failed one was unlike the others. Th was founded by Sir Walter Raleigh, the best known Englishma of his time. He was an admirable leader and a brave soldier, well as the author of some very good poetry and an interestii history of the world. Whatever he undertook he did well, ai he always seemed to know just what to do. There is a sto that one day Queen Elizabeth wished to cross a piece of dan ground. The attendants did not know how to save her Majes from setting her royal foot in the mud, but, quick as thought, ¦ Walter spread his rich velvet mantle on the ground before h and the queen passed over safely. Whether this is true or n the warrior poet was a successful courtier, and Elizabeth w inclined to grant whatever he asked.

He was greatly interested in the New World, and he had sor

BIRTHPLACE OF SIR WALTER RALEIGH AT HAYES IN DEVONSHIRE

ideas that were unlike those of most men of his time. Othe had thought that the chief value of America lay in the gold min that might be found there; Raleigh believed that if colonis would form real settlements and cultivate the ground, their so ing and reaping would be worth more than the vague chance

scovering a mine. Most men thought that if the Northwest Raleigh's
ıssage could be found, Europe would become enormously rich thoughts about
ɔm trade with Asia. Raleigh dreamed of America's becoming America
second home of the English nation. "And when the land is

ll of English towns," he
ought, "what need will there
: of trading with Asia? Will
ıt this American England give
: a market for our manufac-
ıres?"

Raleigh was a rich man, and
: straightway sent out two
.ips to explore the coast of
merica. The next thing to
> was to interest Queen Eliz-
.eth in the plan. A man
ımed Richard Hakluyt knew
ore about America than any
.e else, and Raleigh asked him
 write a book for her, telling
hy it would be a good thing
r England to have colonies in
e New World. Hakluyt gave
any reasons. He brought for-

QUEEN ELIZABETH
(From a portrait in the Queen Victoria collection)

ırd the hope that America would become a market for Eng- Reasons
h manufactures. He declared that England would soon have for planting colonies
:ither food nor work for her people. It was becoming so much
ore profitable to raise sheep than grain that large numbers of
ıglish farmers were turning their farms into sheep pastures.
ıey no longer planted grain, and as one man could care for
any sheep, the men who had been working on farms had nothing
 do. It is no wonder that many people agreed with Hakluyt.

Another strong reason was that England could weaken Spain b
having colonies in America. English vessels, he said, could easil
go forth from these colonies and cap
ture Spanish treasure ships, as wel
as drive the Spaniards from th
Newfoundland fishing ground
Spain would no longer receiv
the vast amounts of gol
that had been coming t
her from her American pos
sessions. "Then is there n

QUEEN ELIZABETH'S COACH

doubt," said Hakluyt, "but the Spanish empire falls to the ground
and the Spanish king shall be left bare as Æsop's proud crow."

Elizabeth was much interested in the plan, and on the retur
of Raleigh's exploring vessels suggested that the land which the
Objections to planting colonies had visited should be called Virginia in honor
of her, their virgin queen. When she was asked
to send out a colony, it was a different matter.
No doubt it would be a good thing to have
powerful settlements in America from which
vessels could be sent out to capture Spanish
ships, but it would be some years before
these settlements would be strong enough
to do anything of the kind, and in the
mean time England needed all her
money and all her ships to meet an
attack that was threatened by Spain.

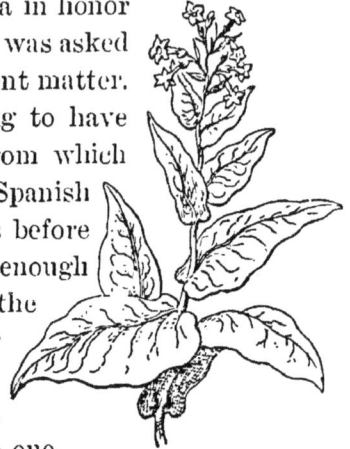

Finally Raleigh sent out more than one
hundred emigrants at his own expense. The

TOBACCO

queen had granted him a generous tract of land, for "Virginia
was to extend from Cape Fear to Halifax, and she had promise(
that American colonists should have all the privileges of men born

nd living in England, and that they should make such laws as hey thought best. England claimed this vast area of land because f the discoveries of the Cabots. Elizabeth said that Spanish laims were nothing where Spain had no settlements, and as for ny rights that the Indians might have, no one thought f them at all. In 1585 the colony went to Roanoke Island, off the coast of North Carolina. It failed utterly. The promised ship with provisions was delayed, he men were homesick, they preferred to search for gold rather than o work, and the governor declared that they talked too nuch! An English vessel ame to the island, and hey all went home. They carried with them potaoes and tobacco, and from hat day to this, as has een said, "the air of England has never been free rom tobacco smoke."

Two years later Raleigh sent out a second olony to the same lace, this time of men, women, and children. Not

Raleigh's colony fails

SPANISH TREASURE SHIPS

ong after they landed, there was born to the governor's daughter . little girl, who was the first child born in America of English arents. She was named Virginia Dare. No one knows what ecame of this little American girl, for the governor had to return o England; and when three years later he was able to go back o the colony, the little granddaughter and all the other colonists

His second colony

had disappeared. There is a tradition that some Indians were at first kind to them, but afterwards murdered nearly all. It was rumored that one young girl was among the few that the savages spared, but whether it was the child Virginia, no one can tell.

Raleigh had not forgotten the colonists during those three

SPANISH ARMADA ATTACKED BY THE ENGLISH FLEET
(From an ancient tapestry in the House of Lords)

Why Raleigh did not help the colonists

years. He tried to send a vessel to them, but it was driven back to port by the Spaniards. He tried again, but the English government had need of every ship in the kingdom, and his vessel was seized for the service of his country. This was in the famous year 1588. Spain was determined to conquer England, and she had fitted out a great fleet of warships. The Spanish word for fleet is "armada," and Spain was so sure that no other vessels could resist her onslaught that she called the fleet the Invincible Armada. This attack was not for money or possessions; the king of Spain meant to become also king of England. The whole land was aroused. Every one who owned a vessel went out to fight the Armada, and the end of the matter was that the Spanish ships were so shattered by the English attacks and by storms that not more than one half ever returned to Spain.

Before this time England had always been afraid of contests with the Spaniards, for Spain was a rich and powerful country. English vessels were so often captured by Spanish men-of-war that even if English colonies had been planted in America, the colonists could not have been sure of receiving food and supplies from England; but after the victory over the Armada, England was "mistress of the seas" and could plant her colonies where she would. Spain was thoroughly subdued and seldom ventured to interfere.

England is "mistress of the seas"

This contest took place while Queen Elizabeth lived; but when she died, King James, the next sovereign, seemed to care for nothing else so much as winning the friendship of Spain. Now Spain hated Raleigh, not only because he had fought against the Armada, but because he had tried to plant a colony and to find a gold mine on what she claimed was Spanish soil; and to please Spain this great man was kept in prison for twelve years, and finally executed on a false charge of treason. Prisoner as he was, he never gave up his interest in America. "I shall live to see Virginia an English nation," he said, and he did see the beginning of a new home for part of the English people across the ocean. If he could look upon America now, he would think that his dream had come true, though it would surprise him greatly that the colonies planted by Englishmen were no longer under English rule. Americans should never forget Sir Walter Raleigh, for he was one of the first men in the world to believe in the wonderful future that lay before our land.

SPANISH GENTLEMAN OF THE ARMADA PERIOD

In 1600 America had been known for one century. People had by that time a fair idea of the shape of South America, but,

Ideas about North America in 1600

although explorers had coasted along the eastern shores of North America, and also along the western shores as far as what is now

SEEKING THE NORTHWEST PASSAGE
(The Hudson River explored during the search)

called Oregon, no one had any notion of the shape or size of the northern half of the New World. From Florida to where New York now stands might be a solid mass of land, they thought, extending to California, but

Canada and all the northwestern part of what is now the United States many supposed to be one great sea broken by islands. From Virginia across the land to this vast northern ocean they thought was perhaps one hundred miles.

Explorers hoped to find a strait through this land, and when-

Search for the Northwest Passage

ever a mariner came to the wide mouth of a river, he would say to himself, "Surely I am the fortunate man who has discovered the Northwest Passage." If he sailed up the river, he found the water less salt with every mile, and at last he would turn his ships about and sail back, saying, "The Northwest Passage must lie farther north, or it may be farther south." Never would he say to himself, "There is no Northwest Passage."

Although Raleigh saw farther into

SASSAFRAS

the future of America than most other men, he was not the only

ne interested in the New World. Valuable woods and dyestuffs Increased
had been found; sassafras had been discovered, and sassafras was interest in the New
he fashionable medicine of the day, the remedy that would cure World
ill diseases. Merchants began to feel that there were as good
opportunities for gain in America as elsewhere in the world.

Other books than Hakluyt's were written to show that it was
worth while to plant colonies. One strong reason for making
settlements in America was that by founding colonies England
might have a larger share in the American
fisheries. Great quantities of fish were
caught off the shores of Newfoundland.
Many more Frenchmen than Englishmen
had taken advantage of this fact; but if
only there were colonies near the fishing
grounds, the English fishermen could be

CODFISH
(The most important of the American fishes)

protected from their enemies, and the colonists could salt and
dry fish and have it ready to send home to England.

SUMMARY.

France, England, and Spain all claimed a share in the New World, but in
1600 there were only two permanent colonies, — Saint Augustine in
Florida, and Santa Fé in New Mexico. Both were Spanish.

Raleigh believed that America would become a second home of the English
nation. He planted two colonies on Roanoke Island, but both failed.

England's defeat of the Armada enabled her to plant colonies without fear
of Spain.

In 1600 the shape of North America was unknown. The continent was
thought to be much narrower than it is. It was also believed that a
passage led through it to the Pacific.

England was feeling interested in the Newfoundland fisheries, and merchants were finding that there were opportunities for gain in the New
World.

SUGGESTIONS FOR WRITTEN WORK.

Raleigh writes a letter to Queen Elizabeth, asking for help to found a colony.
One of Raleigh's colonists writes a letter home describing the potato.
What became of little Virginia Dare?
What Raleigh would think of America to-day.

IV

THE INDIANS AND THEIR WAYS

The different Indian tribes

INDIAN DWELLING IN THE SOUTHWEST
(The Pueblo of Wolpi in Arizona)

For many centuries before Columbus came to America the country was inhabited by a copper-colored people whom he called Indians, because he supposed that he was on the coast of India. There were many different tribes, and each tribe had a name, but for their race as a whole they had no other name than a word meaning "Men," or "Real Men."

The Indians of the northwest never had any settled homes, but roamed about from place to place and lived on fish and game. Those of the southwest lived in fortresses of stone, often built four or five stories high up the face of a cliff, and each of them large enough to make a dwelling for two or three thousand persons. Those of the east, the ones with whom the early English colonists had most to do, gathered into villages.

They lived partly by the chase, and partly on some of the vegetables that are most easily raised, — corn, beans, pumpkins, and squashes.

The Indians who dwelt in villages some-times built long houses large enough for many families, with a division for each family. Sometimes they made wigwams. For these they drove poles into the ground in a circle and fastened the tops together for a frame-work. Then they spread over this framework the bark of trees, or skins fastened together with the sinews of animals. Sometimes, like the people who lived in England in the early

Long houses and wig-wams

SQUAW CARRYING A PAPOOSE

days, they wove slender twigs back and forth among the poles. The fire was on the ground in the middle of the wig-wam, and the smoke made its way out as best it could.

Each family had its own wigwam. The husband, or brave, must protect his wife and children from their foes, and he must procure whatever meat and fish were used. The wife, or squaw, must provide the vegetables. She must not only cook them, but she must plant the seed and give them what-ever care was needed while they were growing. A brave would work to make bows and arrows, but he would not hoe the corn. If his family moved, he would stalk on ahead with his weapons, while his wife followed as best she could with the household goods.

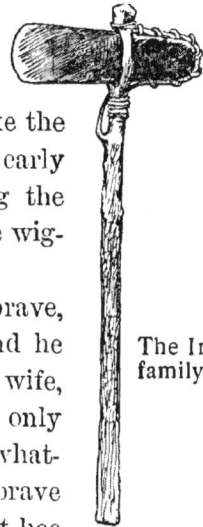

The Indian family

A STONE AXE

This seems at the first glance like a most unfair division of labor, but it must be remembered that when the brave fished, he

The brave had something more to do than to bait his hook and drop it into the water. He must make his hook before he could bait it, and he must make his line from the fibrous bark of some tree. If he needed a pole, he must cut it, not with a sharp steel hatchet, but with a dull stone knife, and he must also make the knife. His boat was either a birch-bark canoe, or a "dug-out," which was hollowed out of the trunk of a tree. Making a boat, as well as almost all other work that the Indians did, was long, slow, and wearisome.

The household goods of the Indians were few. There was per-

MAKING A CANOE WAS SLOW AND WEARISOME WORK

haps a basket or two, some skins to sleep on, a bowl made of clay hardened in the fire, and not much else. If there was a baby, or **The papoose** papoose, in the household, it was not allowed to lie on the ground or creep about as white babies do. An Indian mother would have thought it very careless to treat her precious child in such a fashion. The Indian baby was carefully wrapped in the softest of skins and tied to a framework of wicker or wood. Then baby and framework were stood up in any safe place, or swung to the

ranch of a tree, where the wind would rock the child better than
cradle, and the bright green leaves, gleaming in the sunshine ·
nd waving in the breeze, were prettier playthings than
ny that are found in the toyshops. The Indians of
-day who have not adopted the ways of the white
eople treat their children in the same manner, and
ie babies always look contented and happy.

When the children grew older, the girls were
ught to do all the kinds of work that their
others did. They learned to make baskets and
ottery, to plant corn and cultivate it, and to cook in the
ay bowls. If they had only dishes of wood, they would fill
iem with water and heat the water by dropping in hot stones.
1 this way they could boil their meat and vegetables : or they
could broil the meat over the open fire and
roast the potatoes and squashes in the hot
ashes. They had no way of grinding corn,
but they pounded it into a coarse meal,
mixed it with water, and made cakes of it.

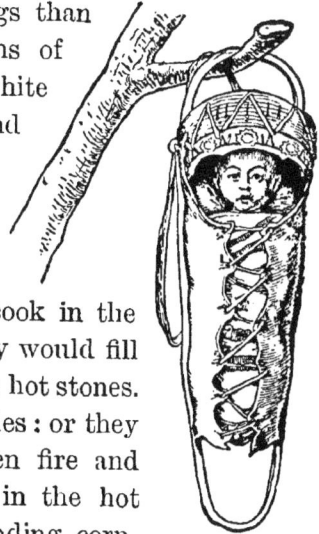

THE INDIAN
BABY'S CRADLE

Making the clothes of the family did not re-
quire much time, for no one wore very many. Indian
A rudely woven garment of cotton or grass- clothing
cloth was enough for the summer, while
leggings of skin and a fur cloak were a
wardrobe for many winters. The Indian
women liked pretty things as well as white
women do, and they gave a great deal
of attention to the shoes of the family.

BOILING FOOD IN AN
EARTHEN POT

hese shoes were called moccasins. They were made of soft,
iick deerskin, and were embroidered with porcupine quills and
ny shells. It was partly because of this embroidery that the
idians were so delighted when the colonists gave them beads,

for beads were easier to use than shells and of much more brilliant colors.

Weapons

As the boys grew older, they were taught to do what their fathers did. They learned not only to fish and shoot, but to make their own fishhooks of bits of bone, and their own bows of wood with the sinews of deer for bow-strings. The heads of the arrows were made of stone, and the Indian boy must work patiently hour after hour, chipping off a little bit of stone at each blow, until he had brought the head to the proper shape. Then it was bound fast to the wooden arrow. He must make his knife by rubbing a bone on a rock until it had an edge. The tomahawk was made of stone, and that, too, was shaped and sharpened by being rubbed on a rock until it slowly came to be of the right form.

The Indian boys did not have an easy time by any means. Even their games were not what we should call play, for many of them were only tests to see who could endure most. It is said that one game was played by the boys putting red-hot coals under their arms. The boy who dropped his coal first was laughed at and despised, while the one who bore the pain longest was the hero of the day and was honored by the boys and by their fathers.

INDIAN WEAPONS

The scalp-lock

As soon as the boy was old enough to become a warrior, his head was shaved, except for one long lock of hair called the scalp-lock. When an Indian killed an enemy, he always "scalped" him, that is, he cut off a round piece of the skin of the scalp. This lock was left to make it convenient to cut off the piece of skin and carry it away. An Indian would

FISHHOOKS OF BONE

ıve thought it exceedingly cowardly to remove his scalp-lock
ɪfore going to fight, and when he looked upon an enemy's, it
ɪemed to say, "Take me if you can."

Their fighting was carried on in quite a different fashion from
ıat of Europeans. The Indian had no idea of two lines of war- **Method of**
ors facing each other and shooting till the men of one side had **fighting**
ther fallen or run away. That would have seemed to him a
ost ridiculous thing to do. The proper way to
ʒht, according to his ideas, was to shoot from
ɪhind rocks and trees, or to come suddenly
ɪon his enemies with a horrible war-whoop,
ɪrhaps in the middle of the night, and kill
ıem before they were fairly awake.

The Indians often tortured their prisoners,
ıt perhaps not wholly from the fiendish
ɪlight, that some races have shown, in see-
g the sufferings of others. To bear torture
ithout a groan was their test of a great man.

AN INDIAN SCALP-
LOCK

the prisoner contrived to get the better of his captors by some
ɪed of bravery, they showed him all honor. Only a few years
ʒo, a young missionary won over a group of Indians in Dakota
ɪ riding a "bucking" pony that they had not been able to man-
ʒe. "After that," said he, "I could preach to them all day if I
ıose, and they would listen to every word."

Each tribe had a chief, but all important questions were talked
ʳer in a general council of the braves of the tribe. The records **Wampum**
these councils were carefully kept, only the Indian way was
ɪt by pen and paper, but by the use of small shells made into
ɪads and called wampum. Belts were made of this wampum,
ıd as shells of different colors were used, sometimes pictures of
en and animals were formed ; but even if there were no pictures,
ıe Indians could tell by the arrangement of the shells what had

been done at a council, or what treaties had been made. This
wampum was not only a record, but the shells took the place
of money, and for some time even the colonists used them for
that purpose. After a while the Indians made their wampum of
beads, and a handful of beads was to a red man what
a handful of gold dollars is now to a white man.
With this in mind, the price paid for Rhode Island,
forty fathoms of white wampum, does not seem so
ridiculously small.

Religion

The Indians thought that if they were brave
warriors they would go to the "Happy Hunting
Grounds" when they died. That they might be
able to follow the chase in this world of happiness,
their weapons were usually buried with them, and

INDIAN
WAMPUM

sometimes a dog was killed and laid at the feet of his dead
master. They are thought to have believed in one Great Spirit
who was more powerful than all other gods, though they also
worshiped the sun, rain, wind, lightning, or anything else that could
help or harm them. They were honest and truthful with members of their own tribe, and they had a great admiration for any
one among the whites who kept his word with them. Long after
the early colonial days,
man in Pennsylvania was
called among them "He
that Tells the Truth;" and even now the Indians of Minnesota speak of the late Bishop
Whipple as "Straight Tongue," because he never
broke his word to them.

AN INDIAN PIPE

Treatment of the Indians by the whites

In their dealings with the whites, they always remembered
kindness, though they never forgot to avenge an injury. Almost
all of the early explorers say that the Indians were at first gentle
and friendly. The whites looked down upon them as heathen

it it was often the Europeans that behaved like savages. Their
eatment of the red men brought upon the colonists many of the
tacks that filled their lives with fear and suffering. If there
as any difficulty with the Indians, the whites would generally
and by one another; and for this reason the Indians felt that
one group of settlers had done them a wrong, they had a per-
ct right to avenge it on any other group.

Such were the people whom the early settlers in America had
meet. If from the first coming of the dis-
verers the red men had been treated with
ndness, taught and not despised, many a
ory of suffering and bloodshed would have
en unwritten. To the Spanish founder of
int Augustine the Pope wrote: "Have a
re that you show not bad habits and vices
the Indians, and so prevent them from be-
ming Christians." It is to be regretted that
is advice was not always followed.

The red men looked upon the first white
en that they saw as angels come down
om the skies to counsel them and teach
em. It was a sad thing for them and for

THE WARRIOR'S WAR DANCE

e whole country that their first century of acquaintance with
uropeans should have often shown them the white man, not as
e kind teacher, but as the savage conqueror, ready for the sake
gold to torture, enslave, and murder the people who had wel-
med him and trusted him.

SUMMARY.

lumbus called the natives of America Indians, because he thought he
was on the coast of India.
e Indians that had settled homes lived in stone fortresses, in long houses,

or in wigwams. Their food was vegetables, fish, or the animals tha
they shot. Their tools and weapons were made of stone or bone. Thei
boats were canoes or dug-outs.

The papoose was protected by a wooden framework. The girls learned t
make household utensils, to cook, raise corn, and make the clothes c
the family. The boys learned to hunt, fish, and make their ow
weapons. Their games were often tests of endurance.

The warrior always had a scalp-lock. He shot from behind rocks and tree
He often tortured prisoners.

Wampum was used for money and for keeping the records of the tribe.

The Indians believed that after death they would live again. They remen
bered a kindness, but never forgot an injury. They welcomed the firs
white men as teachers come from the skies.

SUGGESTIONS FOR WRITTEN WORK.

An Indian boy tells a white boy how to build a wigwam.

An Indian girl tells how her mother cooks the dinner.

The Indians held a council about making war upon the whites; what di
they say?

V

VIRGINIA, THE FIRST PERMANENT ENGLISH COLONY

SIR WALTER RALEIGH at last concluded that planting colonie
Plymouth and London Companies should be the work of a king or of a company of men, and h
gave up his claim to the American lands. While he was in prison
two companies were formed to send colonists to Virginia. The
were named the Plymouth Company and the London Company
King James gave to the Plymouth Company the land betwee
Nova Scotia and Long Island, and to the London Company, th
land between the Potomac and Cape Fear. From the Atlanti

o the Pacific is about three thousand miles, but no one supposed
hen that it was more than one or two hundred, and King James
eclared that these grants were to extend from ocean to ocean.
'he strip between the two claims was to belong to the company
hat could colonize it first. The Plymouth Company did little
more than to coast along the shore and trade with the Indians, but the London Company founded the first permanent English settlement in America.

The London Company's first colony

In 1607 the London Company sent out one hundred and five men. Many prominent persons in England were interested in this colony, and Hakluyt wrote them a long letter of advice. He told them to be kind to the "naturals," as he called the Indians, but not to trust them. An English poet wrote a poem about "Virginia, earth's only paradise." In the plays of the time there was much talk

Ideas of Virginia

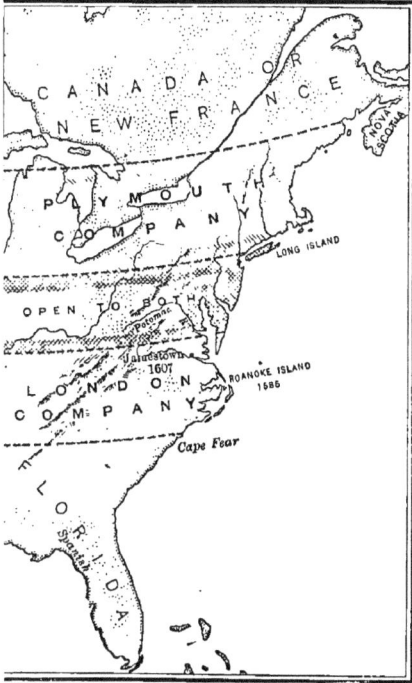

GRANTS TO THE LONDON AND PLYMOUTH COMPANIES

bout this marvelous country. One character says : —

'I tell thee, gold is more plentiful there than copper is with
s. . . . All the prisoners they take are fettered in gold; and for
ubies and diamonds, they go forth on holidays and gather them
y the seashore to hang on their children's coats and stick in their
hildren's caps."

The little company sailed for America. Up the coast they

went; between two points of land, which they named Cap
Charles and Cape Henry in honor of the two sons of Kin
James; and up a river, which they named th
James River in honor of the king himself. On
peninsula which extended into the stream the
decided to make their settlement. They called i
Jamestown.

Everything was against the colony. They ha
thought more of defense than of good air, an
they had settled where it was damp and un
healthy. The river water was not fit to drink
They had so scanty a supply of food that on
pint of wormy
wheat and
barley a day

ENGLISH SOLDIER OF 1603

**Sickness
and other
troubles**

was all that could be allowed
to a man. Such a hot sum-
mer they had never known.
Fever broke out, and more
than half the company died.

Some of these troubles
might have been avoided if
the colonists had been a different kind of men, but half
of them had no idea how to
work with their hands. Some
had come to see what adventures they might meet with,
some to search for gold, and

CAPTAIN JOHN SMITH

some with the hope of winning glory and a royal reward b
finding the Northwest Passage. All these men needed house:
and there were but four carpenters in the party.

With sickness and hunger and helplessness there would have been little hope for the colonists if there had not been among their number one man, Captain John Smith, who knew what to do. Early adventures of John Smith He wrote the story of his life, and it is full of adventures almost as wonderful as those of Sindbad the Sailor. When he came to Virginia, he was only twenty-seven years of age, and in those twenty-seven years he had served as a soldier in three or four countries, and had been tossed into the sea as one whom a company of self-righteous pilgrims thought would bring them bad luck. Three times he had engaged in single combat with a Turkish champion, while two armies watched the contest with delight. He was taken prisoner by the Turks and made to wear a heavy iron collar. He escaped to Rus-

SMITH DEFEATS THE TURKISH CHAMPION
(From a rare print. The crescent and cross above distinguish the Turk from the Christian)

sia, and finally made his way back to England just in time to join the Virginia expedition. His story is a strange one, but in those days of wild adventures it was not impossible for such things to come to pass.

Some of the Indians about Jamestown were hostile, others were inclined to be friendly. Smith contrived to compel the hostile tribes and persuade the friendly ones to sell the colonists corn. John Smith and the Indians After a while he set out on an exploring trip up one of the rivers. He was taken prisoner, but he showed the Indians his pocket-compass, and they hardly dared to kill a man who had such a wonderful article; he might bring some terrible evil upon them. After much discussion, however, it was decided to run the risk. His head was laid upon a stone,

Pocahontas and the warriors were ready to strike, when Pocahontas, the little daughter of the chief, claimed the prisoner as hers, and his life was saved. This is the story that Smith tells, and there is no special reason for doubting it. It was not uncommon among the Indians for one of the tribe to rescue a prisoner in this way. The chief, Powhatan, was perhaps a little amused to see the child claiming the rights of a grown person; and then, too, he was half afraid to put the man to death, and it may be that he was glad to find a way to

A GENTLEMAN OF 1610

avoid it. Powhatan told Smith that he was now a member of their tribe and might go back to his white friends whenever he chose.

On the day of Smith's return another shipload of men arrived from England, but they would do nothing except to search for gold. Before long some earth was found that was full of bright yellow grains of metal. "That is gold" they cried in delight, and the ship was sent back across the ocean with what proved to be worthless dirt. A third shipload of men came, but they were like the others,—eager to search for gold, and with no idea of doing any work. John Smith was now governor of the colony, and he wrote to the London Company: "Send us but thirty carpenters,

A VIRGINIA INDIAN
(From John Smith's map)

husbandmen, gardeners, fishermen, blacksmiths, masons, and diggers up of trees' roots, rather than a thousand of such as we have."

The third ship had also brought a letter from the Company. Three de-
he men who had paid for carrying the colonists to Virginia mands of the
lought it was time for them to receive some return from their Company
ivestment. Their demands seem like the three feats required of
le hero of a fairy-tale, for they said that the colonists must either
:nd them a great lump of gold, or discover the Northwest
assage, or else find what had become of the English who had
isappeared from Roanoke Island nearly twenty years earlier.
The Company are fools," said Governor Smith bluntly; but
robably the Company thought that they had asked no more than
·as fair. They may have reasoned, "Where a substance so
early like gold is found, there must be gold not far away,
ld it is mere idleness and laziness not to discover it."

What the colony would have done without the common
:nse of John Smith is a question. The plan had been
lat whatever money and food could be obtained should
: divided equally. The lazy ones knew that they would
.re as well whether they did any work or not, and so
ley idled their time away. Governor Smith put an end
> that, and now if a man would not work six hours a
ly, no food was given him; and these idle gentlemen
ld to learn to hoe corn and cut down trees. The
ces blistered their fingers, and they seemed to fancy
lat the pain would be less if they swore about it. The
)vernor had an account kept of their oaths, and at night INDIAN CORN
le can of cold water was poured down each man's sleeve for
·ery oath that he had uttered during the day. This punishment,
:cording to John Smith's "History of Virginia," was so success-
il that " a man would scarce hear an oath in a week."

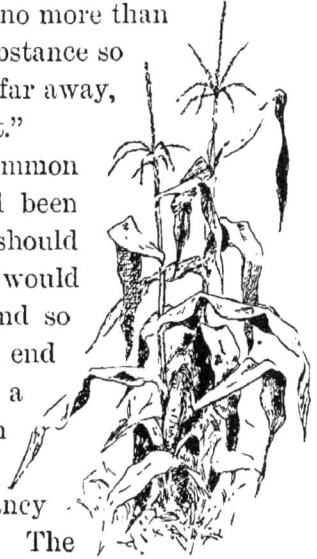

The Indians began to see that the white men meant to stay in Powhatan is
merica, and they were not pleased. Even Powhatan refused to unfriendly
ll corn, but the child Pocahontas was friendly, and often the

lives of the colonists would have been much harder if she and her companions had not brought them corn and venison.

The starving time

Three years passed. Governor Smith was badly injured by an accident and had to return to England. Then came a terrible winter known as the "starving time," when the colonists suffered so severely from cold and famine that in the spring only sixty were alive out of five hundred. "It is of no use to try to live in Virginia," said they. "We will make our way to Newfoundland if we can, and then cross to England." They went aboard their small boats and were far down the river when, behold, three stately ships came into view, full of provisions. The colonists turned back joyfully, and Jamestown was saved.

On board the vessel was a new governor who ruled in much the same way as John Smith. He gave every man a piece of land and said, "You must work if you wish to eat." After a while the settlers became more willing to work, for they found that it paid better than searching for gold. A far-seeing man named John Rolfe had begun to raise tobacco. Smoking was now common in England, and smokers would pay a large price for Virginia tobacco, so before many years the poor Virginians were becoming the rich Virginians.

One chapter of the history of the colony might have come from a story-book. When the little girl Pocahontas was about twenty years old, she married the planter John Rolfe, who took his bride to England. The "Lady Rebekah," as she

A VIRGINIA PLANTER

The Lady Rebekah

was there called, was received as a princess, the daughter of a great king, for even then people in Europe could not seem to understand that Powhatan was not a mighty sovereign governing a nation, but a naked savage ruling over a ittle tribe in the wilderness. John Smith went to see the tall, handsome, dignified young woman, but when he addressed her as "Lady Rebekah," she was grieved and said: "But you must call me your child and let me call you father, just as we did in Virginia."

Powhatan sent several of his tribe to England with Pocahontas. He was anxious to know how many people there were in the distant land across the ocean, and to one of his men he gave a bundle of little sticks, telling him to cut a notch every time he met a white man. When the Indian landed in London, he took

Counting the English

JAMESTOWN IN 1622
(From an early Dutch account of Virginia)

one look at the crowds waiting to see the ship come in, grunted in amazement, and threw away his bundle of sticks.

In 1619, when the settlement was twelve years old, three important events took place. The first was the arrival of a shipload of women. The London Company knew that unless the colonists had homes of their own, they would come back to England as soon as they had made their fortunes. It was much better for the Company to have permanent settlers than to have the land cultivated first by one man and then by another, so they brought over ninety respectable young women who were willing to live in the new country. There was many a suitor for the hand of

A shipload of women

every girl. The one whom she chose must pay the cost of her passage,—one hundred and twenty pounds of tobacco,—and soon there were ninety marriages and ninety homes. The coming of these women and of those who followed them was what made Virginia a permanent colony, for when the men had homes in the new land, they were no longer eager to make their way back to the mother country.

In England no one was allowed to tax the people except the House of Commons, and members of that body were not appointed by the king, but were chosen by the people. Thus far Virginia had been ruled by a governor appointed by the London Company. The settlers did not object to this, but they said that there ought also to be an assembly chosen by them, just as members of the House of Commons were chosen by the people of England, and that only such an assembly should have the right to tax them. The London Company agreed, and an assembly met, called the House of Burgesses, or citizens. This was the beginning of self-government in America, and was the second great event. A demand for similar rights of taxation, made by the American colonies a century and a half later, led to the Revolutionary War.

The House of Burgesses

SLAVES AT WORK

The third event was the beginning of slavery. The Virginians were cultivating great plantations of tobacco, and they needed many laborers. It became the custom in England to send over hiploads of criminals to serve the planters for a term of years. kidnappers would steal children and even grown persons, if they ad no friends to make trouble, and sell them to the planters. ometimes poor people who wished to come to America would sell hemselves, that is, they would agree to work a certain time for ny one who would pay their passage. Even this supply was ot enough, and in the year 1619 a Dutch ship brought twenty egroes to Virginia from Africa and sold them as slaves. So egan that slavery which, two centuries later, had so much to do ith bringing about the great Civil War that came near making ur United States the divided states.

Thus in the same year an English colony first began to be permanent, the ideas that led to the Revolution were first manifested in America, and the slavery which brought about the Civil War made its first appearance.

SUMMARY.

1 1607 the first permanent English settlement was made at Jamestown in
    Virginia by the London Company.
he colonists suffered greatly from sickness, scarcity of food, ignorance of
    how to work, and unwillingness to labor.
y the wisdom of John Smith even the hostile Indians were induced to
    furnish food, but after his return to England seven eighths of the colo-
    nists died of starvation and cold. Only the arrival of ships with
    supplies saved the colony.
he culture of tobacco was introduced.
1 1619 : —
    Women came from England, and the colonists began to have homes.
    The House of Burgesses, the first representative assembly in America,
        was established.
    Negro slavery was introduced.

Powhatan tells a friendly chief about Pocahontas's saving John Smith' life.

John Smith's reply to the letter from the Company mentioned.

One of the colonists describes the punishment given to a profane person.

VI

PLYMOUTH, THE FIRST COLONY IN NEW ENGLAND

In 1620 the first settlement in New England was made a Plymouth in Massachusetts. The Virginia colonists came t America to make their fortunes; the Massachusetts colonist came that they might be free to worship God in the way tha they believed would be most pleasing to him.

First settlement in New England

In those times most people thought that ever person in a country ought to belong to the sam church as the king, and to pay taxes for the sup port of that church. King James belonged t the Episcopal Church, or Church of England and he declared that he would make all his sub jects attend it. Those who were not Episcopa lians were fined and imprisoned without merc Among them were the Puritans and the Sepa ratists. "Puritans" was a nickname that wa given to those who said that they wished t make the church purer. The name "Separa tists" was given to those who wished to leav the church, and these were the people whom w call the Pilgrim Fathers.

THE PILGRIM DRESS

The king forbade them even to hold meetings at one another's The Pilgrims go to Holland ouses, and whenever one of his officers found them doing this, hey were either fined or imprisoned. They knew that ı Holland men were free to attend whatever hurch they chose, and they determined to go ɔ Holland to live. King James had said hat he would "harry out of the land" all rho would not attend his church, but rhen the Separatists were ready to go, is officers found out their plan and rrested the whole company. They made second attempt, and a second time the ing's men discovered the plan. At ıst they succeeded in making their ay to Holland. They were in a brange land with a people whose cus- ɔms and language were new, but ley were free. For a while they rere happy, but as their children grew

WINDMILL IN HOLLAND

lder, the parents found that in spite of all that could be done, he young folks were learning the ways of the children around hem and were talking in their language.

Badly as the English government had treated them, they still rished to live under its rule, and they began to think of America. They decide to go to America 'hey talked about Guiana, but decided that it would be too warm. n Virginia the Episcopal Church was in power. John Smith had xplored the coast of New England and had given it its name, but e had reported that it was exceedingly cold. They concluded hat the best place was somewhere between the Potomac and ong Island. The London Company would gladly allow them to ettle on their land, but the king's permission must be gained.

When they asked King James for a charter, or written agree-

THE PILGRIMS' DEPARTURE FROM HOLLAND
(From an old Dutch painting)

ment that they might settle in America, he said no, he would give no charter, but they might go if they chose. and so long as they behaved themselves no one should disturb them.

To England they went, and then set sail for America in two **The May- flower sets sail** vessels, the Speedwell and the Mayflower. The Speedwell sprang a leak; and it is possible that the captain's report made the injury greater than it was, for he had agreed not only to carry the Pilgrims to America, but to remain there with them for a year and he was sorry for his bargain. Over one hundred passengers **The voyage** crowded into the Mayflower. Nine weeks they were on the ocean There was an accident. Severe storms drove them out of their course, and forced them to take refuge in Massachusetts Bay instead of going farther south as they had planned. The land about the bay belonged to the Plymouth Company, but the Pilgrims knew·that the Company would be only too glad to have a settlement made on their territory, so they decided to stay where they were.

Before they landed, they met in the cabin of the Mayflower and wrote a paper promising to obey whatever laws should be made. After the paper had been signed, a party went ashore to explore the country and find a suitable place for their home. It was November. The shores were barren, "of a wild and savage hue," wrote one of the Pilgrims. No place fit for a settlement was found. For many days they explored the coast. The captain and the sailors grew more and more impatient. "Choose your place soon," said the captain, "for I shall keep enough food to carry my men to England." The sailors muttered, "We'll put your goods on shore and leave you." *In search of a home*

Another party went out to explore. John Carver, the first governor, William Bradford, the second, and the fiery little soldier, Miles Standish, were of this party. Such troubles as they had! It was so cold that the spray froze to their clothes. A heavy storm began to rage, the rudder broke, and the mast snapped into three pieces. At last they reached land, but what land it was they knew not, for night had come upon them. They contrived to kindle a fire in the driving rain, and waited for the morning. When morning came, the sun shone bright and clear. They were on Clark's Island, and there they kept

THE MAYFLOWER
(From the National Museum model)

their Sunday with prayer and singing, for great as was their need, they would do no exploring on the Lord's Day.

Monday morning they sailed to the mainland, and went ashore at a place that John Smith had named Plymouth, and that they now agreed to call Plymouth in remembrance of the English town from which they had sailed. This was the best place that they *Plymouth chosen*

had seen, and it did not take them long to go back to the ship and report that they had decided upon a home. In Plymouth there is a rock which is carefully protected and guarded, for people believe that on this rock the explorers stepped ashore. December twenty-first, the day of their landing, is called Forefathers' Day, and is celebrated in their honor. There was quite a number of children on

PLYMOUTH ROCK

board, and after being crowded into the ship for so many weeks they must have been glad enough to go ashore.

There was no room to spare, even when they were on land, for after they had been in Plymouth all winter and all the following summer, there were but seven houses. For a while they had only one house into which they crowded their goods and as many persons as possible. Some had to remain on the Mayflower for several weeks.

The story of the winter seems almost like that of the starving time in Virginia, though the Pilgrims were somewhat better supplied with food. One after another fell ill, and at one time only six or seven were well enough to take any care of the others.

Hardships of the first winter

PILGRIM CRADLE
(It belonged to the Pilgrims' doctor)

The minister, William Brewster, and the brave soldier Miles Standish, were the most tender nurses that could be imagined; but in spite of their care, more than half the company died in the first three months, sometimes two or three in a day. Before they left the Mayflower a baby was born to Mrs. White, and was named Peregrine from the Latin word *peregrinus* meaning a wanderer. Strangely enough this little child was one of the survivors of the hard winter. The graves of those who died were leveled with the ground and sown with wheat, for Indians had been seen, and there was danger that they would attack the little settlement if they knew how many had died and how few were left to defend it.

One morning in the spring an Indian appeared who did not skulk behind the trees like the others, but walked straight into the centre of the village and called out, "Welcome, Englishmen, Welcome!" The Pilgrims must have felt very much pleased to have a word of greeting in the strange land. The Indian's name was Samoset. He had been among the fishermen farther north and had learned a little English. It was only a very little, but he made the Pilgrims understand that he had a friend, Squanto, who had been carried to England by one of the early explorers, and that Squanto could speak English well.

Samoset and Squanto

STANDISH'S SWORD

Before long the Indian chief, Massasoit, came with a number of attendants and Squanto for interpreter. Massasoit had dangerous enemies, — the Narragansetts, — and he wished to make a treaty with the white people so that he might have aid if he was attacked. The Pilgrims gave the chief and his attendants some presents and feasted them. Then the two parties made a solemn promise that they would assist each other, and that if a member of either party injured one of the other, he should be punished, whether he was an Indian or a white man. This treaty was kept for more than fifty years.

Treaty with the Indians

The Pilgrims did not waste their time searching for gold; they cleared the land and planted corn. Squanto showed them the Indian way of making sure of a rich soil for the corn by putting a small fish into each hill, and he taught them many other things that helped them to live in the new country. When the first autumn came, they

WILLIAM BRADFORD'S ARMCHAIR

PILGRIMS GOING TO CHURCH
(From a painting by G. H. Boughton)

The first Thanksgiving

were so happy at having a good harvest that Governor Bradford appointed a day for Thanksgiving, and invited Massasoit and ninety of his men to a three-days' feast.

Not all the red men were as friendly as Massasoit. One day a Narragansett Indian strode into Plymouth and asked for Squanto. "He has gone fishing," was the reply. Then the Indian threw down a queer looking object and stalked away. This proved to be a rattlesnake's skin wrapped around a bundle of arrows. There was little difficulty in guessing what that meant. The Narragansetts were a large tribe, but it would not do for the little company

Trouble with the Indians

of colonists to show that they were afraid, and Governor Bradford stuffed the snakeskin full of powder and bullets and sent it back with the message, "If you want fighting, come whenever you like, and we will give you enough of it." Canonicus, chief of the Narragansetts, knew that powder and bullets did much damage in some mysterious way, and he was afraid to have the dangerous things about. He contrived to have them taken away from his lands, and for a long time there was no trouble with the Narragansetts. Other tribes threatened the colony, but the valiant Miles Standish went out with his

> "Great, invincible army,
> Twelve men, all equipped, having each his rest and his matchlock,"

and came back victorious.

Plymouth was five hundred miles from the nearest English settlement, and three thousand miles from its king, but the colonists seemed to get along very well without a king. Whenever they needed to decide any important question, they held a meeting to talk it over. Then they voted, and the matter was decided as the greater number wished. This assembly was the beginning of the New England town meetings of to-day.

Town meeting

In England there had often been such wild revelings on Christmas and other church holidays that the Pilgrims had decided to make no difference between these days and others. After a while, some people joined the Plymouth colony who did not agree with this decision; and on Christmas morning, when the governor called the men out to work as

GOVERNOR BRADFORD DEFIES THE NARRAGANSETTS

usual, they said it went against their consciences to work on Christmas Day. "Very well," said the governor, "no one shall force you to act against your consciences, and I will spare you until you are better informed." At noon, the governor found these men having a fine time playing ball and other games. He stood looking at them a moment; then he said, "It goes against

Christmas in Plymouth

your consciences to work, but it goes against *my* conscience to see you play while others work; so if you wish to keep Christmas as a church day, go to your own houses." He took away their ball, and they gave up their attempt to celebrate Christmas. Such were the Pilgrim consciences.

MILES STANDISH'S ARMY

The Pilgrims suffered almost as much as the settlers of Jamestown, but when trouble came to Jamestown, the colonists would say, "Let us go away. We shall never make our fortunes here." When trouble came to Plymouth, the Pilgrims would say, "We have come here to worship God in freedom, and He will not forget us." This is why the Pilgrims were never discouraged, and why they were happy in spite of all their hardships.

Why the Pilgrims were happy

SUMMARY.

Persecution in England drove the Pilgrims to Holland and then to America.

They founded a settlement at Plymouth, but more than half the colonists died the first winter.

The neighboring Indians were friendly, and the white men were victorious over the hostile tribes.

The Pilgrims cultivated the ground instead of searching for gold.

The New England town meeting originated in the Plymouth assembly for the discussion of important questions.

SUGGESTIONS FOR WRITTEN WORK.

What the last body of explorers reported to the Pilgrims waiting on the Mayflower.

The best way to celebrate Forefathers' Day.

One of the older children tells Peregrine White about leaving England.

VII

THE MASSACHUSETTS BAY COLONY

ONE day some Puritans were talking of what the Pilgrims had done to find a home where they could worship God as they thought right. Some one suggested, "Would it not be well for us also to make a settlement in America?" The longer they talked, the more interested they became in the plan. Then they wrote to several of their Puritan friends in different parts of the country, and a number of them agreed to unite in forming a colony. *The Puritans plan a settlement*

The Pilgrims were not rich people, and they had been obliged to borrow money to carry them to America, but many of the Puritans were wealthy, and every year their party in England was becoming stronger. They formed the Massachusetts Bay Company and bought of the Plymouth Company what is now the greater part of Massachusetts. They induced King Charles, son and successor of King James, to give them a charter, allowing them to make laws for the colony. Only one year after the little company of friends had talked about America,

KING CHARLES I

a shipload of Puritans were ready to cross the ocean. They landed north of Boston, and settled at a place to which they gave the name Salem. "Salem" is a Bible word meaning peace, and they hoped that here they would find peace. *Founding of Salem*

The Puritans in England were becoming more and more troubled. King Charles meant to rule the country just as he chose without the least regard to what any one else thought, and he was so untruthful that no one could trust his promises. Some people began to fear that there would be war between those who stood by the king and those who were against him. No one knew how such a war might end. If the king should win, he would be more opposed to the Puritans than ever; but if they had flourishing colonies in America, there would be one place where they could live in safety. In the king's charter not a word had been said about where the Massachusetts Company should hold their meetings. They decided to hold them, not in England, but beside Massachusetts Bay. It is quite possible that the king knew nothing about their decision until they had gone. Even then, he did not object, and it may be that he was glad to have so many who did not agree with him go out of the country.

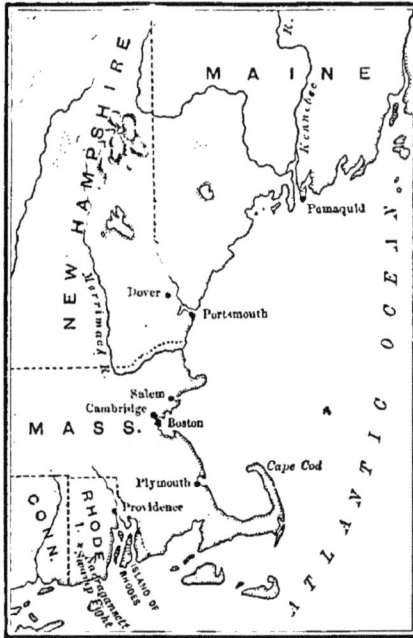

THE NEW ENGLAND COAST SETTLEMENTS

A little later the English Puritans were pleased and encouraged, because John Winthrop, a man whom they greatly respected, said that he would go to America. He was not only rich and well educated, but he was so wise that almost all who knew him felt that whatever he advised was the best thing to do. He set out in 1630 with a great company of

ARRIVAL OF THE WINTHROP COLONY IN BOSTON
·(From W. F. Halsall's painting)

early one thousand persons. They brought cattle, goats, pro-
isions, arms, tools, and farming implements. Several ships were
eeded to carry so many people, and among them was the May-
ower, that had brought the Pilgrims to Plymouth, and had also
iken the settlers to Salem. Governor Winthrop and his party
ecided to make their home where Boston now is. They called
he place Boston, because many of the colonists came from Boston
1 England.

These people had been accustomed to living in comfort, and in
pite of all their careful preparations the first winter was almost Early hard-
s hard for them as it had been for the other colonists. Provi- ships
ons became scarce, and Governor Winthrop was obliged to
ppeal to the Pilgrims for help. A generous supply of food came
·om Plymouth. When that was gone, he asked the people of
oston to spend a certain day in fasting and prayer that God

would help them. The help came, for a ship laden with provisions sailed into the harbor, and instead of fasting, they kept a day of thanksgiving.

The lives of the Puritans were hard, but nevertheless Governor Winthrop wrote to England that he had never felt more contented

Contentment of the Puritans

than in Massachusetts. Another governor of the colony wrote home to his Puritan friends that if they wished to make money, Massachusetts was not the place for them; but if they wished to have plenty of wood to burn and to build their houses with, pure air to breathe, good water to drink, ground to plant, seas and rivers to fish in, and if, above all, they wished to be free to worship God as they thought right, all these good things were waiting for them in Massachusetts.

WINTHROP CUP
(Given by Winthrop
to the First Church,
Boston)

Governor Winthrop was so honest and truthful in all his dealings with the Indians that they called him "Single Tongue," meaning that he never told two stories about anything. He was always ready to do a kindness. It was reported to him one day that a poor man was stealing his wood, and he declared sternly, "I'll soon put a stop to that;" but to the poor man he said, "Friend, I fear that you have not wood enough for the winter. Help yourself from my pile whenever you choose." Then he went to his informer and said, "Didn't I tell you I would put a stop to it? Find him stealing if you can!"

The great fault of the Puritans was that they could not under-

Puritan narrowness

stand how any one else could be as earnest as they in wishing to serve God and yet not go about it in the Puritan way. They had borne a great deal for the sake of living as they believed right, and they meant to govern the new land as they thought best, and to allow no one to stay among them who did not agree with their ideas. They had town meetings like those of the Plymouth people, but they would let only members of their church vote.

The ship that brought them food when they were in such great
ed brought also a talented young clergyman named Roger Roger Wil-liams
illiams. He too wished to serve God, but he had some ideas
at seemed to the Puritans very wrong. He said that King
arles had no right to give away the land of the Indians unless
ey were willing. "What would the king say to that?" whis-
red the colonists to one another. "He might even take away
r charter." Still worse, Roger Williams de-
ared that it was not right to compel a man
attend church or to pay for the support of
church against his will.

The Puritans did not wish to be obliged
attend the Episcopal Church, but they
d wish to oblige whoever came to
oston to attend their church. It
ould not do to have such ideas as
oger Williams's in their colony,
ey thought, and they told him
at the following spring he must
ave Massachusetts. John Win-
rop contrived to send word to
m that they were intending to
nd him back to England; so
stead of waiting for spring, he
ent away from the colony in
e bitterly cold weather. The

FIRST TOWN HOUSE IN BOSTON, 1658

le of his life in the forest in snow and storm will be told in the
ory of the founding of Rhode Island.

To have their children grow up without good schools was some-
ing that the Puritans could not bear. At first the parents Harvard College founded
ught their children at home as well as people who were so busy
uld teach, but only five years after the settlement in the wilder-

ness was begun, a public school was opened in Boston. Many of the Puritans were graduates of English universities, and they wished to make sure that when their ministers died other educated men would be ready to fill the vacant places. They talked the matter over in town meeting, and finally, in 1636, they agreed to give four hundred pounds to found a college.

At that time spending public money for instruction was very unusual in Europe. This generous appropriation shows how much the Puritans cared for education. They used to go to the college to hear the boys declaim in Latin and in Greek, and when one did especially well, his father was happy, and he would say to himself, "Perhaps my son will some day be a minister and preach in our church."

JOHN HARVARD
(From French's statue in Cambridge)

John Harvard

A clergyman named John Harvard died soon after the college was founded, and when his will was read it was found that he had left his books and half his money to the new school. The name "Harvard" was given in his honor. There were other gifts. The state gave a year's rent of a ferry. Plymouth and the other settlements that began to be scattered through New England were ready to help, and once each family gave a peck of corn or its value in wampum. A law was soon made that in every Puritan village of fifty families there must be a school; and if there were one hundred families, a school master must be engaged who could prepare the boys of the town for the university.

John Eliot teaches the Indians

Another reason why the college was founded was that the Indians might have an opportunity to be educated and to learn Christianity. A clergyman named John Eliot was especially

terested in them.   He not only preached, but he translated the
ible into their language.   He did even more; he lived in the
igwams and taught the Indians as if they were his children,
d tried his best to answer all the questions that they asked.
ome of these questions were not easy.   "If the soul is shut up
 iron," said they, "can it get out?"   Another question was,
When you vote and make a man your governor, how do you
now that he will be a good governor?"   Another was, "Ought
wise man to obey an unwise chief?"

John Eliot was never weary of helping them in every way that
e could.   He taught the women to spin, and he showed the men   **Progress of**
etter ways of tilling the ground.   Many Indians learned to read   **the Indians**
d write English, and finally one of them delighted the Puritans
y graduating at Harvard.

Life was growing a little easier for the settlers.   There was
lenty of food, they had schools and a college, and they had
nt away Roger Williams, whose ideas about the church dif-
red from their own.   Their next trouble came from the
uakers.   The Quaker idea of what was right and what was
rong sometimes differed greatly not only from the Puritan
ea, but from that of all the other English people: for in-
ance, a Quaker would not take off his hat even to the king,
cause he thought that to do so would be showing to man a
verence which belonged to God alone.   Other people thought
at this refusal showed scorn of the king's authority, and
e village of Boston was much alarmed when it was known
at a few Quakers had come from England.

These early Quakers were so different from those of later
ys, and even from those who lived in Boston soon after
ese times, that it seems as if their minds must have been

QUAKER DRESS

balanced by the persecutions in England.   They certainly
d strange things.   One man forced his way into the court and

The Quakers and the Puritans accused the judge of putting innocent men to death. Anothe went into the church with a glass bottle in each hand, and in the midst of the service broke the bottles before the people, and cried, "Thus will the Lord break you all in pieces."

The Puritans banished them, but they refused to stay away, fo they said that they should obey God rather than man, and Goc wished them to preach to the people of Massachusetts. Then they were imprisoned or whipped or branded with hot irons. These penalties were brutal, but they were less severe than those in flicted in England upon men who disobeyed the laws for while to-day a man is hanged only for wilful mur der or for treason, there were then in England two hundred offenses for which one might lose his life Finally, four Quakers who returned a second and even a third time after being ordered to stay away were pu to death. The Puritans wrote to the king that these four were hanged because they persisted in refusing tc obey the laws of the colony. This was true, but if the Puritans had not been quite so sure that their belie was the only right one, it may be that they would have had more charity for the Quakers and would not have made such severe laws against them.

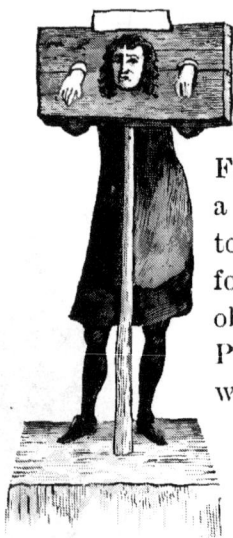

THE PILLORY
(One of the Puritan pun-
ishments)

In 1675, almost twenty years after the coming o the Quakers, there was a terrible war between In dians and colonists. Massasoit was always true tc the English, but after he was dead, his son, "King Philip," as he was called, had different ideas. Many more white King Philip's War men had come, little villages were everywhere, and Philip fel that if the English were not driven out at once, the country would be lost to the Indians. He persuaded other tribes to join him, and they made fierce attacks upon one village after another in Massachusetts, Rhode Island, and Connecticut. In Massahusetts more than half the towns were either partly or wholly destroyed. One thousand men and large numbers of women and children were slain.

At last King Philip was besieged at Mount Hope in Rhode Island. One of his men advised him to surrender, but Philip was so angry that he struck the man dead in a moment. In revenge, the dead man's brother crept away to the whites, and told them where to find his chief. Philip was slain, and his head was fastened to a pole and set up on the green in Plymouth. After this war, southern New England had no more trouble from the Indians.

Death of King Philip

When the Puritans had been in America more than half a century, they became greatly alarmed, because they believed that there were witches among them, and witches were thought to be special friends of Satan. Some nervous girls played various pranks, and declared, probably more in fun than in earnest, that they could not help it, for they were "bewitched." When they saw that the matter was taken seriously, it is very likely that they became so excited that they could not control themselves, and began to believe their own stories. These girls and others began to point out those who had bewitched them, and before the colonists came to their senses, nineteen innocent people had been hanged.

KING PHILIP
(After Paul Revere's picture)

Witchcraft

All over Europe people thought that there was such a thing as witchcraft. A century before the Puritans crossed the ocean, five hundred persons were put to death in three months on the charge of being witches. Fifty years after this alarm in Massachusetts a new law was made against them in England, and many people were executed.

SUMMARY.

English Puritans formed the Massachusetts Bay Company to insure then a refuge in time of persecution and a place for freedom of worship.

Under the leadership of John Winthrop they founded Boston in 1630.

They did not wish to have any one in the colony whose belief differe from theirs; therefore they drove away Roger Williams, and later th Quakers.

Harvard College was founded in 1636 to educate both whites and Indian: John Eliot did much good as a missionary to the Indians.

King Philip's War in 1675 caused many deaths and was the last of th Indian troubles in southern New England.

The Puritans executed nineteen persons for supposed witchcraft.

SUGGESTIONS FOR WRITTEN WORK.

A Puritan tells a friend why he wishes to go to New England.

The reply of the Pilgrims to Winthrop's appeal for food.

King Philip tells his men why he wishes to make war upon the whites.

VIII

MAINE, NEW HAMPSHIRE, RHODE ISLAND, ANI CONNECTICUT

MAINE AND NEW HAMPSHIRE.

The kidnapping of Squanto

WHEN the Indian Squanto, who was so good a friend to th Pilgrims, was a young man, he lived on the coast of what is now called Maine. One day a ship came to anchor near the shore, an the Indians paddled out in their birch-bark canoes to see the whit men and sell furs to them. Squanto and four others were seize and carried away across the ocean, for the captain thought tha after they had learned English they could be brought back an made to serve as interpreters when the white men wished to trade.

It was an unpardonable crime. The only good thing about the whole story was that these five Indians were very kindly treated in England. Squanto and two others were taken into the family of Sir Ferdinando Gorges, who was a friend of Sir Walter Raleigh. Sir Ferdinando was only a few years older than the Indians, and he was much interested in them. It was not long before they could talk with him, and they told him so much about their friends and their home, the clear air, the pure water, and the great forests, that Sir Ferdinando and others began to be eager to found a colony. Squanto in England

Sir Ferdinando had no trouble in finding sailors who would go to Maine and bring back a cargo of fish or furs, but colonizing was a different matter, for the men who first tried to make a settlement had reported that the place was too cold to live in. Still he was not discouraged. He sent out ship after ship to fish and to Attempts to found a colony in Maine

THE BEAVER
(An important New England fur-bearer)

trade, and finally he persuaded one captain, who was also a physician, to spend the winter near where Saco now stands. This captain went home in the spring and said that the climate was perfect, and that not one of his men had even had a headache.

A few years after John Smith returned to England from Jamestown, he sailed as captain of one of Sir Ferdinando's vessels. Sixteen men were with him who had agreed to become colonists, and with such a leader to help and advise them, it is probable that they would have succeeded; but wherever John Smith went, he met with adventures, and so it was on this trip. England and John Smith again

France were at war, and a French vessel took the captain and his sixteen men prisoners, and carried them to France.

Still Sir Ferdinando did not give up. He united with a brave resolute man, Captain John Mason, who had been in Newfound land and was not afraid of the cold weather of Maine. These two men and others who joined with them published glowing descrip tions of the new country. They said the climate was the mos delightful in the world, the soil was so rich that generous har vests could be raised with little work, the forests were full of fur-bearing animals, and the great trees were the best timber for ship-building that could be found. Besides all this, the bays and the rivers were swarming with fish.

Colonists began to go to the new province, which was after wards named Maine, or the *mainland*. The colonies were hardly more than fishing stations, and were scattered about over the southwestern corner of what is now Maine, and the eastern part of what is now New Hamp shire. It is probable that the first settle ment in Maine was made at Pemaquid Point in 1625. This soon became a busy place. Indians who had furs to sell came to Pemaquid, and ships came from England not only to bring tools

THE OLD SOUTH MEETING-HOUSE[1]

and other things that the colonists needed, but to carry back to England lumber and furs, and the fish that had been caught and cured. The Pilgrims were culti vating corn, and they used to send boatloads of it to Pemaquid to

Dover and Portsmouth

exchange for furs. The earliest settlements in New Hampshire were made at Dover, 1623–1627, and at Portsmouth in 1631.

[1] This brick structure, still standing, was erected in 1729 on the site of th wooden building mentioned on page 73, of which there is no picture.

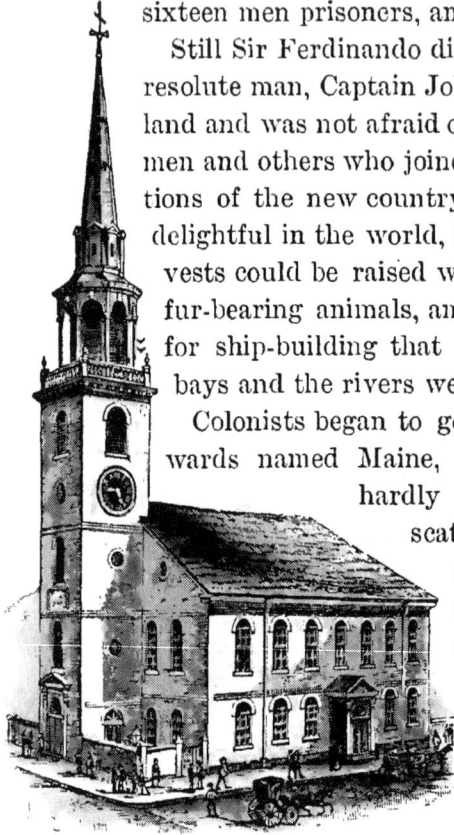

After a while Sir Ferdinando and Captain Mason concluded to divide their land; the former took Maine, and the latter took the land to the west of the Piscataqua River. Captain Mason was once governor of a town in Hampshire, England, and in memory of this he named his land New Hampshire. How far west this land extended was uncertain, and what is now called Vermont was claimed at times by both New Hampshire and New York.

In 1641 the few scattered settlements in New Hampshire asked the protection of the Massachusetts Bay colony. As for Maine, after Sir Ferdinando died, his grandson offered to sell the land to the English king, Charles II. The king was a little slow in giving his answer, but Massachusetts was quick, and before Charles II. had decided whether he could raise the money or not, Massachusetts

The colony divided

BLOCKHOUSE IN MAINE
(Built near the junction of the Kennebec and Sebasticook rivers)

had bought the land and paid for it. The king was angry that a colony should dare to do such a thing as to buy land that he wished to have. Boston wrote him a letter saying that she was sorry to have displeased his Majesty, but she made no offer to give back the purchase. One man in Boston wrote indignantly to a friend in England that the king's letter was worth no more in Massachusetts than an old London newspaper.

Maine joined to Massachusetts

This was hardly true, but it was true that more than once when the king had made a law which would injure the colony, Massachusetts had quietly disobeyed it. More than that, the Puritans would not allow the Episcopal Church in their colony, and this did much to arouse the wrath of the king. Charles sent over and demanded their charter. The Puritans held a town meeting in the Old South Meeting-House, and every man voted

Massachusetts loses her charter

not to return it. Then the king declared that whether the char
ter was in England or in America, it should no longer hold good
He planned to send over one of the most cruel, hard-hearted mer
in England as governor; but before this could be done, the king
died. The charter, however, no longer had any value.

New Hamp-
shire and
Massachu-
setts royal
provinces
New Hampshire had been made a "royal province," and nov
the new king declared that Massachusetts, Plymouth, and Maine
should form another. These colonies could no longer choose thei
own officers, but must be ruled by whatever governor the king
chose to send them.

RHODE ISLAND.

FIRST MEETING-HOUSE IN SALEM
(Where Roger Williams is said to have preached)

When Roger Williams was ordered to leave Massachusetts, the
court told him that he might remaii
until spring. They thought that he
would keep still if they showed him so
much favor; but instead of keeping still
he preached oftener than ever. Ther
the court said he must be taken to Eng
land, and a boat was sent to Salem to
bring him to Boston. However, wher
the officers landed in Salem, Roger Wil
liams was nowhere to be found. Some
one had warned him secretly, and he hac
slipped away. The one who warnec
him was, as has been said, no less a mai
than John Winthrop, and with the warn
ing had come the advice to go to the
Indians about Narragansett Bay, because that place was fre
from any English claim.

Roger Wil-
liams leaves
Salem
It was a cold, snowy night when the message came, but ther
was no time to lose, so Roger Williams said good-by to his wif

and children, took his staff, and went out bravely into the wilderness. When he was an old man, he said he could "feel yet" the winter snow of that journey.

For more than three months he lived in the forest. Sometimes he had a guide, but oftener he found his way alone as best he might. Sometimes he slept in a hollow tree; often he had no fire. He had friends in the forest, however, for he had always been kind to the Indians and had learned their language. They were glad to repay his kindness, and when he came to the wigwam of Massasoit, there was a warm welcome awaiting him. Canonicus, too, the fierce warrior who had sent to Plymouth the bundle of arrows bound together with a rattlesnake's skin, gave him tender greeting, and "loved him as a son." *His wanderings*

Possibly Roger Williams had no thought of founding a colony. He had always cared for the Indians, and now that the whites would not listen to him, perhaps he meant to live among the red men and teach them. Five friends came to him from Massachusetts, however, and they paddled down the Providence River in search of a place to settle. Some Indians saw them and called out in friendly welcome, "What cheer? What cheer?" an old-fashioned form of greeting that they had learned from the whites. He ran ashore and had a little talk with these Indians. Probably they told him of a good place for his house, at the foot of a hill near a spring of water. This was in 1636, and was the beginning of the city of Providence, so called because, as Roger Williams said, it was by the providence of God that he had made his way thither. *Providence founded*

The exile's wife and children soon came to him. Governor Winslow of Plymouth visited him and gave him a piece of gold. The Puritans wished people to worship God in their way; Roger Williams wished every one that came to his colony to be free to worship God in any way that he thought right. Before two years *Growth of the colony* had passed, many had come. He was in the country of the Narragansetts, and Canonicus was glad to sell his friend what land he wanted for a colony.

Among those who came from Massachusetts was a company

Rhode Island and Providence Plantations

that meant to go farther south, but Roger Williams urged them to stay near him, and Canonicus was willing to sell them the Isle of Rhodes, or Rhode Island. The two colonies made a kind of agreement to help each other. That is why the smallest state in the Union has the longest name, for the name that must be used in legal documents is "State of Rhode Island and Providence Plantations."

This tiny state was almost the only place in the world where some one form of worship was not favored. It is no wonder that people with all kinds of ideas came to settle beside Narragansett Bay. It has been said that "if a man had lost his religious opinions, he might have been sure to find them again in some village of Rhode Island."[1]

ROGER WILLIAMS
(From the statue in Providence)

A few years later, Massachusetts, Plymouth, Connecticut, and New Haven agreed to defend one another if there was need. Rhode Island would have been glad to join the league, but the others said this could not be unless the colony would be-

The New England Confederacy

come a part of either Massachusetts or Plymouth. Maine, too, was shut out, because the laws of Maine favored the Episcopal Church.

Rhode Island asks for a charter

It seemed impossible for the little state to stand alone without some protection, and the Rhode Islanders sent Roger Williams to England to ask for a charter. The story of what he had done for the Indians had gone before him, and the English government

[1] Bancroft's *History of the United States.*

rillingly gave him a charter, allowing the Rhode Island colonists
:eedom to make whatever laws they thought best and to choose
1eir own governor and other officers. Roger Williams crossed
1e ocean again, happy in the news that he was bringing to the
ɔlony. When he came to the bank of the river that flowed by
is house, he saw that the whole shore was lined with canoes, for
1e people of Providence had all come out to welcome the man
rhom they respected and loved. His canoe was placed in the
1idst, and so they paddled to the farther shore.

It is no wonder that they welcomed him, for Roger Williams
'as one of the most lovable men that appear in all the colonial
istory. The Puritans had driven him into the wilderness, and
1en had made him lose many thousand pounds by forbidding him
ɔ send goods from the port of Boston to England, but even of
1em he had not a hard word to say, and when the opportunity
ame to do them a favor, he did it as eagerly as if they had been
is warmest friends. *Roger Williams's character*

CONNECTICUT.

A colony that is only sixteen years of age seems hardly old
1ough to begin to found other colonies, but this is just what
[assachusetts did. Not long after the coming of the Puritans,
1e chief of the country along the Connecticut River had asked
ɔth Massachusetts and Plymouth to send Englishmen to settle
n his lands. Some of the colonists began to think of going there
ɔ trade. It was an especially good place, for the Indians could
1uch more easily float down the stream with their canoes full of
1rs than they could make their way through the forest and bring
1e furs on their backs. *English invited to settle on the Connecticut*

The English were not the only ones who saw that it was worth
·hile to get possession of this valuable river. The Dutch were
ɛttled in New York, and they had forts in New Jersey. They too *Trouble with the Dutch*

wished to hold the Connecticut. The Plymouth people thought that the English had a better right to the territory than the Dutch, and a few of them set out for the mouth of the river. They carried with them the frame of a house, and, although the Dutch threatened to fire upon them from the fort at Hartford, kept on up the river. When they were where Windsor now is, they set up their house, and began to trade for furs as calmly as if there was not a Dutchman in the land. Others came, the Dutch were driven out, and in Hartford, the very place where the Dutch fort had stood, there was soon a small company of Englishmen.

INDIAN FUR-TRADERS

It was a hard winter, and it may be that report made the

Puritans decide to settle in Connecticut

sufferings of the settlers even worse than they really were, for several hundred people who lived near Boston were thinking about moving to Connecticut, and the other colonists did not wish to have them leave Massachusetts. Those who wished to go said that the towns in Massachusetts were so near together that there was not pasture for their cattle. "But you have made a solemn promise to support and aid our commonwealth," said the court. "That is true," answered they, "but how better can we support it than by keeping both the Dutch and the English who do not think as we do from settling so near us?" There was also another reason for moving, but little was said about it. In the Massachusetts colonies no one was allowed to vote who was not a member of the Puritan church; and most of the people who wished to move to Connecticut thought that every man should have a right to vote. At last the court agreed that they might go.

The first settlers were led by their pastor, Thomas Hooker, of Cambridge. There were about one hundred in this company, and they must have had a delightful journey. It was June. The trees were green, and the flowers were in bloom. Through the forest they went, making their beds of the boughs of trees, sleeping under the stars, and waking to the singing of birds. Two weeks they spent on the journey, and it must have seemed almost like a picnic two weeks long. There was no fear of hunger, for before them they drove one hundred and sixty cattle, and there was sure to be plenty of milk, even if all other food failed.

A forest journey

These were the people who in 1636 founded Hartford. Others came, and within a few months Wethersfield and Windsor were settled by colonists from other towns near Boston. A few people had come to these places before, but until 1636 there were not enough to call their coming the founding of a town.

Settlements established

Three years later the three towns formed a union and decided upon the laws that should govern them. These laws allowed every man to vote, whether he was a member of the church or not. There was one thing that would certainly have aroused the king's wrath if he had not been too busy to pay any attention to it, and this was that these laws did not even

FIRST MEETING-HOUSE IN HARTFORD

mention his Majesty. Evidently the Connecticut settlers thought that they could manage their own affairs without any help from the king.

Before the colonists were fairly settled in their new home, there was trouble with the Pequots. These Indians did not make any general attack, but they would come as near the settlement as they dared, and seize one man or a small group of men and put them to death. Roger Williams learned that the Pequots were trying to persuade the Narragansetts to join them in making war upon the whites. He did not stop to remember how Massachusetts had treated him, but without a moment's delay he sent word to Governor Winthrop of the danger. He did much more than to send a message. He knew that the Pequots would try to persuade the Narragansetts to join them, and in wild, stormy

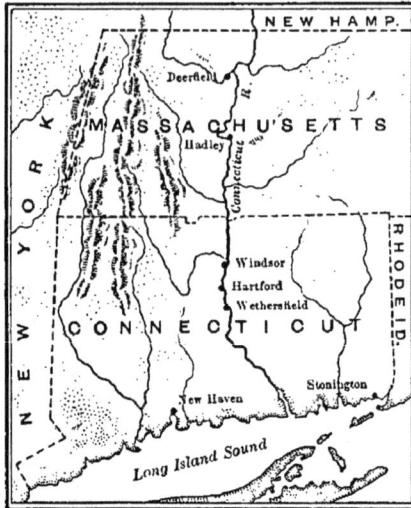

CONNECTICUT VALLEY SETTLEMENTS

weather he paddled his canoe across Narragansett Bay, and went straight to the wigwam of Canonicus. There stood the Pequot messengers, and Canonicus was on the point of yielding

They knew why Roger Williams had come. They glared at him angrily, and would have killed him if they had dared. Canonicus, too, would have killed any other man who had come so boldly into his wigwam ; but he was very fond of Roger Williams, and he listened closely to what he had to say. It was several days before the chief would decide. Roger Williams talked, and the Pequots talked. When they lay down to sleep at night, the white man hardly expected to be alive in the morning. At last Canonicus told the Pequots that he would not unite with them.

In the wig-
wam of Ca-
nonicus

The Pequots decided to make war without help, and all through the winter they put to death every colonist that they could seize.

Then Connecticut appealed to Massachusetts and Plymouth for The Pequot War help. Near where Stonington, Connecticut, now stands was a Pequot village. Around it was a stout palisade, or fence of tree trunks set close together in the ground. There were but two

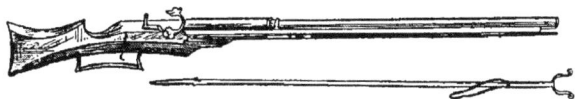

MATCHLOCK AND REST

openings, and those were very narrow. The colonists closed them and threw lighted torches over the palisades. The wigvams blazed, and out of seven hundred Pequots only five escaped. For nearly forty years no Indians dared to attack the English.

One month after this terrible fight, New Haven was founded, in 1638. Hartford had been settled by men who thought the Founding of New Haven Bostonians were too strict. New Haven was settled by a company from England who feared that Boston was not strict enough. This company was made up chiefly of wealthy merchants; and just as the Reverend Thomas Hooker had led his church to Hartford, so the Reverend John Davenport led his church to New Haven. Boston would have been glad to have them stay in Massachusetts, but they had landed just after the banishment of Roger Williams, when Boston seemed to be full of new opinions, and religious matters were being discussed more freely than Davenport thought was right; and that is why he made his way through the forest to Connecticut. He paid the Indians ten coats for a piece of land on the coast, and here he founded New Haven.

A NEW ENGLAND STOCKADE

From almost the first Connecticut had good schools, for these people were as eager as those in Massachusetts for the education

Education in Connecticut of their children. In 1700 ten men from the different settlement came together to found a college. Each laid a few books on table and said, "I give these books for the founding of a colleg in this colony." This little pile of books was the beginning o Yale College.

The land about the river was rich, and there was plenty o

HOUSE WHERE YALE COLLEGE WAS FOUNDED ·
(It was the home of Rev. Samuel Russell, in Branford, Conn.)

food. The laws wer strict, but no man wa persecuted for thinkin; what he would on re ligious subjects. I was a quiet, happ) peaceful country, an(later it was nickname("The Land of Stead; Habits."

When Massachusetts Plymouth, and Main were united as a roya province, the first governor was determined to seize the charte of Connecticut, and he went to Hartford with a company of sol diers to get possession of it. He and the Connecticut official discussed the matter all one afternoon. The governor would no yield, and at last the charter was brought in and placed upon ; table. It grew dark and candles were lighted. Then, tradition The Charter Oak says, the candles were suddenly put out, and when they wer lighted again, no charter was to be seen. Long afterwards, Con necticut presented one Captain Wadsworth with a sum of money saying that he had cared for the charter "in a very troublesom(season." It is thought that he hid it in an oak-tree, and a tree ii Hartford which fell half a century ago was often pointed out as the "Charter Oak" in which the charter was concealed.

SUMMARY.

Maine and New Hampshire. The kidnapping of Squanto aroused the interest of Sir Ferdinando Gorges in Maine.

Gorges and Mason made their first settlements at Pemaquid Point in Maine and Portsmouth in New Hampshire.

Massachusetts bought Maine from Gorges, and Maine, Massachusetts Bay, and Plymouth were united in one crown colony.

Rhode Island. Roger Williams, driven from Massachusetts, was befriended by the Indians. He founded Providence in 1636, and gave religious freedom to all who came. A company from Massachusetts settled Rhode Island, and Williams obtained a charter from the king.

Connecticut. Wethersfield, Windsor, and Hartford were settled from Massachusetts, in spite of the claims of the Dutch.

They were quiet, peaceful colonies, save for the war with the Pequots. They established schools and Yale College.

SUGGESTIONS FOR WRITTEN WORK.

Squanto tells Sir Ferdinand about his capture.

Describe Roger Williams's setting out into the forest.

Describe the Connecticut colonists traveling through the forest.

Describe the scene when Roger Williams entered the wigwam of Canonicus.

IX

EARLY CUSTOMS OF NEW ENGLAND

WHEN a settler comes to a new land, his first thought is to make some kind of shelter for himself. The first houses in New England were built of logs, for wood was plenty and easy to work. The chinks between the logs were filled with chips and clay. Glass was expensive, and in the earliest days oiled paper was used for windows. Since wood was to be had for the cutting, the fireplaces were made large enough for the great logs that were brought in from the forest. There was plenty of heat, but so large a share of it went up the chimney that people cannot have been very comfortable, according to our ideas of comfort.

It was the custom to "bank up" the house for winter, that is, to pile up a bank of earth around it to keep out the cold.

AN EARLY SETTLER'S HOUSE

Stoves were not used until long after the Pilgrims came, and they cannot have been very good for one writer of those days said that he could hardly keep his ink from freezing even when it was close beside the stove. There was no way of heating the meeting-houses. Babies only a few days old were brought into these frigid buildings to be baptized with water in which the ice had to be broken. Women sometimes carried little foot-stoves, which cannot have given out much warmth; and there the people sat through the long sermons. They would have thought themselves exceedingly wicked if any discomfort had made them wish to go home.

In the house the important place was the kitchen. There was the great fireplace with its iron crane, a long arm that stretched out over the fire and could be moved back and forth. "Pot-hooks" were hung to this, and from these hung kettles. Tin "bake-ovens," like small cupboards open at one side, were set up before the fire, and in them were baked biscuit; or on hooks inside pieces of meat were fastened to roast. Strong hooks were fixed into the beams that ran across the top of the room. Poles were laid on these, and from them strings of dried apples or pumpkin were suspended. Sometimes a chain hung from these hooks in front of the fire and held a turkey or a chicken to be roasted before the blaze. "Brick ovens" were made after a while. They were little brick caverns beside the fireplaces. A fire was built in the oven, and when it was well heated the coals were

A FOOT-STOVE

raked out, and the beans and brown bread and chickens and pies and cakes were put in to cook.

The early settlers had stools and benches, but few chairs. They ate from wooden "trenchers," or dishes made by hollowing out pieces of wood. Miles Standish bequeathed twelve of these trenchers in his will. A trencher generally served for two persons, and one large drinking cup was enough for a table. There *Furniture and dishes* were no forks, for they had hardly been introduced into England, but there were knives and wooden or pewter spoons. Pewter dishes were looked upon as elegance itself, and even the poorest housekeeper would not have dared to risk the scorn of her neighbors by leaving her pewter unscoured.

NEW ENGLAND KITCHEN
(Showing crane, brick oven, and beams in the ceiling)

Bedrooms

The bedrooms were icy in the cold New England winters, and it is no wonder that every household had its long-handled warming-pan. This was filled with coals, the cover was shut down and then the pan was drawn back and forth between the sheets. Beds and pillows were valuable articles, and even so great a man as the governor of a colony did not scorn to make a will that bequeathed his daughter a feather bed and a bolster.

The parlor

The parlor, or "best room," had no carpet until the later colonial days, but both it and the kitchen had "sanded" floors; that is, sand was thrown upon the boards, and sometimes so carefully as to make almost a regular pattern. As soon as the colonists became at all comfortable, every house must have a parlor, though it was rarely used except for weddings and funerals and the minister's calls. In the summer the parlor fireplace was filled with sprays of asparagus, or sometimes with laurel leaves.

TINDER BOX
(Showing curved steel, box for tinder, and candle in the cover)

In this parlor there was sure to be a corner cupboard, a buffet, sometimes with glass doors; and when the days of china came, the rare bits were displayed in the upper part, while in the closet below was often the "company cake" and the home-made wine. If a member of the family had died, there was a "mourning piece" on the wall. This was the picture of a gravestone whereon was written the person's name. A woman weeping usually bent over the stone, and a drooping willow filled one side of the picture, or canvas, for sometimes these "pieces" were worked on canvas with silk or worsted.

Home manufactures

The home of the colonist was a real manufactory. There were no "department stores" in those days, and few of the settlers had much ready money. Flax and wool were spun and woven and dyed and made into clothes, all in a man's own house. Stockings and mittens were knit by hand, and hats were made of home-braided straw. Soap was home-made. Butter and cheese were always made at home. To be called a "good butter-hand" was a great honor. For lights, the first settlers had pine-knots. There was no tallow in the earliest days, so candles were made of the beautiful and sweet-smelling pale green bayberry wax.

The men bore their part in these home manu- **The Yankee** factures. In farming implements wood was used **jack-knife** wherever it could be employed, and in the long evenings the jack-knives of the masculine part of the family were kept busy whittling out teeth for rakes, handles for hoes, reels for winding yarn, wooden spoons and dishes, tubs, pails,

FLAX WHEEL

buckets, yokes, flails, snowshoes, skimmers, and handles for axes, and numberless other things. The men made the brooms, sometimes of birch twigs and sometimes of hemlock branches. A Yankee with his jack-knife could almost furnish a house and a barn.

The children did their part of the work of the house. The girls helped their mother, and the boys helped their father. If **Self-reliance** the boys wished for playthings, they made them. If a boy must **of children** have a basket, he made it of birch bark; while for paint he used elderberry or pigeon berry juice. A boy who grew up in this way learned to depend upon himself, and to know what to do if he found himself in any difficulty.

When the Revolutionary War broke out, these boys had become men who were not afraid to try to do things they had never done before. They knew little about military drill, but they could invent new ways of making their attacks, and they could capture forts in ways not laid down in the books. In some of the WOOL SPINNING WHEEL little hamlets away from city life, the old customs lingered far into this century. Many a man, not yet fifty years old, ate in his

Effect of this training boyhood dinners that were cooked in a brick oven, prepared "quills," or pieces of the hollow elder stem, to be wound on the little "quilling wheel" with yarn for use in the shuttle of his mother's loom, and set off for college in a suit of his mother's spinning and weaving. These were the kind of boys who knew an unearned diploma was not worth the parchment it was written on, the kind of boys that the college and the country were proud to possess.

SUMMARY.

The New England colonists lived in log houses, cooked before open fires had simple furniture and wooden or pewter dishes.
They manufactured most of their clothes, tools, and household utensils.
The children learned to be self-reliant, and their training showed in the Revolutionary War.

SUGGESTIONS FOR WRITTEN WORK.

Describe an evening in a colonial kitchen. Tell what each member of the family was doing.
Describe a cold day in a colonial house.

X

NEW YORK, DELAWARE, AND NEW JERSEY

Henry Hudson ABOUT the time when the Pilgrims were planning to leave England and go to Holland, a company of English merchants were making ready to send a ship to search, not for a Northwest Passage, but for a Northeast. They thought there might be a way to sail north of Russia, and then south to eastern Asia. They chose for the captain of their vessel a friend of John Smith, brave English sailor named Henry Hudson. He set out on the voyage, but he had to come back and report that the ice kept him from going to Asia. He had been "farthest north," however, and he found himself famous.

A Dutch company then induced him to command one of their ships. Again the ice prevented him from sailing farther to the northeast, but he made up his mind to go in search of the Northwest Passage instead of returning to Holland. He had with him a letter from John Smith saying that he believed the Passage might be not far north of Chesapeake Bay. One bright September morning Hudson sailed into the mouth of the river that is named for him, though he spoke of it as the "River of Mountains." Up the stream went the little vessel, the Half-Moon, but the water was more and more fresh. Still he kept on, until just beyond where Albany now stands the stream began to grow shallow. This was no Northwest Passage.

THE HALF-MOON LEAVING AMSTERDAM
(Showing the Weepers' Tower, where mariners took leave of their friends)

Hudson made another voyage to Hudson Bay and Hudson Strait, this time for an English company. His crew rebelled, and finally turned him and a few others adrift in a small boat, and no one knows his fate. *Hudson's last voyage*

Hudson had called the country about the "River of Mountains" "as fair a land as can be trodden by the foot of man;" but the Dutch were more interested in the thought that the

Dutch traders in America

North River — as they called the stream, since the Delaware was known as the South River — was convenient for the Indians to float down with canoes full of furs. Furs could be bought for beads, jack-knives, red cloth, and trinkets of various kinds, and could be sold in Europe at a high price. It is no wonder that Dutch traders hastened to send ships to America.

Beginnings of New York

There must be forts to protect the traders, and in 1614 a fort was built on Manhattan Island. That was the beginning of the city of New York. Another name for Holland was the Netherlands, or the lower lands; and the Dutch called their possessions in America New Netherland, just as John Smith called the land north of them New England, and the French named the land that they claimed New France. More forts were built, and one stood where Albany now is. One of the early writers called it "a miserable little fort, built of logs."

FIRST VIEW OF NEW AMSTERDAM
(Sketched by a Dutch officer in 1635)

Settlers on Manhattan Island

Even if the settlers were protected by "miserable little forts," many of them were making fortunes by trading in furs. This was a good thing for the traders, but the Dutch West India Company wished to have permanent settlements, and they began to think of sending colonists to the Hudson. The Indians were delighted to sell Manhattan Island for twenty-four dollars' worth of beads, brass buttons, ribbons, and red cloth. The settlement around the little fort was named New Amsterdam. The settlers lived in log houses, one story high, with roofs made of bark.

People came from most of the countries of Europe. To buy urs for beads and sell them for a generous amount of gold was n easy way to make a fortune, and after making a fortune, the .ext thing was to go back to Europe to spend it. The ompany discussed the matter, and concluded that farm-rs who had been forbidden to deal in furs would be he best settlers. There was rich land all along the 「orth River, but it paid so much better to trade in furs han to manage a farm that the Company knew they ıust make especially good offers to induce people to

DUTCH FLAG

emain farmers. They formed a plan that was entirely different from anything that had been attempted in America.

SETTLEMENTS ABOUT THE HUDSON RIVER

Long before this time it had been the custom in various countries of Europe for one man to hold a large amount of land, and to allow other men to use such parts of it as he chose. These men must work for him so many days every year, and they could not leave one man's land to work for some one else. This custom had gone out of use in Europe, but the Dutch Company thought it might be introduced into America. They offered to give sixteen miles of the Hudson River shore with an indefinite amount of land behind it to any member of the Company who would bring fifty settlers to America.

Patroon system

The owner of this land was called a patroon, r protector. He must clear the land, build houses and barns, nd provide cattle and tools. He was to receive as rent a part f each crop. The colonists were to be free from paying taxes ɔr ten years, but they must agree to remain on his land for that time. The patroon held a court of his own, and had the right to punish any one who broke his laws. Indeed, he could do just about what he chose except to trade in furs. The Company would not give up that right to any one.

In the New England settlements most of the settlers had the

How New Netherland was governed

same ideas of what was good for the colony, and were ready to give up their own wishes for the gain of all. It was not so in New Netherland. The Dutch had come to make money, and in their settlement, if a colonist was becoming rich, he did not care much what became of the colony. In Massachusetts, even after it became a royal province, every member of the church had a vote, but New Netherland was ruled by governors sent over by the Company.

Governor Stuyvesant, the last of these governors, was the best of them, for though he meant to have his own way, he was honest and kept the colony in order. Just as Virginia had demanded a House of Burgesses, so the people of New Netherland wished to elect a council of men to tell what their taxes should be, and to decide how the money should be spent. Stuyvesant finally yielded so far as to allow them to elect the council, but the councilors had no power, for he would pound on the floor with his wooden leg and tell

WALL STREET PALISADE FROM THE EAST RIVER

them what was to be done — and it always was done.

Governor Stuyvesant had in New Amsterdam a great farm, or

The Bowery and Wall Street

bowery, as it was called in Dutch. The lane leading to it was Bowery Lane, and even now the street that is where the lane used to be is called the Bowery. Before New Amsterdam was

;hirty years old, a war broke out between England and Holland; ind lest the English should invade the Dutch city, Governor 3tuyvesant built a stout wooden wall, twelve feet high, directly icross the island. Where this wall ran is now called Wall Street.

The Dutch had good reason to fear being driven away by the English. Holland said, "We were first in the North River." England replied, "Yes, but an Englishman was captain of your vessel; and what is more, John Cabot brought an English ship to America more than a century before you

Dutch and English claims to New Nether land

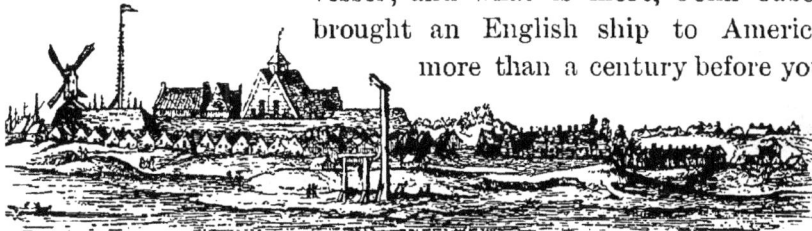

NEW AMSTERDAM
(From a Dutch map published in 1656)

:ame." "True," retorted the Dutch, "but if our captain was an Englishman, yours was an Italian. Moreover, it was your own Queen Elizabeth who said that discovery of a land is nothing; it s colonizing that gives a right to the country. We have had men iere almost ever since Hudson's voyage was made, and the land s ours." But the English said, "King James granted this land to :he London and the Plymouth Companies before Hudson crossed :he ocean. If Dutchmen come here to settle, we are willing; but :hey are on our land, and they are subjects of our king."

The matter was dropped for a time because the English king ind his people did not get along very well together and were too ousy with their own quarrels to give much time to American iffairs. England left the Dutch in peace for a while, but trouble was arising from another direction, and they could not make butter and cheese and smoke their pipes in quiet very long. The <ing of Sweden had been eager to found a colony in America that

Swedes in Delaware

should be open to all Protestants. He died before this could be done, but in 1638 a company of "strong, industrious people" sailed from Sweden to the Delaware River — or South River, as the Dutch called it. Up the wide, beautiful stream they went until they were where Wilmington now stands. There they built a fort and named it Fort Christiana in honor of the little girl, twelve years old, who had become their queen. She was much interested in the colony, and was glad to have her father's plan carried out. This was the beginning of the settlement of Delaware.

DUTCH TANKARD
(Given to the first white girl born in New Netherland, on her marriage)

After a few years, a governor named Printz was sent to rule the colony. He did not mean that any craft should sail up the Delaware River against his will; and when a vessel entered the stream, the sailors must anchor and go on for six leagues in small boats to ask if the governor would allow them to bring up the ship. If his permission was not asked, he would fire upon the vessel, no matter to what nation it belonged.

This was very annoying to the Dutch, for they had a little settlement farther up the Delaware, opposite where Philadelphia now stands, and to be obliged to ask the permission of a Swede whenever they wished to sail up to their own people was rather hard. They said dolefully that the Swedish fort was "extremely well supplied with cannons and men."

DUTCH FLINTLOCK PISTOL

After a while the time came when **The Dutch capture New Sweden** Sweden was too busy making war in Europe to defend her colony on the Delaware. The hot-headed Governor Stuyvesant had borne about as much as he cared to bear, and Governor Printz was greatly surprised one morning to see seven Dutch ships come sailing up his river without asking his permission. There were more men on board, armed and ready to fight, than there were in all the little Swedish settlement, and Governor Printz had to surrender. So it was that the Dutch became masters not only of New Netherland, but of New Sweden. In 1617, only three years after they built their fort on Manhattan Island, they built one where Bergen stands, and this was the first settlement in New Jersey. — New Jersey settled

So far, the Dutch had had matters their own way. They had taken as much land as they chose, and had conquered the Swedes who would not live under their rule, but now trouble was coming upon them. An English fleet sailed into Massachusetts Bay, and the Dutchmen of New Amsterdam were greatly alarmed, but Holland sent a message, "There is nothing to fear. They have only come to oblige Massachusetts to admit the Episcopal Church." There were some Dutch warships

THE STRAND, NOW WHITEHALL STREET, NEW YORK, IN 1673

(The house at the head of the wharf was the first brick house built in the town)

lying off New Amsterdam, but when this dispatch came, Governor Stuyvesant allowed them to sail. The Dutch had made a treaty with the Iroquois, the chief tribe of Indians in that part of the country, but some other red men were making trouble, and the governor and most of his troops had gone up the Hudson to quiet them. One hot August day a messenger dashed into the camp. "The English ships!" he cried. "They have left Boston, and they are coming to Manhattan!" — Trouble for the Dutch

Governor Stuyvesant hurried to Manhattan, and the next day

England claims New Amsterdam

the men-of-war appeared. There were one thousand soldiers on board, and there were six times as many guns as Fort Amsterdam could show. Governor Winthrop came ashore and made it clear to Governor Stuyvesant that the land had been granted to the Massachusetts Bay Company, and must be surrendered. Stuyvesant would not yield, and at last Winthrop presented a letter from the English commander, Richard Nicolls, whom the king had appointed governor of the territory, and went back to the ship. This letter promised that the Dutch might plant as many colonies as they chose and have all the privileges of English colonists, if they would surrender Manhattan.

Nicolls's letter

"Let us read it to the people," said the councilors.

"I won't," roared Governor Stuyvesant, thumping on the floor with his wooden leg; and straightway he tore the letter into bits.

The people heard what he had done, and they demanded to hear

STUYVESANT TEARS UP NICOLLS'S LETTER

the letter. One of the councilors put the pieces together and read it to them.

"The West India Company has done little for us," said one.

"Why should we lose our homes and our lives to hold the land for them?" demanded another.

"We cannot hold the land if we would," declared a third.

'We have twenty guns and two hundred and fifty men; they lave one hundred and twenty guns and one thousand men."

Still Stuyvesant would not yield. The ships sailed into the Vorth River, and the governor marched up the road at the head New York

of his men to prevent the troops from landing. The citizens begged him not to fire. Women and children crowded around him and pleaded with him not to bring war upon them. He yielded, but he said, 'I'd rather be carried to my grave." So it came about that New Amsterdam was no longer a Dutch own. It lost even its name, for the English king gave the territory to his brother, the Duke of York, and in 1664 New Amsterdam became New York.

Nicolls remained as governor. He was a just, kind-hearted man, always ready to please the people. When he was obliged to go back to England, the New York-ers were as sorry as if they themselves had chosen him for their governor. Honest, positive old Governor Stuyvesant and this gentle, courteous Governor Nicolls became warm friends. Stuyvesant lived on

A COMPANION OF
GOVERNOR NICOLLS
(Showing the costume
of the period)

his "bowery" on the East River, and the man whom he would have fought to the death was one of his most welcome guests.

Governor Nicolls was much pleased with the northern part of what is now New Jersey. He sent a colony there when he had New Jersey been in New York only a few months, but before the colonists is given vere fairly settled, he learned that the Duke of York had given away away the land to two noblemen, Lord Berkeley and Sir George Carteret. "Hold on to your homes," said Governor Nicolls. " I am going to England, and I will beg the duke not to give up the and."

The visit was of no use, and one day in 1664 an English vessel appeared in the harbor. The colonists stood in a group on the

Philip Carteret

river bank, not knowing whether they would be treated kindly or driven harshly away from their settlement. A small boat was rowed to the landing, and a young man sprang ashore. Tradition says that he had a hoe on his shoulder. He introduced himself as Philip Carteret, a cousin of Sir George, and made a cordial little speech to the settlers, saying that he was glad to find them there, and he hoped they would stay. He told them how much land he would give them, and promised that every man might worship God as he thought right.

The colonists liked the young man. They had built four "clapboarded houses," and, crowded as they were, room was made for Philip and his men. This is the way in which the town of Elizabeth

STUYVESANT'S BOWERY HOUSE

was begun. The name was that of Sir George's wife. New Jersey's name came from the island of Jersey, of which Sir George Carteret had once been governor.

The Quakers buy New Jersey

Not many years passed before Lord Berkeley sold his share of New Jersey to the Quakers. Some time afterwards they purchased the share of the Carterets also. In 1702 East and West Jersey were united and became a royal colony.

SUMMARY.

Henry Hudson, sailing for a Dutch company, discovered the Hudson River.

New York was first settled by the Dutch fur traders, and was called New Amsterdam. Patroons received large estates along the Hudson.

England claimed the land because of Cabot's voyage, seized it, and gave to both city and province the name New York.

elaware was settled by the Swedes, and afterwards was seized in turn by the Dutch and the English.

ew Jersey was settled by the Dutch, then by colonists under Carteret and Berkeley, then by Quakers. Finally it became a royal colony.

SUGGESTIONS FOR WRITTEN WORK.

uyvesant describes the surrender of New Amsterdam.

patroon tries to persuade a man to come to America.

talk between Governor Printz and some sailors who wished to go up the Delaware.

XI

PENNSYLVANIA AND MARYLAND

PENNSYLVANIA.

SETTLEMENTS had already been made in New England, New York, and Delaware when the boy was born who was to hold more land in America than any other man had ever received. His name was William Penn, and he was the son of an admiral of the British navy. When the boy grew older, he was very handsome. He was an excellent scholar, and spoke five or six languages. He was fond of out-of-door sports, rode well, danced well, was a good swordsman, and a favorite wherever he went.

The boy William Penn

WILLIAM PENN
(When twenty-two years old)

Admiral Penn was exceedingly proud of his brilliant son. He

sent him to Oxford University, and made many plans for hi
career after he had graduated. By and by new
came to the admiral that the young man ha
become a Quaker, and that he was getting int
trouble at the University because he thought i
was wrong to attend the church service and be
cause he persisted in saying *thee* and *thou* instea
of *you*. The Quakers, or Friends, did not thin
it right to speak to one person as *you*, sinc
you is a plural pronoun, although by most pec
ple it was thought as impertinent to say *tho*
to an older person as it would be to-day t
call him by his first name.

A QUAKER[1]

(The Quakers refused to remove their
hats in deference to any one)

The admiral was angry and disappointec
One thing that seemed especially shocking t
him was his son's refusal to take off his hat

**Penn will
not remove
his hat to
the king**

even to the king. The king himself was not at all annoyed. H
thought this whim of young Penn's, as he called it, was ver
amusing, and when the handsome young man stood before him
hat on head, the king took off his own hat. "Friend Charles,
asked the Quaker, "why dost thou take off thy hat?" "Wher
ever I go," answered the king, with a sly twinkle in his eye, "it i
the custom for only one man to wear a hat." William Penn likec
a jest as well as any one, and he must have been amused at thi
speech, but he continued to wear his hat.

**Advanced
ideas of the
Quakers**

In some important matters the Friends were wiser than th
rest of the world; for instance, in England a man might b
hanged for stealing a loaf of bread, but the Friends believed tha
it was far better to punish him in some other way than by takin
his life. In those days most people thought that insane person
could be cured by beating and starving, but Penn believed i

[1] From a portrait of Nicholas Waln in Watson's *Annals of Philadelphia*.

having hospitals for them and treating them kindly. He thought
no one should be imprisoned for debt; and, so far as is known,
he was the first man in the world to declare that criminals ought
to have work provided for them when they were imprisoned, and
not spend their time in idleness and in learning more of evil
from the other prisoners. Another idea of his, which was then Penn's own ideas
almost unheard of, was that nations, instead of going to war when
they disagreed, should let their rulers meet and act as a council
to settle any dispute. It is probable that many who were opposed
to the Quakers did not think so much of the difference of belief
in important affairs as of what seem to us very small matters,
such as refusing to take off the hat, and saying *thee* and *thou*.

There were Quakers in New Jersey, and for some time Penn
thought of founding a settlement in
America where his people could live in
peace and not be fined or beaten or imprisoned. Charles II. owed Admiral
Penn a large sum of money, and when
the admiral died, William Penn offered
to accept instead of the money a tract
of land in America. The king was glad
enough to escape from paying the debt.
He thought it very amusing that this
young Quaker would take wild forest
land instead of such a sum of money,
and it may be that there was a touch of
humor in the name which he gave it,
"Pennsylvania," or "Penn's Woodland,"
though he declared that the name was

CHARLES II

given in honor of the admiral. More amusing still did it seem to
the merry King Charles to send Quakers, who did not believe in
fighting, off among the savages.

"We shall have no fighting," said Penn, "we shall pay the Indians for the land."

"I thought the land was mine," said the king. "Didn't our ships discover it?"

"If some Indians should come over here and discover England, would the country be theirs?" asked Penn.

"Oh good-by, good-by," said the king; "but see to it that you don't take to scalping."

There were to be just laws in Penn's colony and religious free-

Philadelphia founded dom. Ship after ship sailed up the Delaware, full of colonists; three thousand came during the first year. Penn planned his

THE MIDDLE COLONIES

city with wide, straight streets, and gave them the names of forest trees. Some of these names have been changed, but there are still Chestnut, Walnut, Spruce, Pine, and others. The settlers at first lived not *on* the river bank, but *in* it, for they dug into the bluff from the side and top, spread turf and branches over the cave for a roof, and were not at all uncomfortable. So it was that Philadelphia was begun in 1682. The name means the "city of brotherly love," and Penn intended that people of different beliefs should have an opportunity to live there in peace. In a few weeks he asked the settlers to meet him, and together they made laws for the colony.

Soon after Penn's arrival the famous treaty with the Indians was made. Penn feasted them, and they feasted him. They ran

nd leaped to show what they could do. The governor watched
little while, then he showed what he could do. When they
ıw that he could leap as far and run as fast as they, they were
ɔnvinced that he was really a mighty man, and they
ladly made a treaty with him. The treaty
ɪade by the Pilgrims with Massasoit was kept
ɔr more than fifty years, but this famous treaty
f Penn's was faithfully observed for sixty years.

The Quakers paid the red men for the land that they
ɔok, as the whites in New York and New England had
one; but the Quakers were especially fortunate in
aving around them, not fierce, warlike Indians like
ɪose of the east, but tribes that had been completely
ɪbdued by the fierce Iroquois, made to pay tribute,
nd to call themselves cowards. Their conquerors
ɪere friendly to the whites, and were ready to swoop
own upon the Indians of Pennsylvania if they harmed
ɪe Quakers.[1]

PENN'S AUTOGRAPH
AND SEAL

This was what gave Penn safety. But he had more
han safety: he had the friendship of the red men, and this he
ʳon chiefly because he was one of the few white men who treated
ɪem not as inferiors, but as equals, and because he was careful
ɔ do by them as he would have liked them to do by him. Penn
tayed two years in America. He lived at first in a small cottage,
ow in Fairmount Park, Philadelphia, the bricks for which were
rought from England. He was finally obliged to return to Eng-
ɪnd, and visited his "Woodland" but once more.

The city grew. Schools were opened when it was only one
ear old, and — a new thing in those days — they were for girls
s well as boys. Children could be taught to read for four shil-
ngs a term, and for eight shillings they could learn reading,

[1] Fiske's *Dutch and Quaker Colonies in America.*

writing, and arithmetic. The Quaker belief in regard to educa
tion was quite different from that of the Puritans. Both were
eager to understand the Bible aright. The Puritans thought tha
the more of a student a man was, the better chance he would

PENN'S BRICK COTTAGE
(Formerly standing on the west side of Letitia Street)

have of knowing jus
what every verse in
the Bible meant. Tha
is why the Puritans
were so anxious to
found a college. The
Quakers thought tha
if one simply learned
to read, God would pu
into his heart the mean
ing of what was said in
the Bible. That is why

they did not think it was necessary to have a college, although
they wished their children to have a common school education.

Growth of
the city

Philadelphia grew rapidly and soon became the largest city in
the colonies, retaining that distinction for many years. Two years
after Penn's arrival the first printing press in the middle colonies
was established in Philadelphia. There, too, was published the
first daily paper in the United States.

MARYLAND.

English per-
secution of
Roman
Catholics

Maryland is a kind of link between the northern colonies and
those farther south. It was first settled in 1634, the very year in
which Roger Williams was having so hard a time in Massachusetts. The Roman Catholics in England were meeting even
greater troubles than his. If they refused to attend the Episcopal
Church, they were fined or imprisoned, or even tortured. Not a
word could they say about making the laws of the land, and they

could not even send their children away to school in Roman Catholic countries. The queen was a Roman Catholic, but, strangely enough, this fact only made life in England harder for the members of her church. In order to marry her, Charles had promised that the laws against those of her faith should not be carried out. He had no power to bring this to pass, and while the Roman Catholics were indignant that he did not succeed, the Protestants were angry that he even made an attempt, and they watched closely to make sure that the laws were enforced.

In England there was a wise, clear-sighted nobleman called Lord Baltimore. He had been a member of Parliament, and he was a friend of King Charles. This nobleman had become a Roman Catholic, and just as the Puritans wished to found a colony where they could be free to worship as they would, so Lord Baltimore wished to found one where Roman Catholics could have their church. He asked the king for some land north of Virginia, and Charles was more than ready to grant the request. This gift would please the Roman Catholics, the Protestants would not object to their opponents leaving the country, and the only ones displeased would be the colonists in Virginia, who were too far away to make any trouble.

Lord Baltimore plans a colony

Lord Baltimore could appoint his own judges, have his own form of worship, and make very nearly what laws he chose. The only claim that King Charles made upon the proprietor was that one fifth of all gold and silver mined should belong to the crown, and that two Indian arrows should be presented to him every year, to show that the land was under the English rule. The queen's name was Henrietta Maria, and in her honor the tract was to be called Maryland.

CECILIUS CALVERT, SECOND LORD BALTIMORE

The independence of Maryland

106 OUR COUNTRY'S STORY

Just as the papers for this grant were to be made out, Lord Baltimore died, but his son went on with the plan, and carried out his father's ideas. Soon three hundred colonists went to Maryland. A few were rich, and all were well supplied with what would be needed in a new country. Some were Roman Catholics, but many were Protestants, for it was known that men were to attend whatever church they chose. The emigrants came to land on the western shore of Chesapeake Bay. The ship was the largest that the Indians had ever seen, and they sent messengers about to say, "A canoe as large as an island has brought as many men as there are trees in the woods." "Where did a tree grow that was large enough to make it of?" they asked, for they thought it was made of a single trunk like a dug-out. For "axes, hatchets, hoes, and some yards of cloth," the chief sold the whites a piece of land at the mouth of the Potomac, and there in 1634 was founded Saint Mary's, the first settlement in Maryland.

St Mary's is founded

Some wigwams were on this land, and in one of these was held the first Roman Catholic service in that part of the world. This Indian hut is sometimes spoken of as the "Wigwam Church."

A BALTIMORE SIXPENCE
(Issued by Lord Baltimore in 1662)

The governor called the colonists to a meeting, and together they made laws for the settlement. The most famous one of these laws declared that no one who believed in Jesus Christ should be interfered with in his worship. Rhode Island was not founded till two years later, so such liberality was something entirely new in America, and it was almost unknown in Europe. Roman Catholics came to the colony, of course, and Quakers came; and finally some Puritans came who had not been happy in Virginia, and they founded Annapolis.

Religious freedom

The great business of Maryland was raising tobacco. This

DOUGHOREGAN MANOR IN MARYLAND

ork paid so well that people did little else; and while the New
nglanders were spinning and weaving and sawing and whittling,
he people of Maryland were rolling their hogsheads of tobacco
) the wharves, and sending them to England to buy whatever
1ey needed to wear and to use in their houses. With whole
orests at hand, the Marylanders made nothing for themselves,
ut sent the wood to England to be manufactured into tables,
tools, bowls, and brooms, and brought back to them.

People living on large plantations cannot have their houses
ear together, and this is the chief reason why there were so few
owns in Maryland even after many settlers had come. Each
lantation, however, was like a little town in itself. There were
ide fields of tobacco all around, cabins for the workmen, a
hapel, storehouses, and in the centre of all the great, comfortable
ouse of the owner of the plantation. In these rather lonely
laces, the people at the "great house" were always glad to wel-
ome guests. The homes of the planters " are free for all to come
nd go," said one who knew them well.

Why Maryland had no manufactures

Reason for the lack of towns

Puritan rebellion

In a short time there were troubles in Maryland, which arose chiefly because the Virginians did not wish to have a colony so near. Some years later a rebellion broke out among the Puritans against the governor. They were especially ungrateful because, as was said, Lord Baltimore had given them the same rights that he had given to the people of his own church. The Puritans were in power in England, and the man who was then Lord Baltimore was declared to have no claim upon Maryland.

Changes of government

A few years later his rights were restored, and for thirty years every man went to church where he pleased. Then the king took the government into his own hands, and the Roman Catholics were obliged to pay forty pounds of tobacco apiece every year to help support the Episcopal Church. Finally a Protestant descendant of the founder was appointed governor, and his family held the province until the Revolution.

SUMMARY.

The Quaker, William Penn, obtained a grant of land in America and founded Philadelphia. People of all kinds of belief came to enjoy religious freedom. The city soon became the largest in the colonies.

Maryland was founded by Lord Baltimore as a place of refuge for Roman Catholics who were persecuted in England.

Religious freedom was given to all who chose to come.

Maryland had few manufactures because tobacco-raising paid so well that people bought whatever was needed, and few towns because each man wished to have a large plantation for raising tobacco.

SUGGESTIONS FOR WRITTEN WORK.

A Quaker boy describes his cave in the banks of the Delaware.

Penn tells the Indians of his wish to be on good terms with them.

One Indian tells another about the coming of the great ship.

XII

THE CAROLINAS AND GEORGIA

NORTH AND SOUTH CAROLINA.

THE father of Charles II. treated his people so badly that finally he was tried and put to death. For eleven years there was no king in England, and then Charles II. was set upon the throne. The grant of the Caroli-nas The men who had helped him to secure his father's crown expected to be rewarded, but Charles preferred to spend his money in amusing himself. The cheapest thing to do was to give them some land in America, and this he did. To a company of eight he gave the land between Virginia and Saint Augustine. Like the other grants, this terri-tory was to extend to the west as far as the Pacific.

MAP OF THE CAROLINAS AND GEORGIA

Carolina was not all wilder-ness, for a few farmers had come from Virginia and settled near Albemarle Sound, not far from Roanoke Island, where Raleigh had tried to begin his "second home" for the English nation. In 1663 the Company gave the little group of houses the name of Albemarle. This was the first permanent settlement in North Carolina.

Albemarle

The first settlement in South Carolina was made in 1670, near

Charleston where Charleston now stands, by English emigrants whom the Company sent over. Just as Jamestown had been named in honor of King James, so this settlement was named in honor of King Charles II.

South Carolina was especially fortunate in the Huguenot, or The Hugue- French Protestant, emigrants who came to the new colony in the nots early days. The king of France declared that they should not have a church of their own in France, and that if they tried to emigrate, they should be hanged. Those who came to America had to steal away by night and abandon their homes and other property, but when they reached the New World, every colony had a welcome for them. Massachusetts gladly gave them land and money. They were valuable colonists, for they understood various kinds of manufactures, and, more than that, they were brave, upright, intelligent people, a prize for any nation.

In England a learned man named John Locke wrote a body of laws for Carolina. There were laws for everything that could be thought of from the punishment of crimes to the oversight of children's games. There was to be a certain number of noblemen, each owning a certain amount of land. There were also

ENTRANCE TO CHARLESTON HARBOR

to be tenants, who rented land, but could never buy it. They must do whatever the nobleman bade, and they must not leave The Grand his land without permission. The Company were so delighted Model with this body of laws that they called it the "Grand Model," and declared that it would stand forever. In reality, it never stood at all, for the settlers refused to be ruled in any such fashion, and insisted upon buying land and making laws for themselves.

North Carolina had vast forests of pines, and the chief occupation of the colonists was cutting timber and making tar **The chief industries** and turpentine. South Carolina had great tracts of swampy land, and as soon as it was found that rice would grow on it, the raising of rice became the principal work. Long before the Revolutionary War, it was discovered that indigo would flourish in South Carolina, and that paid so well that indigo raising then became the leading industry. It was not easy for white people to work in the swamps, and negro slaves were brought

RICE from Africa. The occupations of the two parts of Caro- **Division of the Carolinas** lina were so unlike and the first settlements so far apart, that what one portion of the country wanted was often quite different from what the other required. The result of this was that the territory was finally divided into two parts, North and South Carolina.

GEORGIA.

There used to be a law in England that men who could not pay their debts should be put into prison. In prison they must stay unless some one paid for them, for there they had no way of earning money. Indeed, they had little food unless their friends gave it to them or they could beg it from those who passed by. **Poor debtors**

GENERAL JAMES OGLETHORPE
(From a print in the British Museum)

Many of these "poor debtors" were honest men who had run in debt because of sickness. Some were even well educated.

The prisons of England were in a wretched condition, and Parliament appointed General James Oglethorpe to visit them and report what reforms ought to be made. General Oglethorpe was a kind-hearted man, and after he had seen the sufferings of these people, he could not rest until he had planned some way to relieve them. This is what he planned. He would pay their debts, set them free, and then carry them and their families to America, and give them a chance to try again.

Oglethorpe plans to help them

Many rich men helped, the English government helped, and it was only a year before a ship set sail with more than one hundred liberated prisoners and their families on board as emigrants. They were to form a settlement between Charleston and Saint Augustine, for Oglethorpe was a good general as well as a kind, generous man, and he knew that Charleston would welcome a strong settlement to the south as a protection against the Spaniards,

Why he chose Georgia

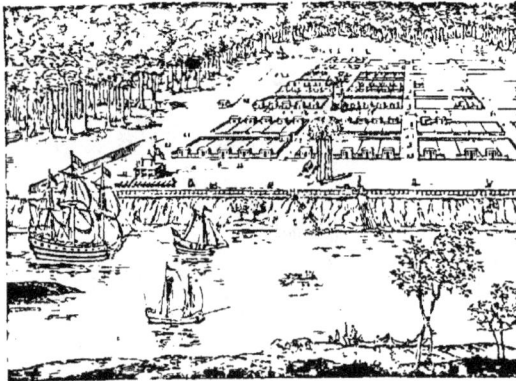

SAVANNAH IN 1741

and that the two colonies could stand more firmly together than either alone. The tract of land given to him "in trust for the poor" was called Georgia, for then King George II. was on the throne.

The first settlement was made at Savannah in 1733. Not many years before this time, the Spaniards of Florida had aroused the Indians to attack South Carolina, and that colony was delighted to have these new neighbors and allies. She gave them cattle, goats, hogs, and rice, besides sending some negroes with them to help build the houses. South

The settlement of Georgia

Carolina was not disappointed in the help that she expected to receive from the new colony, for General Oglethorpe led an expedition against the Spaniards, and after that there was no trouble from them.

Oglethorpe had expected to be able to make wine and olive oil, **Silk-raising** and to produce large quantities of silk, for mulberry-trees, on whose leaves the silkworms feed, grew wild in Georgia. When the colony was two years old, the founder made a visit to England, and carried with him eight pounds of Georgia silk, which was made into a dress for the queen. Silk-raising was not a success, however, one reason being that the raising of rice and indigo paid much better.

Oglethorpe and his friends were to make the laws for the colonies for twenty-one years; but after a little while the settlers were not contented to be ruled by others. There were two reasons why they felt that they had a right to complain. One was that no rum could be brought into the colony, and the second was that slavery was not allowed. The colonists said that men needed rum in that climate, and that besides, they ought to have it to sell to the West Indies. The climate, it was maintained, required the use of negroes, for the settlers said they must have workmen who could endure the heat better than white men.

BRANCH OF OLIVE

The founder and his friends finally granted their requests. Twenty years after the colony was founded, the province was **Georgia is** given up to the king, and until the Revolution it was ruled by a **given up to the king** governor whom he appointed. Georgia was the last of the thirteen English colonies that united, only a century and a half after the first one was founded, to free themselves from Great Britain.

SUMMARY.

The Carolinas were granted to several men as a reward for serving the
king. Among their most valuable colonists were the Huguenots.

The chief industry in the northern part was the manufacture of tar and
turpentine; in the southern, the raising of rice and indigo. The wants
of the two colonies were so unlike that the province was finally divided.

General Oglethorpe founded Georgia as a home for "poor debtors."

The settlers were not satisfied with the government of the colony, and at
last it was given up to the king.

SUGGESTIONS FOR WRITTEN WORK.

General Oglethorpe tells Parliament about the "poor debtors."

One of the prisoners writes his wife about Oglethorpe's offer.

XIII

THE FRENCH EXPLORATIONS IN AMERICA

CHAMPLAIN'S PICTURE OF QUEBEC
IN 1613

A FEW years before Jamestown was settled,
there was in France a brave young sailor who
had become a soldier for the time, and was
helping to fight some of the French king's
battles. His name was Champlain, and he
would have been much surprised if any one
had told him that some day a lake in America
would be named after him.

When the fighting was over, he asked the
king's permission to go to America to search
for the Northwest Passage. He explored
the Saint Lawrence, and on its north shore he noted a rocky pro-

montory. " That is the very place for a town," he thought. " The The found-ing of Quebec river is narrow here, and a fort with a few men could keep any number of ships from coming up the stream." In 1608 he founded a colony on that very spot, and named it Quebec from the Indian word *quebec*, a narrow place.

The Iroquois, the fiercest and most savage of all the Indian tribes, lived in what is now the State of New York, and one day the friendly Indians who were north of the Saint Lawrence came to Champlain to beg for his aid against these Iroquois, who were their deadly foes. Champlain agreed to help them. The white men and the red men feasted and smoked and made speeches. Then they paddled up the river and into Lake Champlain. If they had been one month later and had gone a little farther south, they might have met Henry Hudson and his Dutchmen sailing up the Hud-

A JESUIT EXPLORER

son. All the men that they thought of meeting were the Iroquois, Champlain and the Iroquois and soon the Iroquois came. Champlain's guns won the day, and there was no limit to the devotion of the Indians. To show their affection and gratitude, they gave him the bleeding head of one of their enemies and asked him to present it to his sovereign. This little battle between a few red men in the woods with some white men helping one side was an important event in American history, for ever after this the Iroquois hated the French and were ready to help the English. That is why the French did not venture to found any colonies in New York, although they explored to the westward, up the Saint Lawrence and about the Great Lakes. They claimed all the land that is drained by the river, and called it New France.

The Jesuits The first explorers were Roman Catholic priests called Jesuits Champlain said that he would rather convert an Indian than found an empire, and this was the spirit of these priests. Among the hostile Indians they suffered fearful tortures. They were beaten, they were burned, their fingers were cut off with shells joint by joint, and they were put to death in all the agonizing ways that could be invented. Still, even after the Dutch had ransomed one and sent him home, he made his way back again to preach to his tormentors. One Jesuit, when pursued by Iroquois might easily have made his escape, but hastened back to terrible sufferings because he remembered that some of his Indian converts had not yet been baptized. In all the history of America there are no heroes more brave, more earnest, and more unselfish than these black-robed missionaries of the wilderness.

Another class of people who did much to bring the French and the Indians together were the *coureurs de bois* or forest rangers. The king's officers demanded so much of the profit on furs that many young men went into the wilderness and traded without the royal permission Whenever one was caught, he was severely punished therefore, they went farther and farther away from the settlements. Often they married Indian women Nearly all the English looked down upon the Indians, but the French treated them as equals, and could go among them in safety far from any settlement of whites

A COUREUR DE BOIS

After a while the French heard that beyond their forts and missions there was a great river which the Indians called the Mississippi, or "father of waters." Marquette, a Jesuit priest was eager to go down this stream to preach to new tribes of Indians, and Joliet, a fur-trader, was ready to go with him. The friendly Indians begged them not to go. They said that the distant tribes were fierce and cruel, and that the river was full of "monsters that devour both men and canoes." Nevertheless, the priest and the explorer and five of their friends floated down the Wisconsin and into the Mississippi. The Indians met them kindly, and one tribe, the Illinois, begged that the white men would come back and live among them. They went below the mouth of the Arkansas, far enough to be almost sure that the great river did not flow into the Gulf of California, as had been thought, and then they paddled their way back up the Mississippi.

Marquette was exhausted by the hard journey, but as soon as he was strong enough he went to visit the Illinois. He preached to them and founded a mission. On his way back to the Great Lakes, he died on the bank of the river that is named for him.

To find where the Mississippi emptied was the work of La Salle, another brave French explorer. Nothing could make this resolute man falter. He built a sailing vessel; it was wrecked. A French ship bringing him money was lost. He built a fort; the garrison revolted. He made friends of the Illinois; but when he came to their village a second time, it had been burned, and the heads of his Indian allies were put up on poles. Three times he started on his expedition; twice he failed. The third time, in the bitterly cold winter of 1682, he came to the Mississippi. It was full of floating ice, but the dauntless man never thought of giving up the voyage. Down the stream he made his way. At the mouth of the river he set up a great wooden cross, on which

MARQUETTE
(From the statue in the Capitol at Washington)

Marginal notes: Marquette and Joliet go down the Mississippi. La Salle reaches the mouth of the Mississippi

Louisiana he nailed the arms of France, and took possession in the name o King Louis XIV. of all the land drained by the Mississippi and

SETTLEMENT AT THE MOUTH OF THE
MISSISSIPPI IN 1719

its branches. In honor of the king, he named the territory Louisiana.

He knew that it was of little use to claim the land unless he planted colonies and built forts The king gave him four ships that he might found a colony at the mouth of the Mississippi, but

the pilot made a mistake and sailed to the coast of Texas. There they built a fort, but many of the men died and the rest quar **Death of** reled. Finally, La Salle set out for Canada to find help. On the **La Salle** way he was shot by one of his own men. So died one of the bravest and most resolute of all the explorers of the New World

SUMMARY.

Champlain explored the Saint Lawrence and founded Quebec; therefore France claimed Canada.

He sided with the Canadian Indians against the Iroquois; and, because o their enmity, although the French planted colonies to the west, the founded none in New York.

Marquette, Joliet, and La Salle explored the Mississippi; therefore France claimed the land drained by that river. She named it Louisiana.

SUGGESTIONS FOR WRITTEN WORK.

A Jesuit tells his friends about his life in America.
An Indian tells Marquette about the Mississippi.
La Salle describes his journey down the Mississippi.

XIV

THE STRUGGLE WITH THE FRENCH

A few years after all the colonies except Georgia had been founded, war broke out between England and France. Both nations were beginning to see that it was worth while to hold land in America, and that to destroy one of the enemy's settlements counted for more than to capture one of the enemy's warships.

Who should rule in America

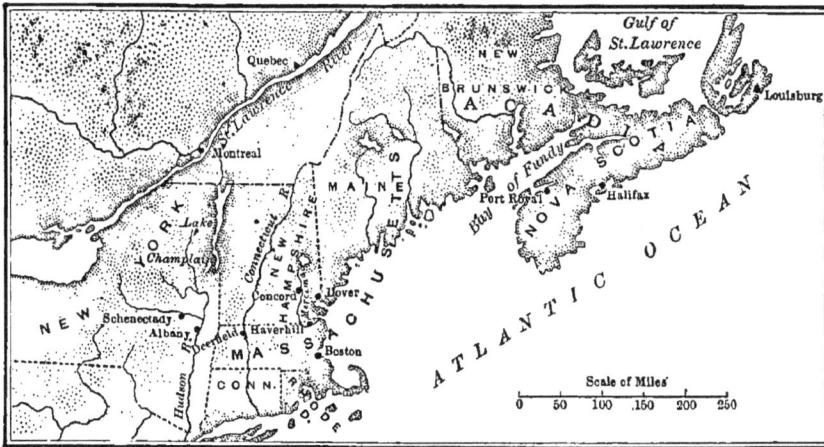

FRENCH FRONTIER IN THE NORTH

This is why there was fighting between the French and English colonies.

In this struggle the colonies that could be most easily reached from Canada suffered most. One of the first to be attacked was Schenectady in New York. The settlers had so little thought of danger that in jest they had put up two snow men at the gates for

Schenectady attacked

sentinels. In the night, through the storm and the darkness, the French and Indians went silently past the watchmen of snow. Not a sound was heard. Suddenly came the terrible warwhoop, and in two hours men, women, and children were slain or carried away as prisoners.

Another raid was made upon a few farmhouses near Haver-

Hannah Dustan's adventures

THE CAPTURE OF HANNAH DUSTAN

hill, Massachusetts. A sick woman named Hannah Dustan was dragged away with her nurse. With the Indians was a boy captured at Worcester long before who had learned to speak their language. "They said that by and by we should have to run the gauntlet," whispered the boy to Mrs. Dustan. "Running the gauntlet" meant running between two rows of men, each man striking at the captive as he passed. "Find out where to strike if one would kill at a blow," whispered Mrs. Dustan. That night they camped on an island in the Merrimack just above Concord, New Hampshire. The two women and the boy each took a tomahawk, and, gliding silently from one sleeping Indian to another, struck the fatal blow. With ten Indian scalps to prove the deed, they made their way back to their friends.

Burning of Deerfield

A few years later an attack was made upon Deerfield, Massachusetts. It was burned and a large number of captives taken on the long march to Canada. Many of them died on the way, or were killed by the savages because they could not travel over the snow and ice as fast as the others. One little Deerfield girl finally

married an Indian. Years afterwards, she and her brave and
their children made several visits to her old home. One Sunday
her relatives persuaded her to put on a gown and bonnet and go
to church; but as soon as she came back, she tossed them off and
went back to her Indian blanket and her Indian wigwam.

After a time of peace, word came across the ocean that France
and England were at war again. The governor of Louisburg, a New Eng-
fortress on Cape Breton Island, heard the news first, and before land expedi-
Boston knew that war had been declared, he burned a little Eng- Louisburg
lish fishing village. The New Englanders were indignant, and in
their wrath they determined to capture Louisburg.

A skilled commander would have hesitated, for Louisburg was

LOUISBURG FROM THE NORTHEAST
(On the right is the Royal Battery, the first French outpost to be captured)

the strongest fortress in North America; but this scheme had "a
lawyer for contriver, a merchant for general, and farmers, fishermen, and mechanics for soldiers." No one in New England knew
anything about besieging such a fort, and in all good faith the
wildest methods were proposed. Almost as an afterthought, some
English vessels were asked to accompany the expedition to prevent French ships from coming to the aid of the fortress. The

New Englanders landed. The cannon must be dragged two miles. The men were up to their knees in mud, and the cannon sank out of sight. There were few tents, and not enough blankets to go around. Shoes gave out, clothes were in tatters, the scaling ladders were too short, two thousand men were sick; and before the troops were the stone walls of the fortress, thirty feet high.

Louisburg taken

Louisburg was captured, but even the colonists themselves who afterwards went within the walls wondered how the deed had been done. It was partly because the French commander was not as bold or as wise as he should have been, and did not make the proper preparations; and partly because, while the besiegers knew nothing of the usual way of attacking a fort, they had had a hard training in finding out how to do things for themselves, and they made their assaults in original fashions that were a continual surprise to the French. "Panic seized upon us," wrote a Frenchman who was at Louisburg; and he added mournfully, "These New Englanders are a singular people." All the fighting on land was done by the colonists without other aid than the instructions of three or four gunners whom they borrowed from the fleet

LOUISBURG CROSS
(Captured at Louisburg and now in the Harvard Library)

to show these daring soldiers how to use the cannon; yet, if the English ships had not kept the harbor clear of vessels coming to help the French, and if they had not captured one with a supply of powder just as that of the besiegers was failing, Louisburg could not have been taken.

Louisburg returned to France

When the terms of peace were arranged, England gave up Louisburg to France. This was done that England might gain some land in Hindustan, but the New Englanders were indignant, for they felt as if their great victory had gone for nothing.

The question, "Who shall rule in America?" was not yet settled, however. Before this, France and England had quarreled about matters in Europe, but trouble now arose about matters

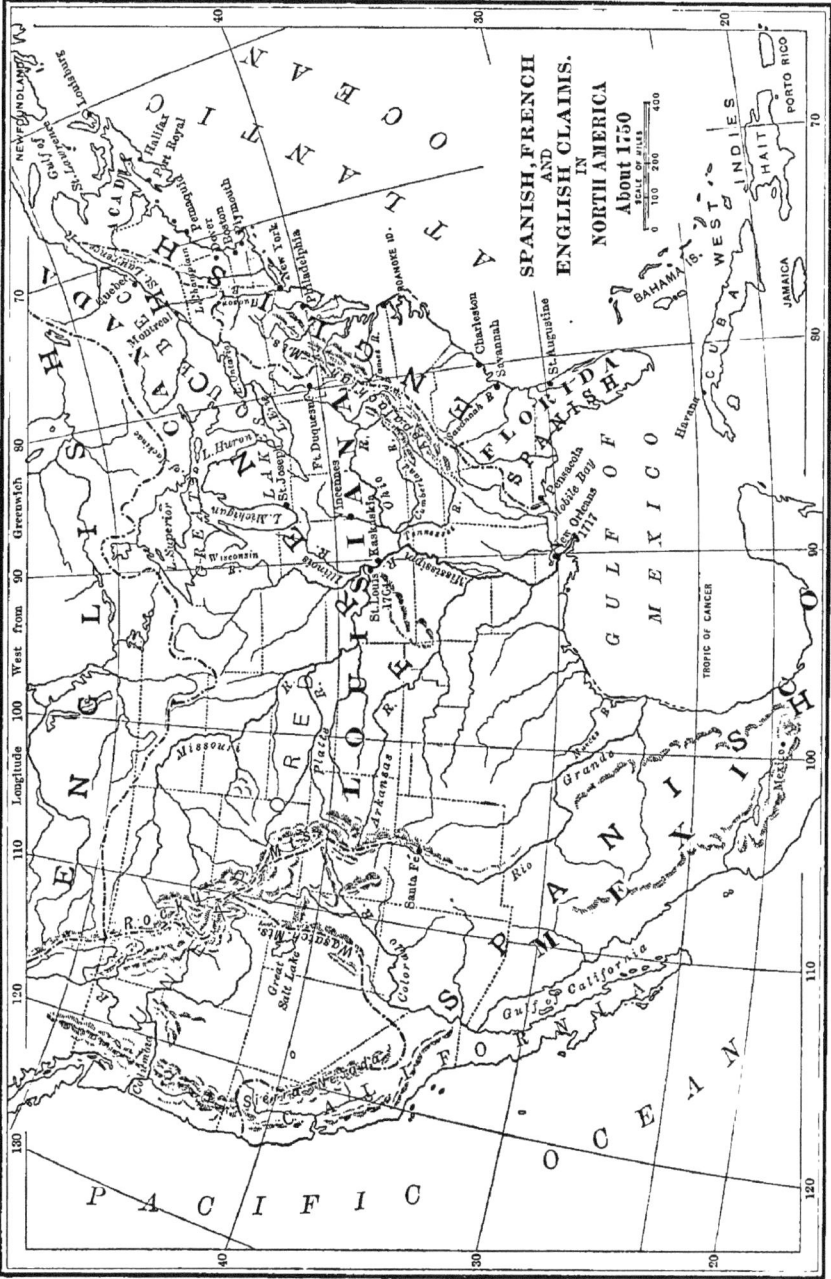

SPANISH, FRENCH
AND
ENGLISH CLAIMS.
IN
NORTH AMERICA
About 1750
SCALE OF MILES
0   100   200   400

in America. France claimed the land drained by all the rivers The French
that she explored. "The French king might as well claim all claim the
land
the lands that drink French brandy," declared an Englishman ;
but France went on building forts and claiming land. The English were not especially interested in the Mississippi, but when the
French claimed the Ohio, they were aroused. Some Virginians
and Londoners formed the Ohio Company and planned to make
settlements on the river. The French began at once to build forts
down the Alleghany.

At length Governor Dinwiddie of Virginia decided to send a
letter to warn them that they were trespassing. A young man of A youthful
twenty-one years was asked to carry the letter, and he set off on a messenger
dangerous journey of nearly one thousand miles. It was winter,
and the path was hidden by the deep snow. The young envoy
would not wait for his party, but with one companion he went
straight through the woods, finding his way by the compass. They
crossed the creeks by felling trees for bridges. The Alleghany
was full of floating ice, and they made a raft. In the middle of
the stream the messenger was jerked into the water. He was
fired at by an Indian not fifteen paces away, but at last he de-
livered his letter and came safely home again. His friends were
very proud of him, and they would have been still more proud if
they had known what he would do for his country a few years
later, for the young man's name was George Washington.

The only answer the French made was that the letter should be
forwarded to Marquis Duquesne, the governor of Canada. Then The answer
Governor Dinwiddie sent Washington to build a fort where Pitts- from the
French
burg now stands. It was hardly begun when the French fell
upon the party, completed the fort themselves, and named it Fort
Duquesne. Washington built a small fort farther south, but
when the French came upon him, he had to surrender and march
back to Virginia.

The next year the English sent over General Braddock to take

command. "I shall capture Fort Duquesne in three or four days,
and then march on to Niagara,"
said he. "The Indians are
skillful in laying snares," mod-
estly suggested a wise colonist
of whom we shall hear more,
for his name was Benjamin
Franklin. "Very likely they
are troublesome to your untrained soldiers," said Braddock a little haughtily, "but
the king's Regulars will have
no difficulty." Washington
tried to make him see that it
would not do to draw up his
men in lines in plain sight
when fighting with Indians,
but Braddock accepted no advice, and wrote home that the
American troops were cow-
ardly.

REGION ABOUT FORT DUQUESNE

Not far from Fort Duquesne there was a sudden attack. Brad-

dock was bravery itself, and the English soldiers would have
stood like a wall against an enemy whom they could see, but
hardly a foe was in sight. The deadly shots came from behind
trees and rocks, and the soldiers had no idea where to fire. They
were panic-stricken, and ran "like sheep pursued by dogs,"
Washington wrote home to his mother. He added, "I had four
bullets through my coat, and two horses shot under me." Then
he signed himself in the formal fashion of those days, "I am,
honored Madam, your most dutiful son, George Washington."

Only the skill of the young Virginian saved any part of the army. Braddock was slain, and Washington buried him secretly at night, lest his grave should be insulted. The Indians strutted about the battlefield, wearing the laced hats and scarlet uniforms of the English officers.

One of the saddest events of the war occurred in Acadia, or Nova Scotia. Nearly all the settlers there were French, and they claimed to be "neutrals," that is, persons who would favor neither party. The English believed that they were aiding the French, and thought that if they were allowed to remain, England would lose Nova Scotia. Suddenly the English troops swept down upon the Acadians, carried six thousand of them away, and scattered them among the English colonies along the coast. In the confusion, husbands were parted from their wives, and mothers from their children. There is a tradition that a young maiden was separated from her betrothed, and wandered for many years in search of him. It is upon this story that Longfellow founded his " Evangeline." The exiles buried many of

EXPULSION OF THE ACADIANS

their possessions, hoping to return. Some of these things have been found, and people have not yet given up digging in search of the chapel bell of Port Royal.

Those who came to Philadelphia were in great need, until a

The Acadians in Philadelphia kind Quaker raised funds to build a row of little wooden houses for them, and to provide a teacher for their children. There was a strange fear of these simple, harmless people, and a young Philadelphia girl wrote that she was frightened because she had to go by the houses of the "French Neutrals" at twilight. This carrying people from their homes was not a new thing, and

THE FORTRESS OF QUEBEC AS IT IS TO-DAY

strangely enough, it is just what the French king had proposed to do some years earlier if he had captured New York.

Quebec The English had won victories, but the one thing that would end the French rule in America was the capture of Quebec. Quebec was built on a great mass of rock that jutted out into the Saint Lawrence. It was one of the strongest cities in the world, and it was commanded by General Montcalm, a brave and successful French soldier. The English were commanded by General Wolfe, a young man who had won glory in previous fighting.

All summer Wolfe tried one plan after another to take the city, but in vain. Autumn came, and he planned a final attempt. He sent part of the vessels with a few men below the town to pretend to be getting ready for an assault, while the other ships with most of the men sailed far up above the town. Montcalm was below, and one of his officers above, each expecting an attack. When night came, Wolfe and his men floated down stream in the deep shadow of the high bank. It was dark, but the stars were out. Wolfe repeated softly his favorite poem, Gray's "Elegy." "I should rather have written those lines," said he, "than to take Quebec." They came near the shore. "Who is there?" called the sentinel. "Provision boats," was the answer. "Keep still, the English will hear!" Provision boats were expected, and the sentinel asked no more questions.

Capture of Quebec by the English

About a mile above Quebec was a high plateau called the Plains of Abraham from a pilot who lived there in the early days. Wolfe had seen with his glass far across the river a rough path up the almost perpendicular cliff, and he believed that his men could climb it. Montcalm, too, had noticed this path, but he said, "They have not wings, and one hundred men posted there could stop their whole army." So they could, but the one in charge was careless, and while Montcalm below the town and his officer above the town were each expecting an attack, Wolfe and his men were climbing up the steep cliff.

In the morning Montcalm found an English army drawn up in line on the Plains. There was a fierce battle. Both commanders were mortally wounded. Wolfe heard his men crying, "They run! See them run!" "Who run?" he asked, and when he knew it was the French, he said, "Now I shall die in peace." Montcalm was carried to a little house in the town. "Thank God," said he, "that I shall not live to see the surrender of Quebec."

ENGLISH SOLDIER OF
WOLFE'S TIME

This victory in 1759 ended in America the war which lasted in Europe till 1763. France gave up to England, Canada, and all

DEATH OF GENERAL WOLFE
(From the painting by Benjamin West)

English rule established in America the land that the French had claimed east of the Mississippi. During the war, England had captured Cuba and the Philippines from Spain, for Spain was helping France. Now England gave the islands back and took Florida in exchange. To pay Spain for this loss, France had to give her New Orleans and all the land between the Mississippi and the Rocky Mountains. The question was settled once for all that England would rule in America.

SUMMARY.

For nearly seventy-five years there were periods of fighting with the French to see who should rule in America.

The latter part of this struggle, brought on by the attempts of the French to seize the Ohio valley, was called the French and Indian War.

'he capture of Quebec gave England the control in America.

ιfter the war, England held Canada and all land east of the Mississippi.

Spain held the land between the Mississippi and the Rocky Mountains.

SUGGESTIONS FOR WRITTEN WORK.

ι New England soldier writes home from Louisburg.

Vashington's companion tells about the journey to the Alleghany.

ιn Acadian girl describes the carrying away of her people.

XV

THE TIMES BEFORE THE REVOLUTION

AMERICA in the eighteenth century was a very different country rom what it is to-day. In the first place, there were probably **Population** ot so many inhabitants in ll the English colonies as here are now in New York nd Philadelphia, and of hese half a million were egro slaves.

Slaves were held in all the olonies. Indeed, England /as making so much money ι the slave trade that she **Slavery** ɔrced slavery upon America, nd ordered her officers in he New World to do all hat they could to encourage

FIREPLACE IN A SLAVE'S KITCHEN

he trade. In the South, a negro could live on cheap food and /ithout many clothes or much shelter, while in the North, if he id not have good food, warm clothes, and a comfortable shelter,

he would die. The result was that people in the northern colonies found that slavery did not pay, and it was gradually disappearing. Even in the southern colonies there was a feeling

A POSTRIDER
(From a print in the Post Office Department)

that slavery would
vanish in time.
The Carolinas were
not at all pleased,
and even a little
alarmed, to have
so many negroes
in their territory.

Newspapers
and mail

There was no daily newspaper, and if there had been, people
would not have received it promptly unless they had lived near
the printing-office, for even between New York and Philadelphia
there was a mail only three times a week, and it took three days
for the mail carrier, or "postrider," to make the journey. Once a
month the mail went to England. Sending mail from colony to
colony was expensive, and a letter of a single sheet sometimes
cost twenty or twenty-five cents, according to the distance that it
was carried. Writing a letter
to a friend was not a business
to be undertaken without con-
sideration, and this is one reason
why the letters of those days
were so carefully and formally
written.

Books

But if the colonists had few
newspapers and few books, they
read all the more carefully what
books they did have, and they
thought about what they read.

BURNING OF MR. JOHN ROGERS
(From the New England Primer)

Most of the books were brought from England, but some were

written in America, chiefly volumes of sermons, discourses on witchcraft, and some rhymes so dreary that no one cares to read them now.

Almost the only book that the children could claim as their own was a tiny volume called the "New England Primer." This con- The New England Primer tained pages of Bible questions, such as, "Who was the oldest man?" or "Who was the meekest man?" There were long lists of hard names, "To teach children to spell their own," said the reading; and the Puritan boys and girls must sometimes have wondered how learning to spell Methuselah would teach them to spell John, but they would never have dared to ask. There was a picture of a man tied to a stake and burning to death because he did not believe in the king's church.

There were verses that this man wrote not long before he was put to death, and there was an alphabet with a picture and a rhyme for every letter. This began, —

A   In ADAM'S Fall
We finned all.

and ended, —

Z   ZACCHEUS he
Did climb the Tree
Our Lord to fee.

There, too, was the children's evening prayer, "Now I lay me down to sleep." This was the children's especial book, and they read it and re-read it till all the early copies were so worn out that there are no more to be found.

A famous book that came once a year was "Poor Richard's Poor Richard's Almanac Almanac," written by Benjamin Franklin. Besides having tides, eclipses, etc., like other almanacs, it had good advice put into rhyme and little stories, and such proverbs as "Great talkers little doers," and "Tongue double brings trouble," "Doors and walls are fools' paper," and "He who pursues two hares at once does not catch one and lets t' other go." There wer often puzzles and riddles to be answered in the nex number. Some households had little other readin; except the Bible. The children must have watche eagerly for the time when the new almanac woul come, and they could have new stories and see i their guesses of the puzzles were correct.

FRANKLIN'S PRINTING PRESS
(Now owned by the Bostonian Society)

Getting new clothes was a weighty matter. I the North the wool or flax must be raised, spur and woven. In the South, even if a gown was t be bought and not *grown*, it generally had to be ordered from England; and as at least three months would have to pass befor the buyer could receive it, deciding what to send for was a seri

Traveling ous business. Traveling was difficult. To go from Philadelphi to New York took three days by stage-coach, and when it wa announced that one was to make the journey in two days, peopl thought the name, the "Flying Ma-chine," was well deserved. Every one who visited a city expected to have many commissions for his friends. Stage drivers and postriders "did er-rands." Only three or four years ago, an old lady on Cape Cod said that in her

EARLY AMERICAN STAGE

youth she and her friends always sent to Boston by the captai: of the packet boat for their bonnets. "And they were prett; ones, too," she added.

Many of the things that the colonists would gladly have mad

or themselves England would not allow them to make, because **England forbids manufactures** he English manufacturers wished to make money selling their goods to the colonists. If the colonists began to make hammers nd axes, straightway the English manufacturers of hammers nd axes would get a law passed that no such things should be iade in America. More than this, no colony was allowed to sell oods to any other colony without paying a tax. 'hey must buy of England, and whatever they pro- uced must be sold to England, even if other coun- ries would pay a higher price. They must not buy paper of pins from any other country, o matter how much better and cheaper ie pins were than those made in Eng- ind.

These laws were unjust, and the olonists broke them just as far as iey dared. Articles were sent from ie colony to another without the lyment of any tax, foreign goods ere smuggled into the coast towns, iips that had never been near Eng- nd went back and forth among the olonies. It seems as if the English

FANEUIL HALL, BOSTON
(Called, on account of the patriotic meetings held there, " The Cradle of Liberty ")

: a century and a half ago might ive seen that if a country was making unjust laws for its colo- ies and the colonies were breaking them, there would surely e trouble before many years had passed.

The French wars cost a great amount of money. France might ossibly try to regain the land that she had lost, and the king and **England decides to tax the colonies** s advisers thought it would be best to keep an army of British ildiers in America to be ready to oppose the French. England ecided to tax the colonies to help pay for the war and the new standing army. The colonists answered, "We do not wish to have a standing army, and we have given more than our share to the war, for we raised and paid as many men as England." The colonists' objections made no difference, and England determined to collect in two ways the money needed. One was by imposing a few new duties and by enforcing the laws in regard to trade. As long as France had power in America, England had not dared to be very strict in demanding the taxes on goods brought from France and Spain, or very severe in punishing smuggling. Now she determined that every penny that the laws allowed should be collected.

Writs of assistance

The king's officers had the right to have a warrant written by the court allowing them to search any special house in which they had reason to think there might be smuggled goods. Now they obtained what were called writs of assistance. These allowed the officers to go into as many houses as they chose without having separate warrant for each one, and if the doors were barred, they could call upon the sheriff to break in. This made the colonists indignant, but it was according to an old English law, and never would have caused the Revolution.

A STAMP ACT STAMP

The second way of collecting money was by requiring every legal document, like a will or a mortgage, to be written on paper stamped in England. An extra price must be paid for the stamp, and if there was no stamp, the document was of no value; for instance, if a man bought a house, he received a deed, or written paper, saying that the property was his, but if there was no stamp on the deed, then he could not defend his right to the house in the courts. The people of the United States have recently been obeying such a law to help pay the cost of the Spanish War; but the men whom we had chosen to make our aws were the ones who decided to raise the money in this way, ind we could find no fault.

It was different with this stamp tax. In each colony there was in assembly of men elected by the people, and only that assembly lad ever imposed taxes. The colonists replied, " This is not just. n England only the House of Commons can impose a tax ; so in America, only the assembly of each colony can tax that colony. 3ut, if the king *asks* us to help England, our assemblies will grant noney as we have often done before."

Right of taxation by House of Commons denied

England was startled that mere colonies should dare to be so ndependent. In these days a nation is proud of her colonies and lad to have them prosper ; but in the earlier times the countries f Europe felt differently. They looked upon a colony as a con- enient place to send men for whom there seemed to be no work nd no room at home. It was also a place where a man whom he king wished to favor could receive a grant of land or hold ome office, and thus make his fortune. In matters of trade, the iother country never thought of trying to help the colony ; and vhen laws were made in old England, they always aimed at etting as much money as possible from the new England across he ocean.

How Europe felt toward colonies

In 1765 the Stamp Act was passed, though many clear-headed tatesmen in England were against it. Edmund Burke said it vas unjust. William Pitt, who was always a friend to America, aid, " England has no right to lay a tax upon the colonies." The olonies from New England to Georgia rebelled. The streets vere full of crowds. Images of the men appointed to sell the tamped paper were hanged or burned or driven about town in he governor's best coach with a figure of Satan for companion. 'he lieutenant-governor of New York threatened to fire upon the ebellious colonists. "You 'll be hanged to a lamp-post if you o," was the answer, and he did not fire. In some places build-

The Stamp Act

ings were torn down, and every scrap of stamped paper tha could be found was burned or tossed into the ocean.

It was not all "mob law." The assemblies met and declare

Opposition by the colonies

Place to affix the

Hereabouts will be the

THE STAMP

NEWSPAPER IMITATION OF A STAMP
(From the Boston Gazette, Oct. 7, 1765)

that it was right to resist tyrann Lawyers agreed that no deed or wi should be called illegal for the lack a stamp. The newspapers came on with a skull and crossbones for a hea ing, or with black borders indicatir the death of liberty. During the Frenc and Indian wars, Benjamin Frankli then editor of a paper published Philadelphia, had printed a picture of snake cut into several parts, labele with the names of the different colonies. It was an old supe stition that if a snake was cut into pieces it would still live if tl pieces were united, and under this picture Franklin printed tl motto, "Unite or die." This design became a favorite emblem.

In one respect the colonists had matters in their own hand They said, "We will not buy English goods." No orders we

Repeal of the Stamp Act

sent to England, and ships that crossed the ocean with goods sell had to carry them back. Then the English manufacturers begged Parliament to give up the tax, and the act was repealed. Parliament declared at the same time that it had the right to tax the colonies, but no one thought much about that, and if King George

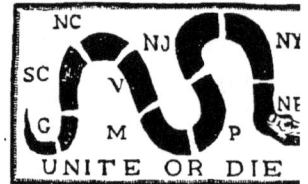

FRANKLIN'S DEVICE
(The initials indicate the colonies)

III. had not been so unwise and so obstinate, there would prob bly have been no Revolution.

After a little while, new taxes were imposed, and Englis soldiers continued to come to America. Some were sent to Bo

:on, and one night a quarrel arose between them and some of
;he citizens. The soldiers fired and killed five. It shows how
iroused the colonists were that they called this the "Boston
Massacre." It shows how anxious they were to be fair that
when the soldiers were tried for murder, they were defended by
;wo prominent lawyers, John Adams and Josiah Quincy, Jr.
Adams said a few years later that this was "one of the best pieces
of service I ever ren-
lered my country."

The colonists re-
fused to buy any of
;he goods on which a
:ax was demanded.
Many of them agreed
:o buy nothing made
.n England so long as
;here were duties on
any goods. One of the
strong men in this par-
ty was Samuel Adams,
who has been called the
"Father of the Revo-
lution."

THE BOSTON MASSACRE IN KING (NOW STATE)
STREET
(From Paul Revere's engraving)

George III. and his "Friends," as those who supported him
were called, formed what they thought a very shrewd scheme.
The Americans used much tea, and a large part of it was smuggled from Holland. It was decided to allow tea to be sent to
America and sold at so low a rate that even with a duty of three
pence a pound it would be cheaper than the tea that was smuggled.
"The people will buy the English tea, and the rebellious leaders
will be left without support," thought the king, and the tea was
sent over to the large cities on the coast.

Charleston stored the tea sent there in damp cellars, where it

soon spoiled. Philadelphia forbade her pilots to guide the tea-ships up the Delaware. New York would not let them enter the harbor. In Boston the matter was more difficult. The ships were in the harbor. They could not leave without the royal governor's permission, and he refused to give it. Nineteen days they lay at the wharf. On the twentieth day, the custom-house officers would have a legal right to unload them, the men who had ordered the tea would pay the duty, and then they would have possession of the goods.

The people of Boston came together in the Old South Meeting-House. All day long they discussed what it was best to do. In the evening two hundred men appeared in the street and marched quietly toward Long Wharf. They wore blankets, their heads were muffled, and what could be seen of their faces was copper-colored. A man who saw them wrote cautiously to a friend, "They say the actors were Indians from Narragansett," but every one knew that they were white men from Massachusetts. When they came to the wharf, they leaped on board the tea-ships. Every man drew out a hatchet from under his blanket, and

PULPIT OF THE OLD SOUTH MEETING-HOUSE

it was not many minutes before Boston Harbor became a vast teapot, for every chest had been broken open and all the tea was in the water. Then the "Indians" went quietly to their homes, and the "Tea-party" was over.

The brig Peggy Stewart brought to Annapolis some packages of tea among other goods. The vessel could not be unloaded till all taxes were paid; therefore the owner paid the tax on the tea. Before this, he had signed the agreement not to buy or import goods taxed by England for revenue, and now the people of Annapolis were so angry that they threatened to destroy the brig. To prevent a riot he burned his own boat, tea and all. This settled the matter in Maryland.

The king was determined to punish these bold colonists. Boston should suffer first, he said, and in 1774 the "Port Bill" was passed, which forbade ships coming to the city or leaving it. Boston would lose the money that she was making from trade, and would soon be glad to apologize and pay for the "Tea-party." So the king thought; but instead of being frightened, the other colonies stood by Massachusetts and sent her all kinds of provisions. Even far-away South Carolina sent ship-loads of rice. Cat-

CARPENTERS' HALL, PHILADELPHIA

tle and sheep were driven into Boston in flocks. England had said that ships should go to Marblehead instead of to Boston; but Marblehead said at once to the Boston merchants, "Use our wharfs and our warehouses without charge."

England's treatment of Massachusetts aroused the colonists to send delegates to a meeting called "The First Continental Congress," which was held in Carpenters' Hall, Philadelphia. The Carpenters' Company knew that the king's officers might take their hall away for allowing the "rebels" to use it; but the only care they took was to mention no names on their record. They said merely, "Voted: That they be allowed to use our hall."

The first Continental Congress

This Congress sent a respectful petition to the king, telling him frankly what rights they thought belonged to them and in what ways they thought they had been treated unfairly.

TEA-PARTY TABLET
(Corner of Atlantic Ave. and Pearl St.)

SUMMARY.

In the eighteenth century there were not so many inhabitants in the English colonies as there are now in New York and Philadelphia.

Slavery was fast disappearing in the North, and was not always looked upon with favor in the South.

Mails were slow, and postage was expensive. There were few books, and England's refusal to permit manufactures was arousing discontent among the colonists.

England decided to tax the colonists because of the expense of the French wars and her wish to station an army in America to guard the colonies against the French.

To raise the money, the trade laws were enforced, new duties were imposed, and the use of stamped paper was required.

The colonists refused to buy English goods, and resisted the Stamp Act. All taxes were repealed except that on tea.

The attempt to force English tea upon Boston resulted in the Boston Tea-party. In retaliation, Parliament passed the Boston Port Bill.

This treatment aroused the colonists to hold in Philadelphia the **First Continental** Congress, which sent a petition to the king.

SUGGESTIONS FOR WRITTEN WORK.

Describe the journey of a postrider from New York to Philadelphia.
A man tells in 1773 why there will probably be war with England.
A description of the Boston Tea-party.
A letter of sympathy to a Bostonian after the passing of the Port Bill.

XVI

THE FIRST TWO YEARS OF THE REVOLUTION

1775.

THE Americans had little hope that the king would pay any regard to their petition, and they were ready to fight rather than yield to injustice. In almost every colony companies were formed and drilled, while in various places arms and ammunition were stored. General Gage, who was at the head of the British troops in America, decided to send eight hundred of his men to Concord, Massachusetts, to seize the powder and cannon that he knew were there. Another thing that the troops were to do was to seize Samuel Adams and John Hancock, that they might be taken to England and tried for treason.

This plan would have succeeded, but the Americans were on the watch, and before the British were ready to start, Paul Revere galloped through the darkness, past the villages and farmhouses on the

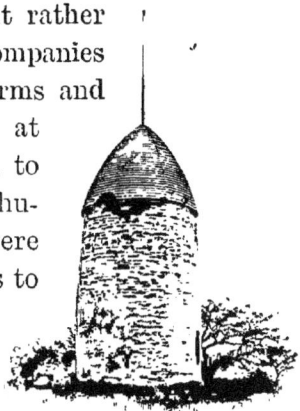

POWDER-HOUSE NEAR BOSTON
(Where the British seized some powder Sept. 1, 1774)

way to Concord, telling every one that the Regulars were coming. Thousands of the Americans had become "minute men," that is, they had agreed to be ready to fight at a minute's notice. When The battle of Lexington

the British troops came to Lexington to seize John Hancock, ther
stood the minute men on the green. "Disperse, you rebels!
shouted the commander. "Lay down your arms and disperse!
Not one laid down his gun. "Fire!" cried the commander. Ii
a moment, seven Americans lay dead, and the Revolution had
begun. This was on April 19, 1775.

The retreat of the British
At Concord the British began to destroy the arms, but so many
minute men were upon them that there was nothing to do but to
retreat to Boston. The farmers pursued. Longfellow tells the
story of the retreat in his "Paul Revere's Ride:" —

> "How the British Regulars fired and fled, —
> How the farmers gave them ball for ball.
> From behind each fence and farm-yard wall,
> Chasing the red-coats down the lane,
> Then crossing the fields to emerge again
> Under the trees at the turn of the road,
> And only pausing to fire and load."

Long afterwards, when Benjamin Franklin was in Eng
land, some one said that hiding behind a wall and
firing was no way to fight. Franklin asked quietly
but with a sly twinkle in his eye, "Did n't those ston
walls have two sides?"

THE MINUTE MAN
(D. C. French's statue at Concord)

Men whose names were to become well-known hur
ried to Boston, and although General Gage was ii
command of the British troops and had been ap
pointed by the king governor of Massachusetts, he was really a

Colonists hasten to Boston
prisoner in the city, for he was surrounded by many thousanc
men. Among these men was Israel Putnam, of Connecticut, whc
had left his plough in the field and started for Boston as soo1
as the news of the battle of Lexington reached him. There wa
also Benedict Arnold with sixty volunteers. Arnold suggestec
that Fort Ticonderoga, at the northern end of Lake George, ough

to be captured, not only because there was in this fort a great supply of powder and guns, but because if no Americans were there to prevent, the British troops could come down from Canada and take New York.

With the permission of Massachusetts, Arnold set out to raise troops in the western part of the state; but much to his surprise, he found there Ethan Allen, a sturdy Vermonter, with his "Green Mountain Boys," and they, too, were on the way to capture Fort Ticonderoga. Allen had more men, and the "Boys" would not fight under any one else, so Arnold went on, not as commander, but as a volunteer. The two men and the "Boys" came upon Ticonderoga when the garrison were fast asleep without a thought of danger. The commander was suddenly aroused by a demand to "Surrender!" He jumped out of bed, not more than half awake, and said, "To whom? By whose authority?" "In the name of the Great Jehovah and the Continental Congress," roared Ethan Allen, and the fort was surrendered. This was only three weeks after the battle of Lexington.

The capture of Fort Ticonderoga

On that same day, the Second Continental Congress was meeting in Philadelphia. John Hancock, whom the king was so anxious to catch, was made president. Benjamin Franklin, Samuel Adams, and his cousin John Adams, Patrick Henry, the great patriotic orator, and Washington, were all members of this Congress. They knew that war must come, and they adopted the forces around Boston as the "Continental Army." A commander-in-chief must be chosen, and every one remembered how skillfully Washington had saved part of Braddock's army at Fort Duquesne

ETHAN ALLEN
(From the statue in the Vermont State House, Montpelier)

Continental Army organized

when he was only twenty-three years of age. He was from the large colony of Virginia, and the election of a southern commander for an army which was as yet made up wholly of northern men would help to strengthen the union among the colonies, so Washington was elected commander-in-chief.

He set out on horseback for the eleven days' ride to Boston, but before he had gone many miles from Philadelphia, he heard what had happened in the east. General Gage was in Boston, and the American troops were in a half circle around the city. Gage knew that if they should come a little nearer and fortify Bunker Hill and Breed's

SAMUEL ADAMS
(From Copley's portrait)

Hill, they could fire into his camp. He decided to seize Bunker Hill. The Americans found out the plan, and when Gage awoke June 17, 1775, ready to send men to the hill, behold, the Americans were putting up earthworks. They were not on Bunker Hill, to be sure, but they had come even nearer and were fortifying Breed's Hill. General Gage and his officers thought just as Braddock had thought, that nothing could withstand British Regu-

The battle of Bunker Hill

JOHN ADAMS
(From a portrait by Trumbull)

lars, and he decided to storm the hill. The Americans had too little powder to waste a single charge. " Wait, boys, wait till you

can see the whites of their eyes," called Colonel Prescott.   Nearer
and nearer came the British.   " Fire!" ordered the commander,
and there was such a volley that the brave, well-trained Regulars
broke ranks and ran.   Again they charged, again the Americans
fired, and again the Regulars fled.   A third time the British

BURNING OF CHARLESTOWN AND THE BATTLE OF BUNKER HILL
(Drawn by a British officer at the time from Beacon Hill)

dashed up the hill.   The Americans' powder had given out; there
was nothing to do but to retreat ; and they retreated, not down-
cast, but jubilant, for they, the untrained farmers and citizens,
had twice driven back the British veterans.

The great elm in Cambridge under which Washington took
command of the army is still standing.   The house in Cambridge
which was his headquarters is the one that was for so many
years the home of Longfellow.   The poet writes : —

Washington
takes com-
mand of the
American
forces

> " Once, ah, once, within these walls,
> One whom memory oft recalls,
> The Father of his Country, dwelt.
>
> .   .   .   .
>
> Up and down these echoing stairs,
> Heavy with the weight of cares,
> Sounded his majestic tread ;
> Yes, within this very room

Sat he in those hours of gloom,
Weary both in heart and head."

It is no wonder that he was weary. Thousands of men we:
looking up to him for orders. They were jubilant over Bunk
Hill; they had not forgotten the glories of Louisburg. Mai
would have been glad to plunge into another battle anywhere :
any moment. Washington saw that bravery alone would n
always win the day, that there must also be drill and trainin
There must be powder and cannon. It was not time to fight.

Meanwhile Congress met again. Samuel Adams said that tl

The last appeal to the king

GREAT ELM IN CAMBRIDGE
(Under which Washington took command of the
Continental army)

colonies had cut loose fro
England, then why not d
clare them independen
Others said, "No; let 1
try once more." A la
petition was sent to tl
king, and the man chos(
to carry it was a descenda:
of William Penn. This d
no good, for the king wou
not even read the paper.
was not easy to get Englis
men to fight their own p(
ple in America, and he hir(
many thousand Germ:
troops called Hessians.

For the king to call

Montreal and Quebec attacked

foreigners to fight his own subjects, who felt that they were as
ing only for justice, made the Americans more indignant th:
ever. They learned that the British meant to come by the w:
of Lake Champlain and seize Fort Ticonderoga, so they decid(
to attack Montreal. Benedict Arnold suggested marching 1

rough the Maine forests to capture Quebec. It was a terrible
urney. The men must make their way over swamps, among
iers, across swiftly flowing rivers, and through the tangled under-
ush. Many died. The others, sick, and weakened by their lack
food in the wilderness, made their way to the city on the rock,
mbed up to the Plains of Abraham, and called upon the garri-
n to surrender or else come out
d fight. The commander would
neither. General Montgomery
d led a second expedition by
ly of Lake Champlain, and he
on came from his victory over
e English at Montreal. There

BRITISH CANNON CAPTURED IN THE REVOLUTION

is fighting, and if Montgomery had not been slain and Arnold
sabled, Quebec would probably have come into American hands.
This was on the last day of 1775. In that year the Americans
d taken Ticonderoga and Montreal, but they had been defeated
Bunker Hill and at Quebec. The greatest gain of the season
is that they had lost their fear of the British Regulars.

Events of 1775

1776.

The year 1776 began. Washington still trained his men and
d his best to collect powder and cannon. The Americans be-
me impatient. "Why does n't he do something?" they com-
ained. John Hancock, who owned many houses in Boston, said,
Burn the town and drive the British out." Washington was
ser than they, and he waited; eight long months he spent
aching his brave fighters to become an army. March came.
any cannon had been dragged all the way across Massachusetts
om Fort Ticonderoga, and now he could "do something." Gen-
al Gage had gone back to England, and General Howe had
ken his place.

Washington drills his troops

One night General Howe had little sleep, for Washington

The evacuation of Boston

cannon roared until morning. When it was light, the astonishe
British commander saw that all this firing had been done onl
to keep him from finding out that the Americans were fortifyin
Dorchester Heights, now a part of South Boston. "Drive the
from the Heights," said the commander of the fleet, "or we mu
leave the harbor." The American fortifications grew strong
every hour. The British remembered Bunker Hill, and, bra

JOHN HANCOCK'S HOUSE IN BOSTON
(On Beacon Street, near the State House. Demolished 1863)

men as they were, they di
not care to storm another hi
with Americans at the to
March 17, 1776, Howe and h
army sailed away for Halifa
This is why Boston celebrat
the Seventeenth of March a
Evacuation Day.

The British did more tha
to take themselves away; the
carried with them nearly
thousand citizens who stoo
by the king, and, either b
cause of haste or because th
boats were crowded, quant
ties of powder and many cas
non were left behind. Th
presence of these articles wa

as welcome to the Americans as was the absence of the Britis
Howe would surely go to New York, thought Washington; there
fore he and his army went to New York to be ready for them.

July 4, 1776, saw the great event of the year. On a table in th
State House in Philadelphia lay a document. Fifty-six men signe
their names to it. That was all, but this act was the beginnin

f the United States, for the document was the Declaration of The Decla-
ndependence. It named one by one the acts of injustice of which ration of Independ-
the king had been guilty. Then it declared, ence
"That these united colonies are, and of right
ought to be, free and independent states."

The man who wrote the Declaration was
Thomas Jefferson, a Virginian, and one of the
youngest men in Congress. He was a lawyer,
a musician, a skillful horseman, a student, a
gentle, kindly man, but firm as an oak in the

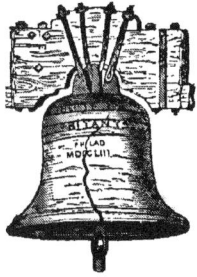

THE LIBERTY BELL cause of liberty. It required much courage to
ign this paper, for if England won, the signers would be looked
pon as the leaders of the rebellion and would receive the most
evere punishment. "We must all hang together, or we shall
ang separately," said Franklin. John Hancock wrote his name
n a large, bold hand, "So that King
eorge can read it without specta-
les," he declared. When Charles
arroll signed, some one jestingly
aid, "You are safe, for there
re so many Carrolls in Mary-
nd that the king will not know
here to find you." "I'll show
im," replied Carroll, and wrote
of Carrollton" after his name.

The colonies, or rather states,
ad declared their freedom, but
uld they force England to ac-

OLD STATE HOUSE IN PHILADELPHIA IN 1789
(This building is now known as Independence Hall)

nowledge it, and could they win the aid of any other country?
o one could tell, but, nevertheless, there was great rejoicing. It The Liberty Bell
egan in Philadelphia with the ringing of the "Liberty Bell," as
e bell of the State House was afterwards called. Strangely

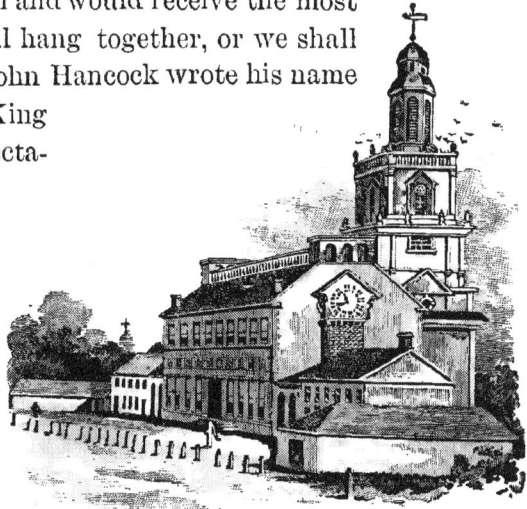

enough, the lettering on the bell read, "Proclaim liberty through out the land, unto all the inhabitants thereof.' This bell was cast just before Washington carried the letter through the wilderness to the French. Another message was to go to them before long, but this time Franklin was to be the messenger.

THOMAS JEFFERSON
(After the crayon portrait by St. Mémin)

South Carolina had some good news to contribute to the rejoicing. British ships had appeared off Charleston, but on an island in the harbor Colonel Moultrie had built a rough fort of palmetto logs and sand. An officer who had fought in Europe sneered at the work, but when the enemy came, the little home-made fort saved the city. Ever after this, the fort was called Fort Moultrie in honor of the leader whose wisdom and bravery had saved his state.

The king's offer of pardon While the Declaration lay on the table in Philadelphia, Admiral Lord Howe, brother of General Howe, was crossing the ocean with more soldiers. He sent a letter to Washington addressed to "George Washington, Esq.," but the American commander would not receive it because he thought it an impertinence to the states that he should not be addressed as commander-in-chief of the army. An envoy came to see

BENJAMIN FRANKLIN
(From a painting by Duplessis)

him, and told him that the letter contained the king's offer of pardon to all rebels who would cease to rebel. "We have committed no fault," said Washington, "and we need no pardon.'

Has your Excellency any message for Lord Howe?" asked the nvoy. " Only my particular compliments," answered Washington ourteously.

Washington had been right in going to New York, for the Washington loses New York british planned to get possession of the city and the Hudson liver. The Americans had no warships, and if the British could eep New England and the outh apart, they could onquer them separately. Washington held New York nd two small forts, one on ne north end of Manhattan sland and one across the ludson. He also held brooklyn Heights on Long sland. General Howe leant to take the Heights. le had many more men, nd there was nothing for ne Americans to do but o flee. In the darkness of foggy night Washington ent powder, cannon, and

CENTRAL SCENE OF WAR

len across the river in any little boats that he could find, and vhen General Howe climbed into the fort, there was nothing here.

Washington could not hold New York now that the British ad Brooklyn Heights. He went farther up the Hudson, and the Retreat to the Dela-ware british pursued. Washington had not nearly as many soldiers as vould be needful to face them, and there was nothing to do but to etreat. Such a retreat as it was. Congress had no money and he men were but half-clothed and half-fed. They marched across

WASHINGTON CROSSING THE DELAWARE
(From the painting by Emanuel Leutze)

New Jersey, stopping now and then to burn a bridge behind them. At last they were safe on the Pennsylvania side of the Delaware River, while on the Jersey side were the British under General Cornwallis. The British could not cross, for Washington had taken every boat that could be found.

Christmas came. It was a sad Christmas for the Americans, but the next day there was rejoicing. Twenty years earlier Washington had crossed the Monongahela in the floating ice, and he was not to be dismayed by the Delaware. "The war is over," thought Cornwallis, and he sent his baggage to New York to be ready to sail for England. The next news that reached him was that this American general, who never would do what was expected of him, had crossed the Delaware in spite of the floating ice, had marched nine miles to Trenton in a fierce snowstorm, had fallen upon the Hessians, half stupefied with their Christmas celebration, and had captured one thousand. Cornwallis did not sail for England.

The battle
of Trenton

1776 was an eventful year. It began with an untried general training his men into an army. Before the year was over, the British had been driven from Massachusetts and South Carolina, the Declaration of Independence had been signed, and the untried general had shown that he could fight, or, if it seemed best, that he could retreat in a masterly fashion, and even in his retreat win a victory.

Events of 1776

SUMMARY.

1775. The first bloodshed of the war took place at Lexington on April 19.
The battle of Bunker Hill and the capture of Fort Ticonderoga and Montreal encouraged the colonists, though they had failed to take Quebec.
Washington took command of the American troops around Boston and trained them into an army.
The king hired Hessian soldiers.
1776. The British troops were forced to leave Boston and were defeated in South Carolina.
The Declaration of Independence was signed in Philadelphia by representatives from the colonies.
The Americans abandoned Brooklyn Heights and were obliged to retreat through New Jersey and across the Delaware River.
Washington showed his ability in his sudden marches and in his successful attack on Trenton.

SUGGESTIONS FOR WRITTEN WORK.

A boy describes the retreat of the British on April 19, 1775.
The commander of Fort Ticonderoga tells about the surrender.
A messenger tells Washington about the battle of Bunker Hill.
A British soldier describes the evacuation of Boston.
Read about the early life of Franklin, and write its story.

XVII

THE LATTER PART OF THE REVOLUTION

1777.

Bagging the fox

THE British pursued the troublesome American general, and found him on a point of land with the Delaware on the west and a little creek on the north. Cornwallis encamped just across the creek. He thought, "My men need rest. The other forces will be here in the morning. Then we can cross the creek and bag the old fox." He slept the happy sleep of the man who sees a successful day before him.

The battle of Princeton

All night long the British sentinels could see Washington's campfires and could hear the Americans digging and throwing up fortifications. When Cornwallis awoke in the morning, he heard cannon; but they were not in front of him across the little creek, they were behind him at Princeton. The "old fox" had marched his troops around in the night, and was routing the forces that Cornwallis was patiently awaiting. The few men that had been left to keep up the fires and rattle the spades had slipped away through the woods at the last minute, and were helping to win the day at Princeton. Cornwallis was too good a soldier not to appreciate the brilliancy of this movement, and long afterwards he said to Washington, "Nothing could surpass your achievements in New Jersey."

Washington in Morristown

It was not easy to follow the Americans, for they had burned the bridges behind them, and Washington made his way safely to the high land of Morristown. So long as he was there, the British could not pass him to go to Philadelphia. They decided that the

GEORGE WASHINGTON
(From the Trumbull portrait at Yale College)

best thing to do was to spend the winter in New York, and this they did.

Washington had to meet other difficulties than battles. When there is war in these days, some favor it and some do not. So it was in Revolutionary times. Some Americans were ready to give their lives and every penny they possessed to win independence. Others thought that it was a wrong and foolish thing to oppose their lawful king. Some believed that war was always a crime,

Differences of opinion about the war

no matter for what reason it was fought. Some joined the army for adventure, some to get the pay that was promised. People were people then as well as now.

FLINTLOCK PISTOL
(Given to Washington by Lafayette)

The lack of money was a great difficulty. Congress had issued paper money, but paper money is of no worth unless the government that issues it is able to give gold for it that will be of value any-

The lack of money

where, and no one knew whether this little company of states would ever be able to pay what the bills promised. Even the truest patriot hesitated to stay in the army with no money to send to his wife and children who were starving at home. Congress had no power to make people pay taxes or to enlist. One man after another gave all that he could. Franklin lent the country his little savings; Washington would accept no salary,

and he agreed to use his own fortune to pay the soldiers, if Congress failed;

Robert Morris

but it was Robert Morris, a rich banker of Philadelphia, who was the real "financial backer" of the Revolution. Washington was the winner of battles, but Robert Morris made it possible for him to have an army. Samuel Adams

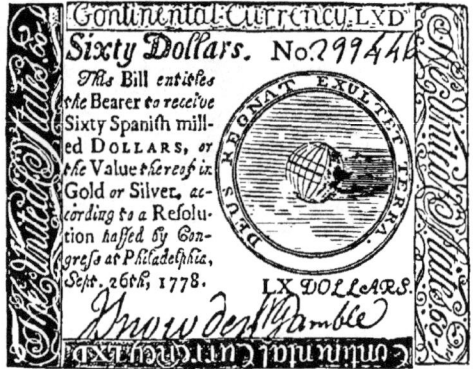

CONTINENTAL PAPER MONEY
(Two thirds of the real size)

was the "Father of the Revolution," Washington was the general, and Morris was the banker.

Franklin fought no battles, and he had little money to give. The thing that he gave was influence, the power to persuade men to do as he wished. Not long after the Declaration, Franklin and two others had been sent to France to try to win the help of the **Franklin in France** French king. So long as the revolt was only a rebellion, the king could have nothing to do with it; but if there was good hope of its being a successful revolution, he was ready to strike a blow at the land that only twenty years before had driven him out of his possessions in America. It began to appear that Washington was a great general. There was once a Roman commander who could not only fight, but who weakened his enemy by "prudent delay." His name was Fabius, and Washington began to be called the "American Fabius." The French king hesitated.

Meanwhile Franklin became the fashion in France. The Parisians delighted in even his whims and oddities. Every one wanted to see how "Poor Richard" looked and to hear him talk. The government moved slowly, but there was a rich young nobleman named Lafayette, only nineteen years old, who would not wait for king or councilors. He bought a ship, fitted it out, invited some veterans to go

Lafayette comes to America

LAFAYETTE
(From a contemporary engraving)

with him, and sailed away for the land whose independence he meant to help win. The Americans rejoiced at his coming, and he was happy with them. "I feel as if I had known them twenty years," this boy of nineteen wrote home. Lafayette was a brave soldier, and the veterans who came with him were of the greatest help to Washington in training his troops; but of most importance was the evidence that friends across the seas would surely help America if she could only endure a little while longer.

During the winter the British government planned for General
Howe to go up the Hudson; for General Burgoyne to come down
from Canada, capturing Fort Ticonderoga on the way, and for
another body of troops to come from Lake Ontario down the
Mohawk Valley. All three would meet, and the British would
control the State of New York.

Burgoyne's invasion

Burgoyne captured Ticonderoga. Food, horses, and ammunition had been collected in the little Vermont village of Bennington, and Burgoyne planned to send some soldiers to take these
supplies. The plan might have succeeded if it had not been for
Colonel John Stark, a New Hampshire man who had fought in
the French and Indian wars and at Bunker Hill. In the promo-
tions Congress had not done him justice. He was too indignant

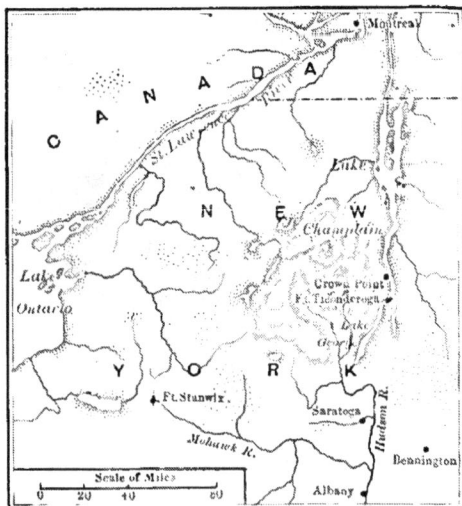

The battle of Bennington

to serve in the army; but
when the British invaded
his own state, for Vermont
was then claimed by New
Hampshire, he raised eight
hundred men, asked an
American officer to lend him
a regiment, and marched
out to fight. "I'm under
no man's command," said
he. "I take my orders from
the State of New Hamp-
shire." His men had no
uniforms, and their weapons
were anything that they
could get, but they carried the day. Congress pardoned Stark for
making war all by himself and appointed him a brigadier-general.

Burgoyne was in great danger, but if the troops could come
down the Mohawk, he would be saved. This expedition had

REGION OF BURGOYNE'S INVASION

me as far as Fort Stanwix, where Rome now stands. There The Ameri-
d already been fighting. The Americans had dashed out of the can flag
rt and captured five British flags. They hoisted them upside
wn, and far above them there floated the most remarkable
nner that ever waved in the New York wilderness. One sol-
er gave a white shirt, another an old blue jacket, and a third
ntributed some strips of red flannel from his wife's petticoat.
it was that the flag adopted by Congress was made, and for
e first time "Old Glory" swung out to the breeze.[1] Benedict
rnold had been sent to assist the soldiers at Fort Stanwix. He
ntrived to spread the rumor ahead of him that Burgoyne had
en defeated. The British fled back to Lake Ontario.

These rumors became true not long afterwards, for General
owe seemed to think chiefly of capturing the "rebel capital," as Burgoyne's
called Philadelphia, and the paper ordering him to go up the surrender
udson and help Burgoyne lay in the desk of a man in London
ho had gone off for a vacation and forgotten all about it. Two
ttles were fought near Saratoga, and Burgoyne was obliged to
rrender. One of the soldiers wrote: —

> "The seventeenth of October
>   They did capitulate;
>   Burgoyne and his proud army
>   Did we our prisoners make."

The main event of 1777, the third year of the war, was the
ilure of the British to gain the Hudson. To prevent this, Wash- Events of
gton had lost Philadelphia; but the enemy could be driven from 1777
iladelphia; while the British, once in full possession of the
udson, could have conquered the country at their leisure. His
illful retreat across New Jersey, his victory at Princeton, and
s masterly fashion of delaying the enemy when he could not
ght them, had won the attention of Europe, and had given his

---

[1] Fiske's *American Revolution.*

soldiers that confidence in their leader without which the most competent general is helpless. Still, if Washington had known what lay before him in the next few months, it seems as if ever he would have quailed.

1778.

The British forces were in Philadelphia,·comfortably housed well fed, giving balls, and amusing themselves. Washington and **Valley Forge** his men were at Valley Forge. A small stone house which is stil standing was the headquarters of the commander. One room i devoted to portraits of him, but in those harassing days he had little thought of his own portrait. It was bitterly cold. The men were in huts o woven boughs, or any rude shelter tha they could make. There was not ever straw enough for their beds, and many a man sat by the fire all night because he had no blanket. Shoes were lacking and the bare feet left blood on the snow Meat failed, sometimes bread failed The country was not poor, but Con gress had little power and none too much wisdom.

The arrangements for providing the army with food were absurd Men were appointed to positions which they had no idea how to fill, and men whose bravery de

A REVOLUTIONARY DANCE

served a great reward were passed over. A conspiracy was formed against Washington. He knew of it, but went on calmly through even the sufferings of that terrible winter.

The great gain of those dreary months was that the army was

ıely drilled for future work. Baron von Steuben, a great German Baron von Steuben drills the American troops ldier, came to America expressly to help Washington train his .refooted, half-naked men. France had sent him, for she had :cided to help the colonies, and she wished the American army

be drilled by a thoroughly competent
ill-master. Baron von Steuben was
ıt-tempered. He would storm at the
en in a mixture of German and French,
ıd call for some one to come and scold
em for him in English. The next
inute he would applaud their quick-
ıss in learning the difficult manœu-
es. The men were fond of the gruff,
nd-hearted old soldier, and were most
illing learners.

When Franklin in Paris heard that
owe had captured Philadelphia, the
ıl philosopher said, "Howe has not
kcn Philadelphia, but Philadelphia has

BARON VON STEUBEN

ken Howe," and that was really the way it seemed. He was

the city, but Washington was only twenty miles away, and Howe in Philadelphia
owe could not well do anything but stay in the city, and feel
happy as possible over the fact that he had taken the "rebel
pital."

Spring came. A French fleet was on its way to help the Amer-
ıns. The British had found that it was of no use to stay in Aid is coming
ıiladelphia, and they started to bring their forces together in
ew York. Washington pursued. There was a battle at Mon-
outh, now Freehold, and had it not been for the insolent disobe-
ence of a jealous officer, it would have been a great victory.

All the summer and autumn of 1778 there were no great
.ttles, but there were skirmishes in many places between small

Indians and
Tories

bodies of troops. In one way some of these attacks were wors
than the real battles, for the British had induced the Iroquois t
join them. Bands of these savages, the most fierce
of all the Indians of the east, were led by Tories,
or men who still wished to be under the king.
They fell upon little settlements in New York
and Pennsylvania, and tortured and murdered the helpless people with the most terrible barbarity.

Clark saves
the North-
west

The "far West," or what is now Indiana
and Illinois, was in danger. There were
forts and old French
towns here and there,
and the English thought
they could unite the
Indian tribes and de-
stroy these settlements.
Unfortunately for their

A BACKWOODSMAN (
THE REVOLUTION [1]

schemes, a young Virginia surveyo
named George Rogers Clark also had
scheme. Thomas Jefferson, and Patric
Henry, who was then governor of Vi
ginia, approved his plan, and he set ou
for Indiana with a few men. When h
messengers returned to Virginia, the
had a thrilling story to tell, for th
adventurous young surveyor had take
Vincennes and other places. He ha
driven back the British, and had actu

A FRENCH FRIGATE

ally won for the United States the vast expanse of country be

[1] From the statue in Richmond of Andrew Lewis, a Revolutionary lead
in Kentucky.

een the Ohio and the Great Lakes, and as far west as the
ssissippi.

The British had failed in their two attempts to win the State
New York, their plans to conquer New England had not suc- The British
ded, and now they decided to begin at the southern end of the attack Georgia
e of colonies and try to get possession of Georgia. They were
ccessful, and they began to feel as if this plan would surely
nquer the rebellious colonies.

The year 1778 began with the sufferings at Valley Forge, and
ded with the loss of Georgia; but, on the other hand, during Events of
is year France had become the ally of America, and the "far 1778
est" had been saved for the states. Such a year could hardly
called unsuccessful.

1779.

There had been many sea fights between English and Ameri-
n vessels. Sometimes one side won, and sometimes the other. The Bon
le greatest naval fight was between the British man-of-war Homme
rapis and the American ship Bon Homme Richard, so called in Richard and
nor of Franklin's "Poor Richard." It took place just off the the Serapis
ist of England. The captain of the American vessel was a
otchman named John Paul Jones. After an hour's cannonad-
g, the captain of the Serapis called, "Have you struck your
ors?" "I have n't yet begun to fight," shouted Captain Jones.
In these days a naval battle is carried on by cannon between
ips a long way apart, but in Captain Jones's time one vessel
metimes clutched the other with grappling hooks, and there was
short, savage, hand-to-hand fight on deck. So it was between
ese two vessels, and the Bon Homme Richard was victorious.
igland could endure to lose a battle on land, but to be so
oroughly defeated on the ocean and just off her own coast was
miliating. It was a little embarrassing to claim to be "Mis-

FIGHT BETWEEN THE SERAPIS AND THE BON HOMME RICHARD
(From a painting by Richard Paton)

tress of the Seas," when in a fair fight one of her new men-of-war, well-armed, and manned with a trained crew, had been beaten by an old American ship with poorer guns and a crew from at least six or eight different nations. It is no wonder that other countries began to feel more and more confident that America would win.

1780.

In 1780 both America and England were in difficulties. America needed money. Had it not been for the gifts and loans of France, she would have had to yield before. The paper money of the Continental Congress was only laughed at, and the old phrase of scorn, "not worth a Continental," has not yet gone out of use. Washington said, "It takes a wagon-load of money to buy a wagon-load of provisions." England needed friends, for France and several other countries had united to oppose her.

England had failed in New York, but she had succeeded in Georgia, and she meant to take South Carolina and work her way north. At first all went smoothly, for Cornwallis captured

Both England and America in difficulties

Charleston and Camden. Soon he wrote home, "But for Sumter Guerrilla warfare in the south and Marion, South Carolina would be at peace." Marion was called the "Swamp Fox," but this would have been as good a name for almost any of the fighters who were such a trouble to Cornwallis. They lived in the swamps and on the mountains, and whenever the English felt especially secure, a band of these men would suddenly dash out, shoot a few "red-coats," rescue a handful of prisoners, and be out of sight before the enemy had a fair look at them. Indian warfare had been a good training for the Americans, and the Regulars never could become accustomed to this exceedingly irregular fashion of fighting.

Among Washington's most trusted officers was Benedict Arnold. He had helped to capture Benedict Arnold Ticonderoga, he had led the march through the Maine wilderness, he had gone to the aid of Fort Stanwix, and he was one of the two men who had forced Burgoyne to surrender. Congress had not pro-

THE SEAT OF WAR IN THE SOUTH

moted him as he — and Washington — thought he deserved. Instead, however, of behaving so nobly that every one would see that Congress had made a mistake, he committed such a crime that people felt that Congress had been in the right.

The one thing that the British wanted most was to gain control of the Hudson. The strongest fort on the river was at West Arnold's treason Point. Arnold asked Washington to give him command of it, and Washington did so willingly, and without the least suspicion that his trusted officer meant to surrender it to the enemy. Major André was sent by the English to make the final plans. He was

captured, papers showing his mission were found in his posse:
sion, and he was hanged as a spy. Arnold escaped to the Britis
lines. He received a large amount of money and was made a
officer in the British army, but he was despised for being a traito
André was risking his life to serve his own country, and althoug
by the custom of war he was hanged, every one was sorry, an

MAJOR ANDRÉ
(From a portrait by himself)

wished Arnold could have been in his plac
The traitor is said to have asked an Amer
can prisoner what his countrymen woul
do with him if they caught him. "The
would bury with the honors of war the le
that was wounded at Quebec and Saratog
and the rest of you they would hang on
gibbet," was the answer.

This terrible treason of the man who
he had trusted was a heavy blow to Wasl
ington. Tears fell from his eyes, but in a
his sorrow and wrath he remembered tl
grief and anxiety of Arnold's wife, and ser
her a message that her husband had escape
So ended the year 1780, saddened by loss

in the South, by the treason of a trusted officer, and by suffe
ings at Morristown, where Washington's army wintered, equal t
those at Valley Forge.

1781.

During the winter of 1780–81 the soldiers were freezing an
A hard win- starving, and seemed almost ready to revolt, but when Britis
ter at Morris-
town   spies offered high pay to any one who would desert and join tl
English army, the men indignantly refused.

Washington was keeping close watch on the Hudson, but in tl
South Cornwallis held South Carolina. General Greene was ser

THE SURRENDER OF CORNWALLIS
(From Trumbull's picture in the Capitol at Washington)

against him. Sometimes one lost and sometimes the other, but, losing or winning, Greene was marching across North Carolina, and the British were pursuing. In the middle of the summer Cornwallis went to Yorktown, Virginia. The English ships would soon bring aid from New York, he thought. So they would, but the French ships were coming, too. Lafayette, whom he called "the boy," was pressing nearer. Washington suddenly dashed across the country and joined his ally. The French ships were on one side, the American forces on the other; there was nothing to do but to yield. October 19, 1781, Cornwallis surrendered. The news came to Philadelphia in the night. It was the custom for the watchman to call the hour and say, "All is well;" but that night he called, "Past three o'clock, and Cornwallis is taken!" Except for a little trouble with the Indian allies of the British,

Cornwallis surrenders at Yorktown

the war was over. The Americans were free, and now it remained to be seen what they would do with their freedom.

SUMMARY.

1777. Washington's ability as a commander won respect in Europe.
Franklin gained friends in France, and Lafayette came to aid the Americans.
1778. The British took Philadelphia, but their plan to cut New England from New York failed, and Burgoyne's army was captured at Saratoga.
The Americans suffered much at Valley Forge from cold and hunger, but France promised aid and Clark saved the Northwest for the United States.
The British planned to take Georgia and work to the north.
1779-1781. The victories of the Bon Homme Richard increased European confidence in the final success of America.
Arnold's treason was a great blow to Washington and to the country.
The surrender of Cornwallis in 1781 practically closed the war.

SUGGESTIONS FOR WRITTEN WORK.

One of Cornwallis's soldiers writes home what happened on the Delaware.
Describe the making of the flag at Fort Stanwix.
A day at Valley Forge.
A British soldier describes one of Marion's attacks.

XVIII

THE YEARS OF WEAKNESS

1782-1789.

Disagreements among the colonies

The thirteen colonies had stood together to resist the king, but now each one began to think what would be best for itself. There were many difficult questions to settle, and no one had any right

WASHINGTON RESIGNING HIS COMMISSION AS COMMANDER-IN-CHIEF
(From Trumbull's painting in the Yale Art Gallery)

to settle them. The most pressing matter was how to raise money. Congress could impose taxes, but if a state did not choose to pay them, there was no power to make it; and some people said, " We would not let Parliament tax us, and we will not let Congress." During the war, the Americans had paid no debts to British merchants, and, indeed, had been forbidden to pay such debts. Congress now requested the people to pay, but they did not obey. England retaliated in several ways, one of which was to pass laws that injured American commerce. The Americans could not make any such laws against England and so force that country to treat them fairly, because a law that might be of advantage to one state might not be of value to another, and they could not agree among themselves what laws to make. Each state was looking out for itself, and there were so many disagree-

Financial
difficulties

ments that few people in Europe believed the union would last "They'll soon come back," thought George III., "and ask to b under our rule again." Some of Washington's officers even begai to plot to have a kingdom and make their commander king, bu he sternly rebuked them for thinking of such a plan.

The North-western Ter-ritory Fortunately there was one thing in which every state was intei ested, and that was the Northwestern Territory. Several state had claims upon it, but at last it was agreed to put the whole are into the hands of Congress in the hope that it could be sold t settlers and the war debt paid. Any state leaving the unioi would lose its share of the vast amount of money that, it wa thought, would be realized from this land.

The Consti-tution Six years after the surrender of Cornwallis, it was decided t hold a convention in Philadelphia "to form a more perfect union, and then it was that our Constitution was written. This was no an easy thing to do, for each state was guarding it own rights, and was afraid of having less power tha: the others.

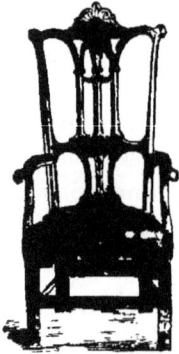

How to represent the people fairly was the hardes question. "A large state should have more represent atives," said one. "A small state has its all at stak just the same as a large one," declared another. A last it was decided that each state, whether large o small, should choose two men to send to Congress, an so the Senate should be made up. Men should also b sent to form the House of Representatives, and th number of these sent from each state should depenc upon the population of the state.

THE PRESIDENT'S
ARMCHAIR IN
INDEPENDENCE
HALL

The Presi-dent's term of office How long the President should be in office was another har question to decide. Some said one year. "That is not long enoug] for a man to accomplish anything," said one party. "Let us hav it seven years." "A dishonest president would gain too mucl

power in seven years," the other party declared. Finally the term
of four years was decided upon. It was also agreed that Congress Congress
should make the laws, that the President should have power to
oblige people to
obey them, and
that the Supreme
Court, formed of
judges chosen by
the President,
should settle all
disputes about the
meaning of the
laws.

The Su-
preme
Court

INAUGURATION OF WASHINGTON

There was much
discussion about
this Constitution
in the different states, but at last all thirteen adopted it. Then
each state chose electors, or men to vote for a president. Every The first
one of the electors voted for Washington, and in 1789 he became President
the first President of the United States.

1789–1817.

The first difficulty for the states to meet was the lack of money.
The Continental Congress had never been able to pay what it The lack of
borrowed, and no foreign nation would lend them a dollar. A wise money
man named Alexander Hamilton was made Secretary of the Treasury, and so it became his business to suggest to Congress the
best way to manage the money affairs of the country. He said,
"Let us tax all foreign goods brought into the United States
for sale. This will make the price higher, of course, but it will
yield revenue and will enable our manufacturers to make many
things that we now bring from Europe." Then he suggested,

"Let us agree to pay all the money that the Continental Congress borrowed." His third suggestion was a little startling, for it was, "Let us promise to pay whatever each state borrowed." Finally Congress agreed. These suggestions of Hamilton's were very wise, for those whom the United States owed saw that if the government did not stand, they would never get their money, and every creditor became a friend to the new nation.

Large amounts of money were soon to come into the country in a way that no one had thought of. A young man in Connecticut was asked to go to Georgia to teach the children of a rich planter. When he arrived, some one else had been engaged, and he was far from home and almost penniless. General Greene's widow had met him on the long journey south, and she invited him to her home. In Georgia the chief business

ALEXANDER HAMILTON
(From Trumbull's portrait in Boston)

The cotton-gin is invented

was raising rice and indigo, though of late years planters had begun to sow cotton. Cotton had been brought from India before this, and the planters were sure of a high price for all that they could send to market. They had little to sell, however, for the cotton clings fast to its small seeds, and all these had to be picked out before it could be woven. One day a planter said to Mrs. Greene, "If we only had a machine that would get these seeds out, we could all be rich." "Here is Mr. Whitney," she said. "He made me this embroidery frame, and if any one can make such a machine, I believe that he can." The result of the conversation was the invention

FLOWER AND BOLLS
OF THE COTTON PLANT

of the cotton-gin, with which a man could clear at least fifty times as much cotton in a day as without it.

Southern planters now began to raise much cotton. They did not weave it, but sold it and bought what- ever they needed; therefore they wanted duties low. The North raised no cotton, and a large share of the northern income came from manufactures; therefore the North preferred high duties on goods that could be made in America.

Effect of cotton-gin o duties and low. slavery

The cotton-gin encouraged negro slavery. Before this, many, even in the South, had felt that it would be good to have no such thing as slavery, but now large numbers of workers were needed, and it was thought that the negroes would not work unless they

WHITNEY'S COTTON-GIN

were slaves. If cotton was not plenty, the mills in the North would make less money, and, therefore, many Northerners were willing to have slavery flourish.

John Adams became president in 1797. Before that time, France declared war against England and wished the United States to join her; but our government refused to have anything to do with European disagreements. France was angry and began to destroy our vessels. The French minister, Talleyrand, suggested that this would be stopped if the Americans would bribe some of the officials of the French government.

Trouble with France

A COTTON-FIELD

Then Charles Pinckney, who had been sent to France to represent the United States, declared that his country had "millions for defense, but not one cent for tribute." These words were in every one's mouth, just as in the Revolution every one was saying, "No taxation without representation." "America is not scared," wrote Adams. "France shall do as she pleases." The thought of another war made the union of the states stronger.

Hail, Columbia

This was when the words of "Hail, Columbia," were written, though the music had been composed several years before. The tune was called "The President's March," and was first played when Washington was going through Trenton on his way to New York to be inaugurated. Our small navy began to attack French vessels, and was so successful that France soon suggested that we should be friends.

In Adams's administration, in the last month of 1799, Washington died. General Henry Lee pronounced the funeral oration, and then it was that Washington was called "First in war, first in peace, and first in the hearts of his countrymen."

While Jefferson was president, there was trouble with Africa. For several hundred years the people living in the Barbary States in northern Africa had been accustomed to de-

BARBARY PIRATE VESSEL

Suppression of the Barbary pirates

mand tribute from all vessels that came their way. If this tribute was not paid, they would seize the vessels. Any wealthy men that might be on board were kept for ransom, and the others were sold as slaves. These pirates were so fierce and savage and had so many vessels that the nations of Europe had paid them tribute rather than run the risk of losing their merchant ships. For the lack of warships, the United States did the same thing at first, but very unwillingly. One officer, sent to pay the tribute, Suppression of the Barbary pirates wrote home that he hoped he should never be sent to pay tribute again unless he could deliver it from the mouth of a cannon. At last warships were sent against the Barbary States, and one of their chief cities was bombarded. Then the ruler thought it was time to ask for a treaty with the United States, and to cease meddling with American ships.

CANNON CAPTURED FROM THE BARBARY STATES

About this time the United States suddenly became more than twice as large as it had been before. When the French and Indian War came to an end, the immense tract of land north of Texas and between the Mississippi and the Rocky Mountains was given to Spain. After a while, France gained possession of it again. France owned also some land on the east of the Mississippi at its mouth; and, therefore, if she chose, she could prevent the Americans from using the river. Jefferson sent two Louisiana Purchase men to see whether Napoleon, emperor of France, would sell New Orleans. Napoleon was about ready to make war upon England. He wanted money, and he did not want this land in America, for England could easily seize upon it. While the two envoys were thinking about New Orleans, he suddenly offered them the whole territory known as Louisiana at two and a half cents an acre. Such a bargain as this was not to be passed, and the land was bought. No one knew much about it, and some said not a settler would go there for

MERIWETHER LEWIS

a century; but the purchase would give the right to use the Mississippi, and it would prevent England from ever holding the land, so that most Americans were glad.

Exploration of the western land

Jefferson sent out a party at once to explore the new territory. The leaders were his secretary, Meriwether Lewis, and William Clark, whose brother George had saved the Northwestern Territory for the Americans. They went up the Missouri, then made their way to a branch of the Columbia, and so down to the Pacific Ocean, which was, as their journal says, "more raging than pacific."

A WARSHIP'S GUN-DECK IN 1800

The Columbia River had been discovered more than a century before this by a Rhode Island captain, who gave it the name of his vessel.

Again the quarrels of Europe made trouble for the United States. France

The Embargo Act

and England were at war. Napoleon gave notice that he should fire upon any vessel carrying goods to England; and England declared that she should seize any vessel carrying goods to France or to any of the countries that were on the side of France. Congress believed that both France and England needed our goods so badly that if none made their way to either country, these declarations would be withdrawn, and so they made a law called the Embargo Act, forbidding any American vessel to leave port. People who depended upon commerce suffered greatly by this act. They spelled its name backwards and called it the O-grab-me act. It hurt the United States much more than France or England had done, and before long it was repealed.

Causes of the War of 1812

Madison became president. He was a gentle, courteous, scholarly man, but it was during his term of office that a second war with England was fought. One cause was the interference with our commerce. Another was England's claim that no Englishman could become a citizen of any other country, and her

exercising what was called the right of search. An English warship meeting an American vessel would signal it to stop, and would
fire at it if the order was not obeyed. Then the English captain
would take from the crew of the American ship all the men that
he thought were Englishmen, even if they had become American
citizens. If he needed sailors, he would not be particular to make
sure that these men were of English birth. He would claim that
no one could tell an American from an Englishman, and so he would
carry off what men he chose, and force them to enter
the British navy. The United States had long been
indignant at this behavior of England, but had not
been able to prevent it for want of an army. England was engaged in the war with France also,
but she had a large and well-trained army and
sixty times as many warships as the United
States. Nevertheless, this country would bear
no more, and war was declared. The
contest is called the War of 1812.

The first aim of the Americans
was to conquer Canada, but they did
not succeed. As the enemy were
invading the Northwestern Territory, it began to be clear that the
only way to keep them out was to
gain possession of Lake Erie. A
young naval officer named Oliver
Hazard Perry was sent to Erie, Pennsylvania, to build a fleet.

OLD IRONSIDES
(Built in Boston, 1797, and now at the Charlestown
Navy Yard)

To keep English ships from sailing up the Saint Lawrence, the
frigate Constitution under Captain Hull was sent at the beginning
of the war to cruise about the Gulf. One afternoon he caught
sight of the British frigate Guerrière, the ship of all ships that he
was most eager to meet, for he had once been chased nearly three

days by the Guerrière and the rest of her fleet, and he meant to have his revenge. The British captain was ready, for he was sure that he could capture any American vessels "with a bit of striped bunting at their mastheads," as he said scornfully. The fight was not half an hour long. The masts of the Guerrière were shot away, and her hull was riddled with cannon balls. There was nothing to do but to surrender. The wreck was not worth saving, and it was set afire. New England had not favored this war, but when Captain Hull appeared in Boston harbor, the city made ready to give him such a reception as she had never given to any man before. To sink an English frigate was enough to arouse the enthusiasm of this little nation with its navy of sixteen vessels. One city gave Hull and his officers swords, another presented silver plate. State dinners and decorations and cheering and illuminations and the waving of flags were everywhere. As for England, this victory was perhaps one of the greatest surprises that she had ever known, and she became more and more surprised as time passed. In the long war with France she had taken hundreds of ships and lost only five; but in the first six months of this War of 1812 she "had had six naval battles, had lost six ships, and had not taken one."

Old Iron-
sides

The Constitution won so many victories and was so little injured that the name "Old Ironsides" was given her. Twenty years afterwards the government decided that she was no longer seaworthy and must be broken up. Then Oliver Wendell Holmes wrote his famous poem, "Old Ironsides," beginning, "Ay, tear her tattered ensign down!" and so many were eager to save the ship that it was repaired and sailed the ocean for many a year. It is now, more than a century old, in the Navy Yard at Charlestown, Massachusetts. It is kept in good repair, and will, perhaps, last another hundred years.

Perry and his company of carpenters were at Erie, cutting down

trees as fast as they could to build a fleet. There was no time to Perry's victory on Lake Erie
wait for timber to season, and the ships were made from lumber
that was almost fresh from the forest. The one that he chose for
his flagship was named the Lawrence, from a brave officer
who had fallen in a sea fight a year earlier. The last words
of Lawrence were, "Don't give up the ship!" and this is
what Perry put on his flag. The young captain had never
seen a naval battle, but he went out boldly to meet the
British fleet. Capturing a flagship is about the same on
the water as taking the enemy's capital is on land; but
even when Perry's flagship was shot so full of holes that

PERRY'S FLAG

she was ready to sink, he did not surrender. He and his twelve-
year-old brother sprang into a boat with the eight sailors who
still lived, and rowed to another ship of the fleet. There was a
storm of bullets and cannon balls around them. More than one
bullet went through the boy's cap, but they reached the vessel in
safety. "Don't give up the ship!" swung out from the masthead,
and in less than ten minutes the British fleet surrendered. Perry
sent a message to the government, "We have met the enemy and
they are ours." This victory cut the Brit-
ish off from further invasion of the Northwestern Territory.

The war was more serious than it other- The Indians and the English
wise would have been because the Indians
of   Canada   united

COMMODORE PERRY'S MESSAGE
(*By permission of Harper & Brothers*)

with the English, and their chief went to Alabama to induce the
red men there to fight against the Americans. The Indians were
suppressed by two men who afterwards became presidents of the

United States, General Harrison, who won victories in Canada, and General Jackson, who was successful in the South.

The burning of Washington When the war with France was over, England sent more soldiers and more vessels. Suddenly word came to Washington that fifty British ships were at the mouth of the Potomac. The city had no fortifications and was helpless. The invaders swept into the town, burned the Capitol, and even the Congressional Library, and took possession of the White House. Dolly Madison, the President's wife, saved the Declaration of Independence and a valuable portrait of Washington. Tradition declares that, like a good housekeeper, she also carried away to safety her work-bag filled with silver spoons. To destroy Washington gave no military advantage. The British said it was done because the Americans had burned Toronto. There was this difference, however, in the two acts: Toronto was burned by soldiers acting without authority and the United States disapproved of the deed, while Washington was burned under strict orders from the British government. Americans may well be ashamed of the destruction of Toronto, but they have no such act of barbarism to regret as burning a national library.

DOLLY MADISON
(From a miniature)

Attack on Baltimore The British ships next appeared before Baltimore. All day the cannon thundered. On board one of the ships was an American

prisoner, Francis Scott Key. The cannonading went on through The Star-
the night. He watched anxiously every "rocket's red glare," lest Spangled
Banner
he should see that the American flag had been lowered. Dawn
came, and the flag still floated. In his relief and joy, he wrote
"The Star-Spangled Banner." It was printed at once; the air
was a familiar one, and soon the song was. sung from one end of
the country to the other.

After more than two years of fighting, England planned to
make a fierce attack upon New Orleans and so gain control of the The battle of
Mississippi. General Jackson was sent to defend the city, and New Orleans
wherever he went something was usually accomplished. The
American troops had had little experience, and they were only half
as many as their enemies. The British soldiers were veterans, but
their knapsacks, muskets, etc., were far too heavy for rapid movement. Both sides fought bravely, but the English were terribly
defeated.

One especially sad fact about this battle, with its great loss of
life, is that it was fought in January.
1815, two weeks after the treaty
of peace was signed. The only
way for news to come from
England to America was
by sailing vessel, and there
were few that even with
fair winds could cross the
ocean in less than a month.
This treaty said not one

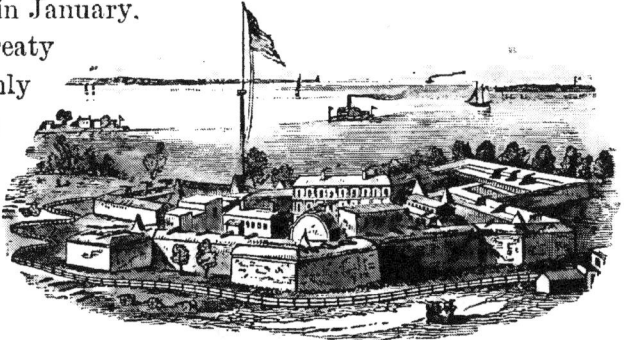

FORT McHENRY, BALTIMORE
(Where " the Star-Spangled Banner " of the song waved)

word about any rights of
the Americans to buy and sell as they chose and did not mention The treaty
the right of search, but after this, England never again attempted of peace
to interfere with American commerce or to search an American
vessel. Before this war the United States had been looked upon

as a few millions of people who had banded together to fr
themselves from England. After the war it was seen that tl
United States was a nation, able to defend its rights, and to ho
an honorable place among the nations of the world.

SUMMARY.

After the Revolution each colony thought only of its own gain. Congr
had no power to enforce its laws. The chief thing in which all t
states had a common interest was the Northwestern Territory.

A convention held in Philadelphia drew up the Constitution, which ga
Congress the power to make laws, the President the power to enfoi
them, and the Supreme Court the power to interpret them.

In 1789 Washington became the first president of the United States.

The government obtained money by duties on imports, and friends
assuming the Revolutionary debts of the colonies.

The invention of the cotton-gin resulted in an increase in the producti
of cotton, which caused disagreement between the North and the Sou
about duties, and encouraged negro slavery.

Our vessels were attacked by the French because of our refusal to aid the
in a war against England. After we had captured many French vesse
France made peace.

In 1799 Washington died.

The Barbary pirates were suppressed by our warships.

The United States bought of France the land between the Mississippi a
the Rocky Mountains, which was soon explored by Lewis and Clark.

The Embargo Act was passed in retaliation for the declarations of Frar
and England which injured our commerce.

The War of 1812 was caused by England's interference with our commer
and by her searching our ships and seizing our sailors.

American attacks on Canada failed; but American victories on Lake E:
and elsewhere kept the British out of our Northwestern Territory.

Our ships won many victories on the ocean.

The British burned Washington, but were defeated at New Orleans aft
peace had been made.

SUGGESTIONS FOR WRITTEN WORK.

A sailor describes the search of an American vessel by the British.
Perry's brother describes the victory of Lake Erie.

XIX

THE WESTWARD GROWTH OF THE COUNTRY

1817–1841.

JAMES MONROE was the next president. Soon after he was inaugurated he made a tour of the country to see the forts and navy
yards. Traveling was easier than
when Washington had to ride on
horseback from New York to Boston,
for a man named Robert Fulton had
invented the steamboat. Steamers
were already on the rivers and the
Great Lakes, and before Monroe's
term of office was over, Georgia sent
one to Europe. Monroe had a joyful
reception wherever he went. He wore
the blue and buff uniform and the

FULTON'S STEAMER, THE CLERMONT

cocked hat of the Revolution. The old soldiers remembered that The " era of
he had been one of them and gave him a comrade's greeting. good feel-
One of the Boston papers called the times the " era of good feel- ing "
ing," and that described the condition of things so well that the
phrase went throughout the country.

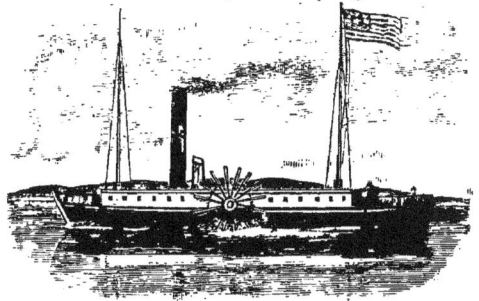

In the southeastern corner of the land there was trouble. The
Creek Indians of Alabama had sided with the British in the War Trouble with
of 1812, because they felt that the Americans were driving them the Semi-
away from their lands. They expected the British to secure the noles

land for them, and when this was not done, they were more indignant than ever. In Florida there were Seminoles, negro slaves
who had escaped from their masters in Georgia, Spaniards, and a
few English, all of whom were willing to unite with the
Creeks against the Americans.

Monroe sent General Jackson to subdue them, and
he succeeded; but Congress was a little startled when
it was known that he had paid no attention to the fact
that Florida was Spanish soil, and that among
the men whom he punished were both Spaniards
and English. There might have been trouble
if Spain had not been in need of money. The
result was that she sold Florida to the United
States. Our country then owned every foot of
what is now United States territory east of
the Mississippi. West of that river the vast
tract called Louisiana was United States soil.
Spain still owned what is now Texas and
Mexico, but she agreed to give up all claim
to the "Oregon Territory," which was the
land north of California.

OSCEOLA, CHIEF OF THE
SEMINOLES

There was much talk about the Pacific coast just then, for
The Monroe Russia had taken possession of the land which we now call Alaska,
doctrine and had begun to build trading-posts along the California coast.
Other nations of Europe were looking for new territory in South
America. Then it was that the President announced what is now
called the "Monroe doctrine." It was that European nations could
not acquire new territory in either North or South America, and
that the United States would not permit any European country
to "interfere with any independent American government."

The Americans were no longer confined to a little strip of land
along the coast. There were twenty-two states, and two others

were asking to be admitted. The new states had been settled Going West
chiefly by colonists from the older ones. There were no railroads,
and the only way for a family to "go West" by land was by wagon
or on foot. The wagon most often used was called a prairie
schooner. It was long and low, and was covered with white
canvas drawn over great wooden hoops. The emigrants would
ride slowly on day after day, cooking their meals in gypsy fashion
over out-of-door fires, and sleeping in the wagon. They would
pick out a good piece of land, build a log house, cut down the
trees, plant corn and potatoes, raise sheep and cattle, spin, weave;
and, if all went well, they
would have a comfortable
home, where the family
would at least be sure of
enough to eat and to wear.
The emigrant would, of
course, be wise enough to
select land that was near
a river, so that as soon as
he had any produce to
sell, it could be taken
to a market and ex-
changed for things that
he could not make.

EMIGRANTS GOING WEST
ACROSS THE PRAIRIES

Other settlers would come, perhaps a village would grow up
around his house; and he might become a rich man.

This is what every emigrant hoped, and it is no wonder that so
many went to the "far West," which then meant states no farther Numbers of
the emi-
grants
away than Ohio or Tennessee. One man in Pennsylvania reported that two hundred and thirty-six prairie schooners went
through his town in a single month. Some of the emigrants had
set out bravely on foot to find the happy land where the poorest

CHICAGO AS IT WAS IN 1832

had enough. One man and his wife were seen in Pennsylvani
on their way to Indiana, having already walked from Maine
They had a little handcart, in which were all of their possessions
and as many of their six children as were too young to make th
journey on foot.[1]

These people came from all parts of the country, and an im
portant question was arising because o
the new settlements. Should slav
ery be allowed in the newly opene
territory? The North sai
"No," not only because man
were beginning to think slav
ery wrong, but because if ther
were more slave states thai
free states, their representa
tives in Congress would vot
against duties, and this woul
hurt the northern manufac
turers. The South said "Yes,
fearing that if there were mor

HENRY CLAY'S BIRTHPLACE, HANOVER COUNTY,
VIRGINIA

[1] McMaster's *History of the People of the United States.*

free states, slavery might be interfered with. She hoped also to The Missouri Compromise gain representatives enough to abolish duties on imported goods. Maine asked to be admitted as a state, but the South said, "No, we will not have another free state." Missouri made the same request, but the North said, "No, we will not have another slave state." Finally Henry Clay, "the great peacemaker," persuaded Congress to admit both states on condition that there should never be another slave state north of the southern boundary of Missouri, that is, 36° 30'. This act was called the Missouri Compromise. People felt relieved and glad. "There will be no more trouble about slavery," they said.

In 1824, four years after the Missouri Compromise, the United States "had company." Lafayette was invited to visit the country as the guest of the whole nation. Such rejoicings as there were, and such welcomes, not only from the old soldiers who had fought under "the boy," but from every one who loved his country and appreciated the help that Lafayette had given so generously to win its freedom. He visited each one of the twenty-four states, and was greeted everywhere as the friend of

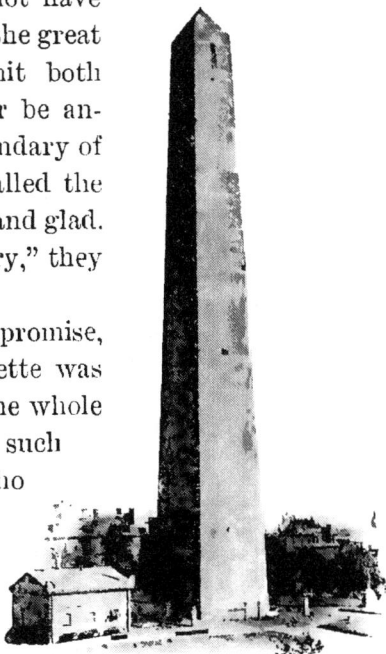

BUNKER HILL MONUMENT

the nation. From each railroad train that comes into Boston from Lafayette's visit the north the tall gray stone monument that stands on Bunker Hill may be seen. Its corner-stone was laid by Lafayette, June 17, 1825, just fifty years after the battle, and many veterans were present who, as young men, had stood on that hill waiting to "see the whites of their eyes."

When Lafayette was ready to return to France, Congress gave him a generous sum of money and more than one half as much land as there is in the District of Columbia. A new frigate was named the Brandywine in honor of the battle in which he was wounded, and this was sent to the mouth of the Potomac to carry him across the ocean.

John Quincy Adams became president in 1825. When July 4, 1826, drew near great preparations were made throughout the land to celebrate the fiftieth anniversary of the signing of the Declaration of Independence. There were speeches and cheers and music. Guns were fired and bells were rung. When night came, the country was ablaze with

STAGE-COACH

bonfires and illuminations. The use of gas was

The fiftieth Fourth of July

beginning to be common in some of the large cities, and its light was so much brighter than that given by candles and whale-oil lamps that it was looked upon as a marvel. Audiences would gaze with wonder and delight when the gas in a theatre or concert hall was suddenly turned up.

The whole land was jubilant, but a few days later word came that on July 4, while the country was happy in its celebration

Death of Adams and Jefferson

of independence, two men who had done much to win that independence had died. They were Thomas Jefferson in Virginia and John Adams in Massachusetts. Grief took the place of joy, and black drapings were hung where such a little while before there had been only brightness.

To-day the death of a famous man would be flashed over the Slow travel-world in a few minutes, but seventy-five years ago news traveled ing slowly, for there were no steam railroads and no telegraph. The only way that a message could be carried from New York to Pittsburg, for instance, was by a man on horseback or by stage-coach. When the people in Ohio wished to send their pro-duce to market, they usually carried it in wagons to Pitts-burg, and then it went by boat down the Ohio and the Missis-sippi to New Orleans. Goods sent from New York to south-

AN OLD-FASHIONED CHAISE

ern Ohio had to be carried by wagon across Pennsylvania, or else by boat up the Hudson and the Mohawk, across Lake Ontario and a part of Lake Erie, and then down the Alleghany to Pitts-burg.[1] The part of this journey that could not be made by water was made in great wagons or ox-carts.

New York and the other Eastern cities knew that there must

FREIGHT WAGON
(From an old freight bill)

be a cheaper way to carry goods to the West, or else the new states The Erie would make all their purchases in New Orleans and bring them Canal

[1] McMaster's *History of the People of the United States.*

up the Mississippi in steamboats. It was proposed to dig a canal from Albany to Buffalo. There was no dynamite for heavy blasting and no steam machinery for digging. Every pound of dirt must be lifted by a man with a shovel. It was a great undertaking. Governor Clinton of New York was much interested in its success, and the people who did not believe in the canal called it "Clinton's big ditch." " How shall you get back the millions that it will cost?" one asked. "We will tax every boat that goes through it," Clinton answered. "You'll have nothing but mud for your pains," another grumbled; but Governor Clinton kept bravely at work, and after eight long years the "big ditch" was done.

There was a great celebration in Buffalo, and the Erie Canal was formally declared to

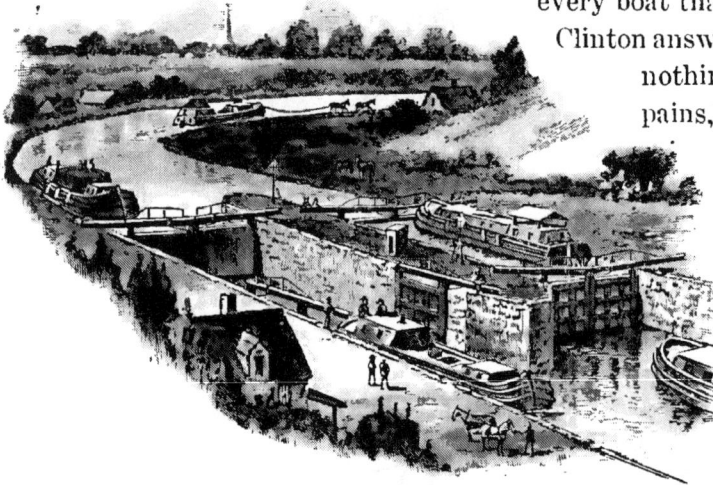

A CANAL SHOWING HORSES, TOW-BOATS, AND LOCKS

Opening of
the canal

be open. A cannon was fired, then another five miles farther down the canal, and so on all the way to New York city. Probably no news had ever before traveled five hundred miles so rapidly. Governor Clinton and others went on board some canal boats, fresh and new, and made gay with flags and streamers. Horses walking the "tow-path" towed the boats along to Albany. Then they went down the Hudson to New York city and out into the bay. Two kegs of water, brought from Lake Erie, were poured into the sea to show that Lake Erie and New York Bay were united.

The canal was used so much that even the first year the tolls paid nearly twice the interest. Freight grew cheaper each year, and it was not long before one dollar would carry as much weight from Albany to Buffalo as fifteen had formerly done. Towns were soon built all along the canal. Other canals were dug, and each one of them made it possible for new towns to be built and new manufactures to be engaged in. There was such enthusiasm over canals that some people declared it would not be long before there would be a waterway from the Atlantic to the Pacific.

KEG BROUGHT THROUGH THE ERIE CANAL

Canal boats were cheap and safe, but their speed was only four miles an hour, and people began to question whether it would not be better to build railroads. The idea of a railroad was not new. Wooden rails had been laid in several places to carry stone or earth, and wagons had been dragged on these rails by horses; but the use of steam locomotives on railroads we owe to an Englishman named George Stephenson. He tried for a long time before any one would believe in his invention. People laughed at it just as they had laughed at the "big ditch." "What should you do, Mr. Stephenson," asked one man, "if your engine was going at full speed

BOSTON AND WORCESTER RAILROAD TRAIN OF 1835

and a cow got in front of it?" "It would be very bad for the cow," said the inventor gravely. The new engines were tried in America. They went very well on level ground, but they could not climb a hill that was at all steep. The road must either go around the hill, or else there must be machinery at the top to pull the cars up by ropes. The speed was not so very much greater than that of a steamboat. The rails were of wood with strips of iron on top. The passenger cars looked almost exactly like stage-coaches, and part of the passengers had to ride backwards. Improvements came rapidly. Every year the trains went a little faster, the roadbeds, rails, and locomotives were a little better. It was easier for people to go about the country. They learned new ways of doing things. They saw new sights and thought new thoughts.

Men had to think new thoughts in those days, for several difficult problems were coming up to be solved. There were the two old ones, about slavery and about duties, and there was a new one, " Who shall pay for these canals and railroads?" The South said, "Let each state pay for its own;" the North said, "They are 'for the gain of the whole country, and therefore the whole country should pay for them."

Who shall pay?

When it was time to elect a new president, Andrew Jackson, the sturdy old Indian fighter, was chosen. He was a straightforward, upright man, with a frank, cordial manner. He liked to please people and to do everything in the simplest way. His good-heartedness led him to do one deed that was an injury to the country. Resolute as he was, it was always hard for him to refuse a friend's request. When he became president, every one who had the least claim upon him begged for some position in the government employ, and he could not say No. The only way to find positions enough was to turn out the men who were then in office. This fashion of favoring one's friends is called the " spoils system" from a remark made in jest that "to the victor belong the spoils."

ANDREW JACKSON

Jackson and the spoils system

The hardest question that Jackson had to meet was in regard

WEBSTER MAKING HIS FAMOUS SPEECH
(From the painting by Healy in Faneuil Hall, Boston)

to what was called "nullification," or making of no force. Con- Nullification
gress voted to impose duties large enough to make imported
goods cost more than those made in the United States. South
Carolina said, "This is an unjust law, for it makes us poor while
it makes the northern manufacturers rich. It is right for us to
refuse to obey it, and therefore we shall nullify the act." This
statement was made in the Senate. Daniel Webster replied in
the famous speech that closes, "Liberty and Union, now and forever, one and inseparable." President Jackson did not like the
large duties, but he meant that the laws of the land should be
obeyed, and he sent forces to South Carolina to see that the
duties were collected. Soon after this, Henry Clay, the "great
peacemaker," persuaded Congress to lessen the duties, and there
was no outbreak.

If a government is strong, and people feel safe and have time
to devote to education, books are sure to be written. In the colo-

Our first great American writers nial days few books were written in America whose reading still gives pleasure. Even after the Union was formed, people across the ocean used to say with a smile, "Not even the Americans read the American books;" but before Jackson's time three American writers became known whose works were read with pleasure on both sides of the Atlantic. They were Irving, Cooper, and Bryant. One great difference between their writings and those of most of the American authors that had come before them was that they did not try to imitate English writers. When Bryant described a landscape, he put in American flowers and trees and birds; while the American poets before him were inclined to put in larks and nightingales and primroses and "crimson-tipped" daisies, without stopping to think whether these birds and flowers could be found in America. Cooper had little to say about lords and princes; he liked best to write about the Indians of his own land. So it was with Irving. When he wrote "Rip Van Winkle," he did not make his hero live in some old

BRYANT'S HOME AT ROSLYN

English castle, but in a New York village; and Rip's strange adventures all took place on the New York mountains.

In 1837 Jackson's term of office was over. He was the last Close of Jackson's term President that had had anything to do with the Revolutionary War. Not one man was living who had signed the Declaration of Independence. The men who had made the country were dead, and the land was left in the hands of those that had come after them.

When Van Buren's name is mentioned, the first thought that comes to mind is "hard times," that is, times when no one seemed to have money to pay his debts. The government had received for public lands and duties many million dollars more than it needed to use, and had deposited the money in various banks. These banks had loaned it to speculators, and to men who wished to build railroads or canals or to buy western lands. Suddenly the government decided to divide this money among the states. and ordered the banks to return it. The banks called upon the speculators and others to bring it back. *Martin Van Buren*

To do this at once was often difficult or impossible; for instance, men who had borrowed money to buy land where they expected a railroad would be built could not sell their land at a fair price till the road was completed, and had no money with which to pay the banks. Another trouble was that the government had declared that men who bought western land must pay for it in gold or silver; and, therefore, much coin had gone West. The banks united, and said that for the present they would not give coin for their bills, and they would make no new loans. No one knew what to-morrow's value of the paper money, or "rag money," as it was called, would be. Every one wanted coin, and whoever had any coin held on to it. Business firms failed, banks failed, mills stopped, work stopped, poverty and suffering were everywhere. The acts that caused the trouble came before Van Buren's term of office, but as the trouble itself appeared while he was president, it was always associated with his name. *Hard times*

After a while the money difficulties passed away, but there was another difficulty that was growing worse all the time, and that was the difference of opinion about slavery. Anti-slavery societies were formed in the North. William Lloyd Garrison had for several years been publishing a paper called the "Liberator," whose object was to arouse people to do away with slavery. "It is wrong," said these societies, "for one man to hold another as his slave." "It is right," said the South, "for us to hold the *Anti-slavery societies*

negro. He is happier and better cared for than he would be as
a free man." The societies sent pictures and pamphlets throughout the land to persuade people that slavery was wrong. The
South declared that these papers would make the slaves rebel
and demanded that the government should forbid such acts in
order to prevent the danger of a slave insurrection.

Differences of opinion in the North

Not all northerners sympathized with the anti-slavery societies
by any means. Probably most men in the North thought that it
would be better if there were no such thing as slavery, but many
believed that each state had the right to do as it chose in the
matter, and some who would have done anything in their power
to keep slavery out of a new state thought that no one had a
right to interfere where it already existed. Anti-slavery papers
were sometimes taken from the mails and destroyed. A hall in
which an anti-slavery meeting had been held was burned, and the
offices of the "Liberator" and other publications of the sort were
raided.

SUMMARY.

During Monroe's term of office, the Seminoles were subdued, Florida was
acquired, Spain gave up all claim to the Oregon Territory, and the
Monroe doctrine was proclaimed. Emigration to the West increased
and the Missouri Compromise postponed the slavery trouble. Lafay
ette became the guest of the nation.

While John Quincy Adams was president, the fiftieth birthday of the
nation was celebrated. Jefferson and John Adams both died on the
day of the celebration.

The success of the Erie Canal brought about the building of many other
canals and railroads, which made new towns and manufactures possible

Jackson's enforcement of the law and a decreased tariff prevented nullifica
tion in South Carolina.

Irving, Cooper, and Bryant wrote the first great American books.

Van Buren's administration was marked by hard times and by increasing
difference of opinion about slavery.

SUGGESTIONS FOR WRITTEN WORK.

Fulton's difficulties in making the first steamboat.
Governor Clinton tells why he favors the Erie Canal.
A ride on one of the early railroads.

XX

TROUBLE ARISES OVER SLAVERY

People suffered so much while Van Buren was in office that, although he was not to blame for their misfortunes, they wished to have a man who belonged to another political party. William Henry Harrison was chosen president and John Tyler vice-president. Harrison was a brave, faithful, upright man, who had always done his best and could be trusted to do well whatever he undertook. Just before the War of 1812, he had subdued the Indians at Tippecanoe in Indiana, and before the election took place his friends used to sing an absurd song, which ran : —

Harrison and Tyler

> "Oh, what has caused this great commotion
>   Our country through?
> It is the ball that's rolling on
>   For Tippecanoe and Tyler, too;
> And with them we'll beat little Van, Van, Van!
> Van! oh, he's a used-up man,
> And with them we'll beat little Van!"

Perhaps what helped Harrison most was a remark made by a newspaper that was opposed to him. It was that Harrison would feel more at home in a log cabin than in the White House. "That is just what we want," said his friends. "A man who can live in a log cabin, plough his own field, and build his own

The "log-cabin candidate"

house — he's the man for us." Pictures of log cabins appear on flags and medals. Re ones were drawn in the torc light processions by sto horses or oxen. Mammo log cabins were built for tl meetings held by Harrisor friends, and the "log-cab candidate" was elected.

Just one month after Ha rison was inaugurated] died, and John Tyler took b place. The chief subject abo which people were talking w: the annexation of Texas. Tl land southwest of the Unit States which formerly b longed to Spain had becon free and taken the name

Tyler succeeds Harrison

PICTURE FROM THE HARRISON CAMPAIGN ALMANAC

Mexico. Mexico was willing that settlers from other natior should form colonies on her soil, and it came to pass that mo: than twenty thousand people from the United States settled c the land between the Red River and the Gulf of Mexico, called Texas. After a while the demands of the Mexican government became too severe to please the Texan-Americans. Just as Mexico had fought herself free from Spain, so Texas fought herself free from Mexico. She then asked to become a state, but for several years her request was not granted, and she was a state alone t herself. This is why Texas is called the "Lone Star State."

The Lone Star State

SEAL OF TEXAS

There were various reasons why people wished or did not wis

to have Texas admitted, but the most important one was the ques- The admission of slavery. Texas held slaves, and if it became a state, the sion of Texas slave states would gain in power because they would have more votes in Congress. There was a long discussion in Congress, but finally the state was admitted. The South was triumphant; but the abolitionists, as those were called who wished to abolish slavery, set to work with more energy than ever.

People were not thinking about slavery alone. Many a man was at work on some invention that would be a gain to the country. Great inventions The sewing machine had been invented long before, but it was a tions clumsy affair. Elias Howe succeeded in making machines that were practical. Rubber shoes had been used, but they were thick and heavy and they had a fashion of melting when they were left in a warm place. Charles Goodyear found a way to vulcanize the rubber so it would not melt. "Daguerreotypes" of buildings had been taken, but now a way was found to take pictures of persons. A vast amount of suffering was prevented by the discovery that by inhaling sulphuric ether the most severe operation would be painless. Samuel F. B. Morse worked for many years to find out the way to send messages by electricity. Even after he was sure that he could do it, so few believed in him that it was a long time before he could persuade Congress to give him the money to build a line of telegraph. At

A TELEGRAPH SOUNDER

last the line was built, and the reverent message, "What hath The first God wrought!" was sent from Washington to Baltimore. telegraph

"Telegraph" means "far-writing," and it was a great mystery how writing could be done so far from where the message was given. Some did not believe any news that the telegraph brought until letters had come to prove that it was true. Some believed that the wonderful invention could not only carry the news, but collect it, and it is said that one woman objected to having a tele-

graph pole set up near her house because, as she declared, sh
did not want people all over the country to know what she wa
doing.

The Oregon Territory While Tyler was in office, there was much discussion abou
what was called the Oregon Territory, that is, the land that now
forms Oregon, Washington, Idaho, and parts of Wyoming and
Montana, and extends as far north as Alaska. A Rhode Islande
had discovered its chief river, the Columbia; a Virginian had
explored the stream; and a New Yorker had sent out a colony
England, too, claimed the land, and for many years the two coun
tries had held it in common.

The southern limit of Alaska is latitude 54° 40′, and when i
was time to elect a new president, one of the political par
ties took for a campaign cry, "Fifty-four forty or fight."
The candidate of this party, James K. Polk, was chosen
president. When he was elected, he declared, "One thing
that must be done while I am in office is to settle the
Oregon boundary." In his inaugural address he said that
the title of the United States to Oregon was clear, that emi
grants were going from the east to the extreme west, and
that the government ought to protect them and their
interests. A little later he urged that an overland mai
should be established to go to Oregon at least once a
month.

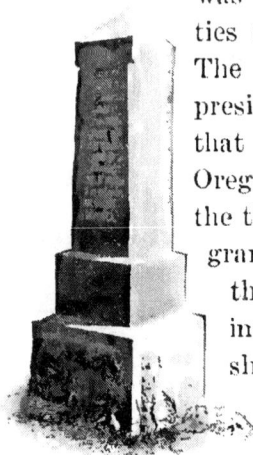

Only a few years earlier it had been a disputed
question whether it was possible to cross the moun
tains in wagons, and whether the Oregon country
was worth the effort. Few had thought that much
of it was of any value. In Congress a senator had
declared, "For agricultural purposes I would not
give a pinch of snuff for the whole Oregon Territory." The pre
sident's address did much to increase the number of emigrants

MONUMENT AT CHAMPOEG, OREGON
(To commemorate the organization there on May 2, 1843, of the first American government on the Pacific coast)

The trains of cattle drawing wagons loaded with furniture, tools, food, and clothing grew longer and more frequent. Many of these trains went to Oregon. It was a long journey; it took six months to go from the Missouri to the Willamette, but the very fact that it was farther from the east than any other part of the country to which emigrants had begun to go was one reason why so many went, for some people had the feeling that the farther they traveled, the more successful they would be.

The number of emigrants increased so that it grew more and more important to both England and the United States that the boundary line should be settled. Both countries were finding out that a part, at least, of the Territory was a rich, fertile land; but after all, the chief thing desired by each country was to get possession of the Columbia River and the inlet south of Vancouver Island. President Polk made it clear that this country would not give up any territory south of 49°. There was great excitement, and again the cry was heard, "Fifty-four forty or fight." After much discussion England offered to surrender all claim to the mainland south of 49°. This was agreed to, and our northern boundary, at 49°, was then completed. From the Lake of the Woods to the Pacific, it was marked by iron pillars placed one mile apart, and by piles of stones.

A MEXICAN BOY

Although there was no fighting with England, the United States did have a war while Polk was in office, and it came about because of the "Lone Star State," for Texas had at last been admitted to the Union. The Texans claimed the Rio Grande as their western boundary, but Mexico declared that the new state extended only to the Nueces. It was because of that strip of land, one hundred miles wide, lying between the two rivers, that the war took place.

The Mexican War

General Zachary Taylor was sent to the banks of the Rio Grande to defend the American claims. The story is told that

before the fighting began the Mexican leader said to one of th

American officers, "If General Taylor will surrender, I can pro

Campaigns
of the war
mise him good treatment." "General Taylor never surrenders

said the officer indignantly, and that speech became the watcl

word of the campaign. In these Me:

ican battles many a man fought who:

name was to become familiar a fe

years later. Among these men we:

U. S. Grant, Robert E. Lee, and Jeffe

son Davis. General Taylor was un

formly successful along the R

Grande. One division of the Ame

ican forces conquered California, ar

another marched from eastern Kans:

to California, capturing Santa Fé l

the way. Finally General Winfie

Scott made a wonderful march fro

Vera Cruz through the enemy's cou

try to the city of Mexico. The ci

was captured, and the war was ende

DISPUTED TERRITORY OF THE
MEXICAN WAR

One condition of peace was th

Acquire-
ment of new
territory
Mexico should sell to the United States California and the land

which Nevada, Utah, Arizona, and part of Wyoming, Colorad

and New Mexico have been formed. American laws and custon

were introduced at once into the new territory, and little attenti

was paid to the wishes of the people who were living on the lan

Even if there had been no question that all American laws we

better than Mexican laws, these changes were made so sudden

and so harshly that they brought about much suffering. M

Jackson's story of "Ramona" was written to picture the life of tl

Mexicans at the first coming of the Americans into the territor

Part of this land was California. It was known to have

delightful climate and a fertile soil. After a while it was dis- covered that bits of gold were to be found in the beds of gravel on the hills and in the valleys. A man could fill a pan with earth, pour on water, wash the gravel over the top of the pan, and find in the bottom grains of shining gold.

When the report of this discovery reached the East, there was a wild rush for the "Golden State." Some sailed around Cape Horn, some risked the deadly fevers of the Isthmus of Panama, others went across the country, in "prairie schooners," in ox-carts, on horseback, or even on foot. The overland route was marked not only by goods that had been thrown away when the horses became too weak to carry them farther, but by skeletons of horses and cattle, and by the headboards of hastily made graves. It was 1849 when these first gold-seekers went, and they called themselves the " Forty-niners."

While the Forty-niners were hurrying to California, Zachary Taylor, who " never surrendered," was chosen president. In a few months he died in office, and Millard Fillmore, the Vice-President, took his place. Fillmore was followed by Franklin Pierce, and after him came James

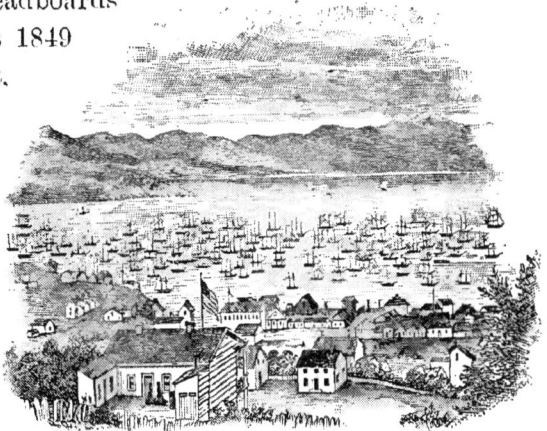

SAN FRANCISCO IN 1849
(From an engraving published in 1855)

Buchanan. During the terms of office of these presidents the laws in which people were most interested all dealt with slavery.

The first one came about because so many Forty-niners went to California that one year later the territory asked to come in as a free state. Much of California was south of 36° 30', and there was the same discussion that there had been in 1820 when Missouri wished to come in as a slave state, but in 1850 it was eve

The compromise of 1850 more bitter. In 1820 "the great peace-maker," Henry Clay, ha proposed the Missouri Compromise, and now in 1850 he brough forward another compromise. "To please the North," he said "let us admit California as a free state. To satisfy the Soutl let us pass a new fugitive slave law, and decree that if a slav escapes to a free state the United States government shall seiz him and return him to his master." The third proposal that h made was, "Let us agree that the rest of the land which wa bought from Mexico shall be free or slave territory, just as th people who may live there shall decide." Men who settled upor land to which they had no title were sometimes called "squatters, and this law allowing the settlers to decide whether slavery should exist in their territory was spoken of as "squatter sovereignty."

The compromise was agreed upon, and California was admitted Daniel Webster and many others who did not believe in slavery

The underground railroad voted for this law, because they feared that the country would be divided if they refused. The slaveholder said, "This negro is my property. I paid for him, and I have a right to claim him wherever I can find him;" but when a negro who had made his escape appeared before the door of a man who believed that slavery was wrong, that man was much inclined to help the fugitive, even if the government did order that he should be given up. Anti-slavery men would hide these runaway slaves, and pass them on from one to another, concealed in all sorts of ways, until they were safe in Canada. This system was so secret and so successful that it was spoken of as the "underground railroad."

People were talking of slavery more than anything else, and

Uncle Tom's Cabin into the midst of the discussion came Mrs. Stowe's "Uncle Tom's Cabin," painting the life of the slave in the darkest colors. The North believed that it was a truthful picture and opposed slavery more than ever.

GROWTH OF THE UNITED STATES
Up to the Civil War

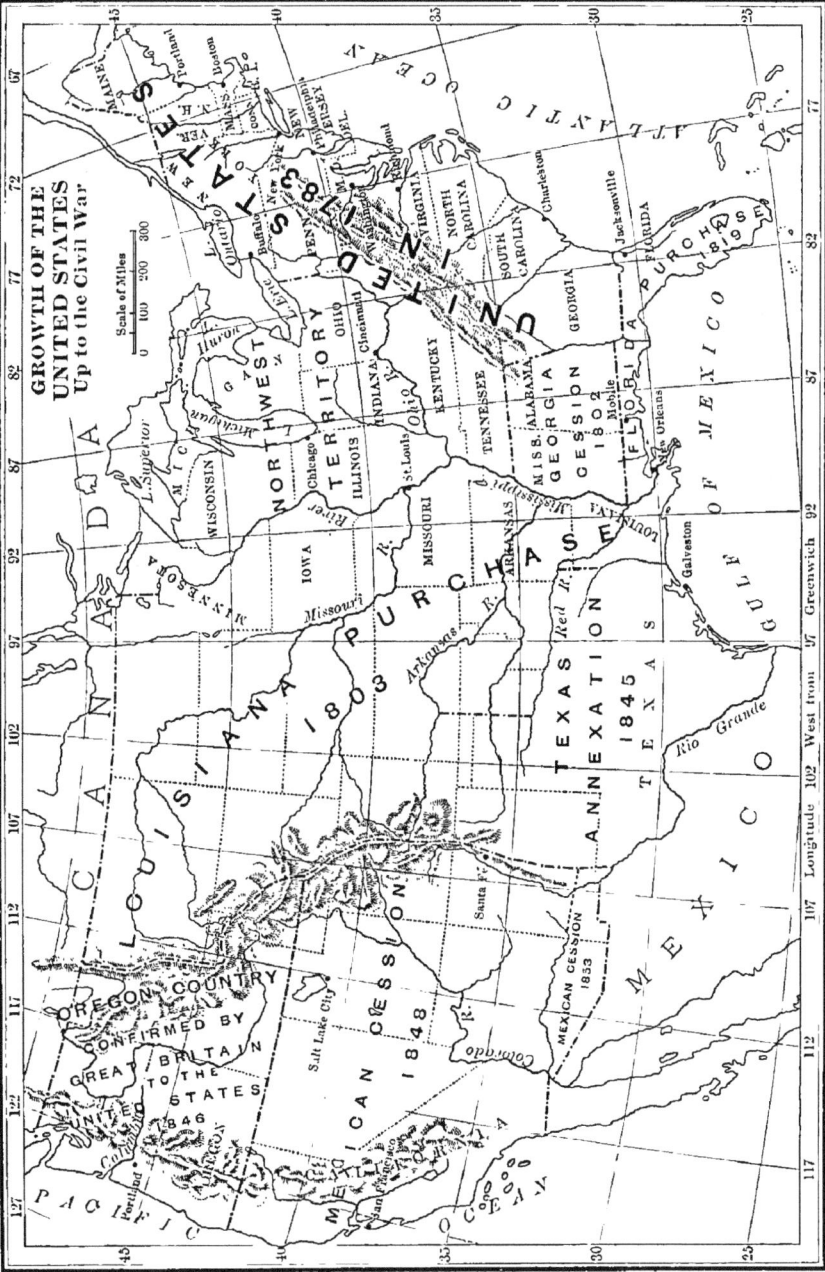

Scale of Miles

100 200 300

The Missouri Compromise declared that all territory north of 36° 30′ should be free; but now, influenced by the friends of "squatter sovereignty," Congress voted that, although Kansas and Nebraska were north of the line, yet when they wished to come in as states, they might be free or slaveholding, as they chose. Then there was a struggle to win the new territories. Settlers from the slave states round about pressed into Kansas. Anti-slavery men in the North became colonists or gave money to help to send others. Both parties were sure that they were in the right; both were eager and excited. There were battles between them, and for several years there was so much bloodshed in the territory that it was called "bleeding Kansas." In a battle at Osawatomie, one of the fighters was John Brown, of Connecticut, who fought so fiercely that he was afterwards often called "Osawatomie Brown." The one aim of his life was, as he said, to wage "eternal war with slavery," and he had gone to Kansas to do everything in his power to make the territory into a free state.

In 1857 James Buchanan became president; in the next four years there was one act that especially aroused the North and one that alarmed the South. The first was what was known as the "Dred Scott Decision." Dred was a slave. His master kept him in Illinois several years, and then carried him back to Missouri. In Missouri, Dred was flogged. He said, "No man is a slave in Illinois; therefore, when I was there, I became free, and my master must pay for flogging me." The case went from one court to another, and at last the Supreme Court of the United States, whose business it is to tell what the laws mean when people differ, said, "A slave is not a person; he is property, and his master may take him anywhere." The North cried indignantly, "That is not only protecting slavery in the states where it already exists, it is forcing slavery upon us;" and the opposition to it became even more determined.

Two years later came the act that alarmed the South. "Osawa

John Brown's raid tomie Brown" had left Kansas to live near Harper's Ferry in Virginia. He thought that with the aid of a few friends it would be possible to fortify some place in the mountains where fugitive might be safe, and that after a while the slaves might be united in a general revolt. To get arms, he seized upon the United

HARPER'S FERRY

States arsenal at Harper's Ferry. A figh followed; John Brown was captured by United States troop led by Robert E. Lee tried for treason and murder, and executed He had broken the law of the land, and hi punishment was law ful; but so much sym pathy was felt in th North with his eagerness to free the negroes that his deat strengthened the northern hatred of slavery.

In the South it was thought possible that John Brown wa supported by many northerners. There might be a general revol

Seven states secede of the slaves, pillage, burning, and murder. The South was fear ful of the horrors that might come, and more angry than eve with the North. It was near the end of Buchanan's term. Man southerners declared that the South would leave the Union the next President should oppose slavery. "Must a state be kep in the Union against its will?" they asked. "Has it not a right t secede?" Abraham Lincoln was elected, and the watchword o his party was "No more slave states." Seven states, South Care lina, Georgia, Alabama, Florida, Mississippi, Louisiana, and Texa left the Union. Franklin's great-granddaughter was present when the senators of these seven states withdrew from Congress. Jefferson Davis was one of the senators, and he told her that the new government and the old would live side by side and be friendly to each other. "The North will never fight the South," he said. "You see how quietly they have let us go."

SUMMARY.

Texas freed herself from Mexico and was admitted to the United States. A quarrel over her boundary brought this country into a war with Mexico.

The telegraph was invented.

The conflicting claims of the United States and Great Britain to Oregon were settled, and the northern boundary of our country was marked.

California and a vast area of land east of California were ceded to the United States by Mexico. The discovery of gold in California caused a great westward migration in 1849. California was admitted as a free state, and to satisfy the South the Fugitive Slave law was passed. Squatter sovereignty did away with the Missouri Compromise.

The question of slavery became more violent. "Uncle Tom's Cabin" and the "Dred Scott Decision" aroused the North; while John Brown's raid alarmed the South. Finally, seven states seceded.

SUGGESTIONS FOR WRITTEN WORK.

Morse tells Congress how valuable the telegraph will be.

A day's ride with a western emigrant.

A Forty-niner describes his journey to California.

XXI

THE CIVIL WAR

1861.

The Southern Confederacy. THE seven seceding states formed a union, or confederacy, and in a little while four others joined them. These eleven were Virginia, North Carolina, South Carolina, Georgia, Florida, Alabama, Mississippi, Louisiana, Texas, Arkansas, and Tennessee. Jefferson Davis, who had fough[t] bravely in the Mexican War, was chosen president. A flag was adopted which had a red field crossed diagonally by wide bars of blue outlined with white. I[n] the bars were eleven stars for the seceding states and two more for Missouri and Kentucky, which the Confederates expected would secede because those states had sen[t] representatives to the Confederate congress.

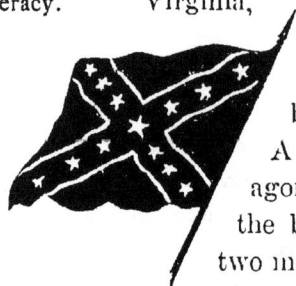

CONFEDERATE
BATTLE FLAG

Lincoln's determination Jefferson Davis had said that the northern states would no[t] fight, and he had much reason to think so, for President Buchanan was not sure that the government had any right to force [a] state to remain in the Union, and many people in the North agreed with him. When Abraham Lincoln was inaugurated, he sai[d] that he should not interfere with slavery where it already ex isted, but that he should protect the Union and the property o[f] the Union.

The attack on Fort Sumter Among these pieces of property were the forts, one of which Fort Sumter, was on an island at the mouth of Charleston harbo[r] In April, 1861, the Confederates demanded its surrender, an[d] when Major Anderson refused, General Beauregard fired upon it

ABRAHAM LINCOLN

(From an original negative made in 1864, when President Lincoln commissioned General Grant Lieutenant-General and commander of all
the armies of the republic)

The Union men held out for two days. So much of the fort was on fire that the defenders had to lie on the ground with handkerchiefs over their mouths to keep from being suffocated. The powder was nearly gone. There was nothing to eat but salt pork. Then Major Anderson surrendered. The flag on the fort had been shot through and through. Anderson saluted the tattered banner with fifty guns, and the little company which had

Surrender of Fort Sumter

formed the garrison marched out with drums beating and colors flying.

The first gun fired upon Fort Sumter aroused the whole country. Before that men talked about what might happen. Now something had happened, and every man in the land must stand for the Union or against

FORT SUMTER IN 1861

The country is aroused it. Lincoln called for seventy-five thousand men to serve in the army, and more than that number offered themselves. Most people in the North supposed that the revolt would soon be suppressed, and Lincoln asked the men to serve for three months.

The South, too, raised an army at once, and made ready to defend the border line of the seceded states. Richmond was chosen as the Confederate capital. If the Union men could take Richmond or the Confederates could take Washington, it would be a great gain to the victors, it might even bring the war to an end. Week after week passed. "On to Washington!" cried the Confederates. "Why does n't General Scott do something?" complained the Unionists. "He could fight in the Mexican War. Why does he stand still now? On to Richmond!"

The two armies pressed a little nearer together. Neither was ready to fight, but each commander felt that he must pay some regard to the wishes of his people.

A UNION SOLDIER

A CONFEDERATE

In Virginia, not far from Washington, is a little river called Bull Run, and just beyond it is a railroad that runs from Washington to the southwest. If the southern army held this railroad, they Battle of Bull Run could bring men and arms and provisions from the South easily and quickly, and thus threaten Washington. The North meant to prevent the capture of the road, and that is why the first great battle of the war was fought near Bull Run. General Beauregard

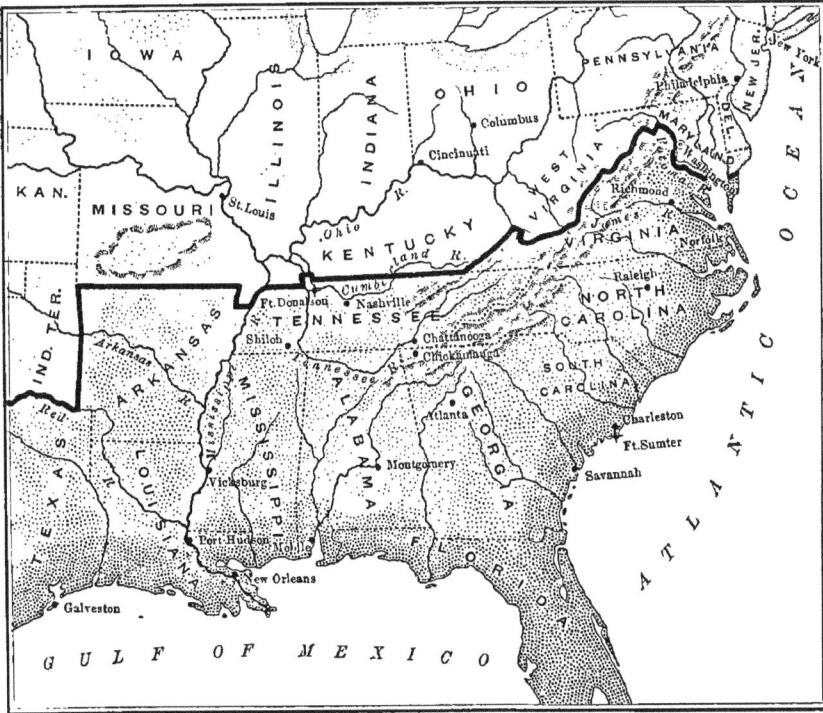

THE SOUTHERN CONFEDERACY AND ADJACENT UNION STATES

had come from Charleston, and was in command of the Confederate forces. He had been educated at the United States Military Academy at West Point. Among his classmates was Irvin McDowell, and it was McDowell who stood on the other side of the little stream, leading the Union army. Another West Point graduate, General Jackson, was on the field, fighting for the Confederacy. It seemed at first as if the Union men would win, and as they pushed forward upon Jackson, an officer shouted to his troops, "Look at Jackson and his men standing there like a stone wall." Soldiers always nickname their favorite commanders, and from that day the brave general was known among them as " Stonewall " Jackson.

Defeat of the Union troops

There was a fierce battle, and thousands of men were slain. The Confederates were victorious, and the retreat of the Union soldiers was a wild stampede. Men, horses, army-wagons, gun carriages, sutlers' teams, dashed along the road in the maddest confusion, while tents, cannon, and provisions were scattered along the way. The two chief reasons for the Union defeat were first, that the soldiers had expected to win the day easily; secondly, that they were "green," as Lincoln said, and had no idea of the training and obedience required of a soldier. General McDowell said that on the march to Bull Run it was hard to keep these untrained warriors from leaving the ranks to pick blackberries.

Making an army

After Bull Run it was clear that the conflict would be long and serious. Lincoln called for seven times as many men as at first. Another thing that was clear was that bravery alone would not make a soldier. The troops must be drilled. General McClellan spent week after week in training his men. In the autumn of 1861 there were thousands of *men* who wished to fight for the Union; in the spring of 1862 these men had become an *army*.

Blockade runners

The Confederates had felt almost sure of the favor and support of England, for English mills were using large quantities of southern cotton, and cotton could not be sent so long as there was war. A Union warship watched every important port, and a vessel trying to enter or leave the harbor was in great danger of being captured. Those that did attempt it were called blockade runners. The risk was so great that an enormous price was charged for the goods that they carried ; and before the war was over a pound of cotton that cost four cents in South Carolina could be sold for two dollars and a half in England. Two men were appointed by the Confederates to go to England and try to persuade both that country and France to help them. They were on board the Trent, a British mail - steamer. A Union captain obliged the Trent to stop, and carried away the two men. Thoughtless people throughout the North rejoiced, but Lincoln declared that

The Trent affair

A CONFEDERATE BLOCKADE RUNNER
(This vessel, the A. D. Vance, was captured Sept. 10, 1864)

this was exercising the right of search, and the men must be given up. They were set free with an explanation to England that their capture was not approved by the United States government.

1862.

The United States government now planned to get control of the Mississippi. That would cut Texas, Arkansas, and most of Louisiana from the other Confederate states, and would make it easy to transport men and supplies from the North. The first step was to take New Orleans, which would prevent blockade runners from landing there arms and ammunition or anything else that would help the Confederates.

The capture of New Orleans

There was a naval officer named David Farragut who had gone to sea as a midshipman when he was only eleven years old. He had stood firmly by the Union, but some were afraid to trust him because he was of southern birth. The government believed in him, and gave him command of the fleet that would, it was hoped, succeed in taking New Orleans. The city was

AN AUGUST MORNING WITH FARRAGUT
(From W. H. Overend's painting showing Farragut in the rigging)

defended by two forts, by sixteen gunboats, by chains stretche
across the river, and by rafts of logs. Flat-boats loaded wit
pine-knots or with cotton were set afire and let loose to dri
down among the ships; but Farragut avoided the fire-boat
broke the chains, cut his way through the rafts, silenced tl
forts, and captured New Orleans. No one distrusted Farragu
after this.

While Farragut was on his way to New Orleans, a new sort (
The Merri- battle was being fought off the mouth of the James River. .
mac   Virginia navy yard had been seized by the Confederates at tl
beginning of the war. The Merrimac, a Union frigate taken ?
that time, was cut down to the water's edge and covered with
sloping roof of iron, pierced with holes for the cannon. This ne
kind of craft attacked the wooden vessels of the Union. On
sank, another surrendered, a third, the Minnesota, ran agroun(

and the iron-clad left her destruction until the morning. Should she be abandoned? Trains of powder were laid that she might be left and blown up. "Wait," ordered the captain. "And he did more than order," said one who was there. "He almost begged us to stay. We had heard about the Monitor, though we did not know

THE MERRIMAC

whether the Monitor was coming or whether it would amount to anything if it did come, but a man does not like to leave his ship, and we stayed." Morning came, and with it the queerest little vessel that was ever seen. "A cheese-box on a raft," the Confederates called it. This was the Monitor, invented by a Swede, John Ericsson. It was made of iron, it carried two guns, and the "cheese-box" could be turned so that the guns might be fired in any direction. The battle was a severe one, but neither vessel was destroyed. Next day the Merrimac came out, but as the Monitor was needed to protect Washington, it did not engage in another battle. Later the Confederates were forced to evacuate Norfolk, and destroyed the Merrimac. This battle made it necessary for all countries to build iron-clad naval vessels instead of the wooden vessels that had been used.

The battle

THE MONITOR

"On to Richmond!" was still the cry, and a plan was made

for McClellan to land near Yorktown, march up the Peninsul
as it was called, between the York and the James rivers, me
McDowell, and press on to Richmond. "Stonewall
Jackson was carrying on a brilliant campaign
the Shenandoah Valley, where small bodies
Union troops were stationed. Up and down tl
valley Jackson swept, making marches as u
expected as Washington's sudden moves, al
so rapid that people called his army "Ston
wall's foot-cavalry." It would not do to l
McDowell and his troops leave Washingtc
for it was possible that Jackson might su
ceed in reaching that city, and therefore M
Clellan had to do as best he could witho
them. Richmond was alarmed, and Jefferson Davi:
niece wrote to a friend, "Uncle Jeff thinks we h:

GENERAL ROBERT E. LEE

McClellan's attempt to take Richmond

better go to a safer
place than Richmond." After
much fighting, McClellan was
driven back toward the sea;
and as there was still fear for
the safety of Washington, he
was ordered to come nearer the
capital.

General Lee

There was reason for alarm,
for the Confederates were evidently planning to carry the
war into the North. General
Robert E. Lee was now at the
head of the Confederate army.
He was the son of a famous
Revolutionary officer, a West

THE SCENE OF WAR NEAR WASHINGTO
AND RICHMOND

Point graduate, and he had served with honor in Mexico. When the war broke out, he knew that a position in the Union army which might tempt any soldier, would be offered him, but Lee was not the man to do what he thought wrong for the sake of posi-

tion. It was a strug-
gle for him to choose
on which side to stand,
but he decided that
as a citizen of Virginia
he ought to follow the
bidding of his state.
This was the man
who was pressing to-
ward Washington. He
thought that the peo-
ple of Maryland would
be glad to join him,
and that with them he
could march against
the capital; but the

Battle of
Antietam

BRIDGE OVER ANTIETAM CREEK
(From Battles and Leaders of the Civil War)

Marylanders did not wish to join him. There was a terrible fight at Antietam in Maryland, and Lee withdrew into Virginia.

During the year 1862, the great gains of the Union forces had been the capture of New Orleans, the securing of the command of the sea, and the withdrawal of Lee from Antietam. On the Confederate side, Jackson had swept the Union troops from the Shenandoah Valley, and Lee had kept McClellan from Richmond.

1863.

Civilized nations have adopted a rule that private property must not be touched in war except in times of great necessity Contrabands unless it is plainly intended to be used for military purposes, of war

as in the case of guns or ammunition. It is then called con
traband, or illegal, and it may be seized by the opposing sid
Wherever the Union army appeared, runaway slaves flocked t
the camp, and what to do with them was a little puzzling. Gen
eral Butler, a shrewd man with a keen sense of humor, finall
solved the problem. When a "master" came to him and de
manded the return of some runaway slaves on the ground tha
they were private property, the general said, "No. You will us
them in making fortifications and in raising corn to support th
Confederate army. They are contraband of war." After thi
the negroes were often called "contrabands."

In time of civil war the President, as commander-in-chief
the army of the United States, can do very nearly what he think
The Emanci- wise, provided the greater part of the people approve of his act
pation Pro- When the first day of 1863 came, Lincoln signed a paper that
clamation   almost as famous as the Declaration of Independence. It is calle
the Emancipation Proclamation, and it declared that all slaves
those who were resisting the Union government were free.

Thousands of slaves did not hear of their freedom for month
but the Proclamation made it clear to the world, and especiall
to England, that whoever helped the Confederacy would be hel
ing slavery; and as England had abolished slavery in all he
colonies, she could hardly support it in America.

She did, however, give much indirect aid to the Confederate
for although she had promised to help neither side, she allowe
them to build at the English shipyards swift blockade runner
and armed privateers to destroy Union vessels. The most powe
The   ful of these was called the Alabama. She destroyed a warshi
Alabama   captured a mail-steamer, and either sank or burned more tha
sixty other American vessels, chiefly merchantmen. She wa
finally sunk by a Union ship.

The year 1863 began with the Emancipation Proclamation. I

May, the Confederates were victorious at Chancellorsville in Maryland; but they met with a loss that was worse than a defeat, for through a mistake "Stonewall" Jackson was shot by his own men. In the month of July there were two great northern victories. The first was at Gettysburg in Pennsylvania, for Lee Gettysburg again invaded the North. Up the valley of the Shenandoah he marched, across the Potomac, through Maryland, and into Pennsylvania. He planned first to take Harrisburg, then Philadelphia. He came to Gettysburg, lying in a peaceful valley, with orchards, green fields, farmhouses, and away to the west the blue mountains. Here he met the Union forces and fought the most terrible battle of the war. For three days it raged. One man out of every four — some say one out of every three

UNION LINE MEETING PICKETT'S CHARGE AT GETTYSBURG
(From the Gettysburg Cyclorama, by permission of the National Panorama Co.)

— was killed, wounded, or missing. Such was the slaughter that men threw themselves on the ground and held up bits of white paper to show that they had surrendered. Lee was driven back, and retreated into Virginia.

The day after the battle was spent by both sides in burying the dead. Four months later, a part of the battleground was set Lincoln's apart as a national cemetery. Lincoln made on the day of the Gettysburg dedication a short, simple speech, so full of thought and feeling, speech

and appreciation of the honor due to those who had given their lives for their country, that it will never be forgotten.

The siege of Vicksburg The second great Union victory was at Vicksburg. If that town and Port Hudson could be taken, the Mississippi would be in the hands of the Union; but it was not easy to take Vicksburg. The city stood on a bluff so high that shot could not be thrown to it from vessels on the river, while the city guns could easily sink any ship that attempted to pass. For three months General

MORTAR FOR THROWING SHELLS

Grant and General Sherman tried to get into a position to attack the town. At last they succeeded, and the siege of seven weeks began. Day and night the shells were falling. People dug caves into the side of the hill to be safe from flying fragments. A lady who lived in one of the caves wrote that even the mules in the

A UNION RIVER GUNBOAT

town seemed wild, and the dogs would howl madly when a shell exploded. Food was scanty. By and by it gave out altogether, and finally the brave suffering, starving people surrendered. The Confederate flag was hauled down, and the banner of the Union run up. The whole Union army witnessed the scene, but not a cheer was given, says General Grant, so

deeply were the courage and endurance of the people respected. One member of the victorious army was the war-eagle, "Old Abe," the pet of a Wisconsin regiment. He was in many a battle, and when the noise and confusion were greatest, he would flap his wings and scream as if war was his chief delight.

A few days later Port Hudson, which lies between Vicksburg and New Orleans, yielded, and the Mississippi was in the hands of the Union. This capture prevented the bringing of troops and supplies from Texas and Arkansas to the aid of the Confederate states east of the Mississippi. The Confederacy had now no way to communicate with Europe. It was shut in upon itself.

The Mississippi in Union hands

The greater part of the Confederate army was now divided between Virginia and the northwestern corner of Georgia. It was in Georgia that the hardest fighting of the last six months of the year took place. One battle was at Chickamauga. The Union forces lost, but it would have been a far more terrible defeat if the bold stand made by General Thomas had not prevented the rout of the army. The Confederates had had a "Stonewall" Jackson. Now the Unionists had a "Rock of Chickamauga," for this was the name that the soldiers gave to General Thomas.

OLD ABE

Several other battles were fought in that part of the country. The last one was called the "Battle above the Clouds." It took place on Lookout Mountain, and the heavy mist settled down so darkly that while the eager watchers in the valley could hear the sound of the cannon, they could only guess who were losing and who were winning. The Union forces won. "God bless you all!" came over the wires to General Grant from the weary, anxious President in Washington, for every victory brought nearer the coming of peace for which he prayed.

The end of 1863 came. During this year the Confederates had been successful at Chancellorsville and Chickamauga, but they had lost General Jackson. Lee had kept the Union soldiers from Richmond, but the repulse at Gettysburg had driven him from Pennsylvania. The Mississippi had fallen into the hands of the Union, and Union troops had been successful in Georgia.

1864.

The plan to end the war

Two men now stood out as the most successful generals in the Union army, Grant and Sherman. Grant was put at the head of all the Union forces. The two generals formed a plan that they hoped would end the war. Grant was to face Lee and try to take Richmond. Sherman was to cut his way through Georgia to the sea.

Grant went into Virginia from the north, swept around to the east of Richmond, then to the south. There were terrible battles. There were two days of fighting in a dark, gloomy forest called the Wilderness. The woods caught fire, and wounded men were burned to death in the blazing timber. There were explosions of trains of ammunition. There were dense clouds of the smoke of powder. Suffering men

Copyright, 1891, by M. P. Rice

GENERAL U. S. GRANT

(From a picture taken in 1864 when he was commissioned commander-in-chief)

Battles of the Wilderness

lay moaning. The underbrush was crackling in the fire. Men shot at their opponents in the darkness, or took aim by the glare of the flames. It is thought that about 30,000 men were killed. Neither side could claim a victory.

In the Shenandoah Valley

General Grant pressed on till he was at Petersburg, south of the Confederate capital. Lee had not men enough to drive him away, but he could keep him from advancing upon Richmond. He even made the government fear another invasion of the North, for he sent General Early through the Shenandoah Valley toward Maryland.

Sheridan marched out to oppose him. Early had once been within a few miles of Washington and had burned Chambersburg, but now his opponent went through the valley with orders to destroy everything which would feed man or beast, that there might be no more raids upon Pennsylvania. It was not long before he reported to Grant, "If a crow should want to fly through the valley, he would have to carry his food with him."

CONFEDERATE CAPITOL, RICHMOND

Sheridan was called to Washington, and when he returned to Winchester, he heard firing far away. He put spurs to his great black horse and galloped on. He met men running to the town. "General Early has attacked us," they cried, "and we are beaten." "Back!" ordered Sheridan. "We'll beat them yet. Face about!" Sheridan's ride

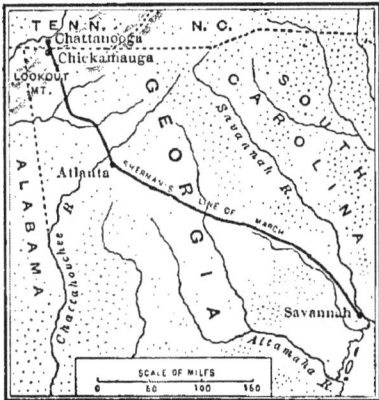

SHERMAN'S ROUTE TO THE SEA

he shouted to the retreating cavalry. They did face about. Early was driven away, and the disaster was prevented. This was the "Sheridan's ride" which the poem by that name has made famous.

But while Grant was before Richmond and Sheridan was in the Shenandoah Valley, where Where was Sherman? He was attacking the Confederate forces in northwestern Georgia. The Confederate general, Johnston, had not men enough to meet Sher-

man, but he retreated after the masterly fashion of Washingtc
in New Jersey. Sherman had to leave guards behind him 1
protect the railroads, and Johnston meant to continue the r
treat until so many men had been left that the two armies coul
fight on equal terms. After two months of this retreating, tl
Confederate War Department gave Johnston's command to Gei
eral Hood. Hood made bold attacks on
Sherman, but was obliged to retreat,
leaving Sherman in possession
of Atlanta. Then began Sherman's famous " march to
the sea." He marched
southeast through the
state in four col-
umns, twenty
miles apart, cut-
ting a swath
sixty miles wide.
He burned At-
lanta with its

CORDUROY ROADS IN SOUTH CAROLINA

mills and foundries. He destroyed railroads and bridges, leavir
a pitiful ruin behind him. The object of this march was not on
to cut the Confederacy in two, but to destroy everything th;
would help the Confederates to carry on the war. Just befo
Christmas he entered Savannah, and sent to President Lincol
the message: —

I beg to present you as a Christmas gift the city of Savanna
with one hundred and fifty heavy guns and plenty of ammun
tion ; also about twenty-five thousand bales of cotton.

W. T. SHERMAN.

So ended the year 1864. The Confederates had burned Chan

bersburg, but Sheridan had devastated the valley of the Shenandoah, Sherman had made a wide path of ruin through Georgia to Savannah, and Grant had pushed on toward Richmond as far as Petersburg.

1865.

The year in which the war was to end began. Sherman had a hard march before him, and he would not leave Savannah until **The end** his men were rested. They were impatient to go on, and when he **draws near**

WASHINGTON MONUMENT AND CAPITOL SQUARE, RICHMOND

rode about the camp, they would call out, "Uncle Billy, Grant is waiting for us at Richmond." Finally the march through South Carolina began. The streams were swollen, the swamps flooded, and the roads were often only long lines of mud. The men waded, they built bridges, they made "corduroy roads." At last they were in North Carolina. Both Sherman and Grant had many more men than the Confederate commanders near them, and they believed that one more battle would end the war.

Lee was one of the great commanders of history, and his soldiers trusted him and loved him; but his army was reduced to
26,000 men, and many of those were so weak from exposure and
want of food that they could not lift their muskets to their
shoulders. The most skilful general is helpless without strong
men and food and supplies. Lee could no longer protect the
Confederate capital. "Richmond has surrendered," was telegraphed to Washington, and on the 9th of April Lee's whole
force surrendered to Grant at Appomattox Court House, a little
village west of Richmond. The two generals met to discuss
terms. It was agreed that the Southern soldiers should lay down
their arms and return to their homes in peace. The horses Grant

Copyright, 1887, by the Century Co.

APPOMATTOX COURT HOUSE
(From a war-time photograph)

left with the cavalry. "I hope this will be the last battle of the
war," he said, "and they will need the horses to work their
farms." Lee's men had been living for days on parched corn,
and not very much of that. Grant's first action was to send a
generous supply of food to the men.

This surrender was the real close of the war. On April 14th, just four years after the fall of Fort Sumter, Anderson was

Copyright, 1887, by The Century Co.
UNION SOLDIERS SHARING THEIR RATIONS WITH CONFEDERATES
AFTER LEE'S SURRENDER

sent to take command of the fort a second time. The same old flag was hoisted, pierced with the holes of the first shots of the war. Late that evening, in the midst of the rejoicings of the defenders of the Union, the telegraph flashed over the country the message, "President Lincoln has been assassinated," and all the joy was turned into sorrow. He was shot by a man who fancied that he was avenging the "wrongs of the South." In reality he was murdering the true friend of the South. Only six weeks before, when Lincoln was made President for the second time, he said in his inaugural speech : —

The assassination of President Lincoln

"With malice toward none, with charity for all, with firmness in the right, as God gives us power to see the right, let us strive to finish the

AN ARMY
CANTEEN

work we are in . . . to do all which may achieve and cherish a just and lasting peace among ourselves."

SUMMARY.

1861. The Civil War began with the capture of Fort Sumter. The Union forces were defeated at Bull Run. The capture of the Confederate commissioners on the Trent nearly made trouble with England.

1862. The Union forces capture New Orleans. The contest between the Monitor and the Merrimac took place. Jackson swept the Shenandoah Valley. McClellan failed to reach Richmond, and Lee withdrew from Antietam.

1863. The Emancipation Proclamation was signed. The Alabama did much damage to Union ships. The Confederates were victorious at Chancellorsville, but Lee was repulsed at Gettysburg. The Union forces gained control of the Mississippi by the capture of Vicksburg and Port Hudson. The Confederates were successful at Chickamauga.

1864. Grant pressed on to Petersburg. Early had burned Chambersburg, and to prevent such raids Sheridan devastated the Shenandoah Valley. Sherman marched through Georgia to Savannah.

1865. Lee was forced to abandon Richmond, and to surrender at Appomattox Court House April 9th. Four years from the day when Fort Sumter fell President Lincoln was assassinated.

SUGGESTIONS FOR WRITTEN WORK.

A soldier writes about the attack upon Fort Sumter.

A boy describes the siege of Vicksburg.

Two sailors on the Minnesota discuss the possible coming of the Monitor.

XXII

THE EVENTS SINCE THE CIVIL WAR

AFTER the war, the government had to decide a difficult question. This was, "Will it be safe to allow the states that wished The position of the seceded states to leave the Union to send representatives to Congress and help make the laws for the country?" Lincoln's belief was, "No state *can* leave the Union. Some persons have raised an insurrection, but this has

THE WHITE HOUSE
(The official residence of the President as it appears to-day. The corner-stone was laid by Washington, Oct. 13, 1792)

been suppressed. These states as states have not forfeited their right to send representatives."

When Lincoln died, the Vice-President, Andrew Johnson, became president. His belief was almost the same as Lincoln's, but Andrew Johnson where Lincoln would persuade men, Johnson would try to compel them, and all through his term of office there were quarrels between him and Congress, and many of the laws made at that time were made not with the President's consent, but in spite of his opposition.

An addition was made to the Constitution which is known as The Thirteenth Amendment the Thirteenth Amendment. It forbids slavery in the United States or in any place governed by the United States. A law

was passed requiring every man who wished to hold office in th
South to take what was called the "iron-clad oath," declaring tha
he had taken no part in the war. This was an unwise deman(
for almost every respectable man in the seceding states had take:

Carpet-baggers

part in the war; and the result of the act was that worthles
men from the Nort]
persuaded or bribe(
the negroes to vot
them into office. Thes
men were called "ca1
pet-baggers," becaus
they usually had n
property, and often n
baggage except a ca1
pet-bag. For a co1

THE GREAT EASTERN LAYING THE ATLANTIC CABLE

siderable time the northern adventurers and the ignorant negroe
were in power in the South.

In order to send representatives to Congress, the Confederat

The negro vote

states had been obliged by the government to grant the negroe
the right to vote; but it was not long before the whites had th
power in their own hands again, for in many places they woul(
either frighten the negroes or bribe them, and so keep them awa
from the polls. United States troops were then sent South t
protect the negroes in their right to vote and to support the me:
who had been lawfully elected; but the soldiers did not like thi
duty, the whites were angry, and the negroes often suffered mor
than before the troops came. Matters were made a little bette
by the pardoning of those Confederates who had taken part in th
war, and restoring to nearly all the right to hold office. Thougl
there are even now some hard questions to settle about the ne
groes, it is probable that very few men in our country, even i1
the South, would be willing to have the days of slavery return.

In 1866, while Johnson was still in office, Europe and America came nearer together. It took Columbus ten weeks to cross the The Atlantic cable Atlantic. The Pilgrims spent nine weeks in sailing from England to Massachusetts. In 1812, even a swift sailing vessel needed a month. Before the Civil War, the invention of steamboats had made it possible to send a message from England to America in ten or eleven days. A persevering man named Cyrus W. Field was now convinced that a telegraph wire might be laid across the Atlantic Ocean. The first attempt failed, the second failed, the third time all went well, but in a few days the cable broke. Field's money was gone, and his friends had no more that they wished to invest. At last Congress voted to help him. This time the cable succeeded. The wire was laid from Ireland to Newfoundland, and instead of the New World and the Old being ten weeks apart, whatever was done in one continent could be known in the other in a very few minutes. Whittier wrote of this new wonder : —

" And round the world the thought
        of all
    Is as the thought of one."

So it was that in Johnson's time the Atlantic grew narrower ; but at the same time the United States grew wider, for Alaska was bought of Russia. Every time that the country has bought a piece of land,

Photograph by W. H. Partridge

SITKA, ALASKA

there have been citizens who opposed the purchase for one reason The purchase of Alaska or another ; and when Alaska was bought, some declared that it was a foolish, extravagant deed, that the country could "keep house" without a "refrigerator." This "refrigerator," however, is just the place for fur-bearing animals, and in a few years the fur companies had paid for the right to collect furs much more than Alaska had cost. The recent discovery of gold in the Klondike district of Alaska has greatly increased the value of this possession.

The Alabama claims

Few were pleased with Johnson's management, and in 1868 General Grant was elected to succeed him. While Grant was in office, an important war question was settled in regard to the "Alabama claims," whether or not England ought to pay for the damage that the Alabama and other privateers built in that country had done to American shipping. For less cause than this, nations have fought long and bloody wars, but both countries agreed that the matter should be left to five men who would not favor either party. The men met at Geneva in Switzerland. They decided that England should not have allowed the boats to be built, and that she must pay to the United States fifteen and one half million dollars to make good the harm that they had done.

THE CONFEDERATE PRIVATEER ALABAMA
(From Official Records of the Union and Confederate Navies)

The Atlantic cable had brought Europe nearer to America, but the Americans had felt for many years that eastern and western America ought to be

Travel in the far West

joined together. Gold and silver had been found east of the Rocky Mountains. Emigrants were going westward by thousands. There were railroads as far as the Missouri, but no regular way of sending letters or goods from the Missouri to the "far

West," now that this "far West" had moved from the Mississippi to the Pacific. The days of the postrider returned, and the "pony express" was introduced. Each mail carrier rode seventy-five miles, finding a fresh horse awaiting him every twenty-five miles. Then another man took the mail and galloped away. The next The Union plan for carrying mail and passengers was by stage-coach; but Pacific Railroad while in Revolutionary days this would have been thought a

luxurious way to travel, it was entirely too slow for the sons and grandsons of the Revolutionary heroes. A railroad ought to be built across the continent, so the people said, and the Union Pacific Railroad was begun. There were mountain ranges to be climbed, vast expanses of prairie to be crossed, and rivers to be bridged. It took seven years to build the road, but at last the golden spike was driven that marked its completion. Every year the

"THE PONY EXPRESS"

trains go a little faster, and to-day one can cross the continent in less time than it would have taken the New Yorker of a century earlier to go to Boston and return.

The time soon came when it was natural to look back a century, for the hundredth anniversary of the days when the thirteen col- The onies were becoming a nation was at hand. In 1873 a tea-party Centennial was given in Philadelphia in memory of the Boston Tea-party of 1773. Lowell wrote a poem about the fight at Concord bridge, and the men —

" Who did great things, not knowing they were great."

One event after another was commemorated in song or in cele-

bration; but the great celebration came in 1876, the hundredtl
birthday of the nation. The Declaration had been signed ir
Philadelphia, and there the Centennial Exposition was held. Al
the nations of the world were invited to come to the celebra
tion of the United States, and to bring specimens of what the
could make or produce. One guest was the war-eagle, "Old Abe.
The exhibition was most interesting, and it was a great help t
our manufactures, for it gave us new ideas, and taught us nev
methods. The United States had no need to be ashamed of he
own exhibit, for although she was the youngest nation repre
sented, her list of recent useful inventions was longer than tha
of any other country.

Greenbacks become as good as gold

In 1877 Rutherford B. Hayes became president. There was no
important treaty while he was in office, there was no war and no
discovery of gold, but a great event took place, for the treasure
of the United States announced that he was ready to exchang
gold for "greenbacks." Just as in the Revolution the colonie

THE TREASURY BUILDING, WASHINGTON

issued paper money, s
in the Civil War, wher
the government needec
money, it issued bills
called "greenbacks," be
cause the backs wer
printed with green ink
These bills were onl

the promise of the government to pay in gold or silver the amoun
named, and people knew that if the government should fall, the
would never be paid. When the Union won a battle, the valu
of the greenbacks would rise, but if the Union lost, it would fall
and at one time it cost nearly three dollars in greenbacks to buy
one dollar in gold. The government needed so much mone
during the war that a clock ticking sixty times a minute woulc

have to run for more than ninety years before it could tick off, once for every dollar, the money borrowed. After the war, the Paying for the war United States began straightway to pay the debt; the greenbacks rose in value, and when finally the Secretary of the Treasury offered to give gold in exchange for greenbacks, people did not care to accept the offer, because the promise of the United States had become literally "as good as gold."

In 1881 James A. Garfield was elected president. A few months later he was shot, and Chester A. Arthur, the Vice-President, became president. This murder was partly due to a mistake made fifty years before by honest, faithful Andrew Jackson. The kind-hearted old warrior could not bear to refuse a friend who asked for a position, and to make room for these friends he turned out large numbers of those who were in office. This act grew into a custom. Every man who had tried to help elect the successful candidate thought he ought to have the reward of a government position. Hayes did not believe in this custom, and Garfield did

JAMES A. GARFIELD
(Died September 19, 1881)

not. Men who had voted for Garfield expected the usual reward, and were angry when it was not given them. It was one of these disappointed seekers after office who shot President Garfield.

This crime aroused Congress, and a law was made requiring many offices to be filled only by men who had successfully passed Civil Service Reform an examination. Another law, which applied to many thousand subordinate positions, provided that men who were working for the government well and faithfully should not lose their places when the party that appointed them went out of power. These laws were a long step in the direction of justice and fairness. They were passed while President Arthur was in power, so that

his term of office was marked by the beginning of what is calle
Civil Service Reform.

It was at this time that two expositions somewhat like th
Centennial were held in the South, and the whole country wa
glad to see the prosperity of the southern states. The Sout
had feared that the negroes would not work if they wer
free, but now it was proved that far more cotton was raise
in proportion to the number of the negroes than befor
the war. More tobacco and sugar were also raised an
much more corn and wheat. Manufacturing was no
carried on in the South. The southerners were also look
ing below the surface of the ground as they had neve
done before; and, behold, there were great beds of coa
and of iron. Cotton seed used to be thrown away, bu
now every state that raises cotton receives a large income fro
the sale of the oil that is pressed out of the seed.

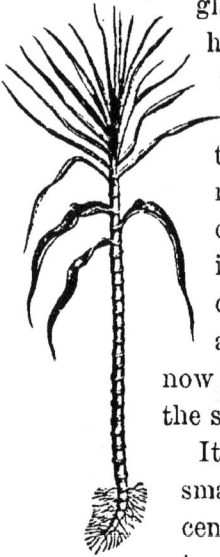

It was in Arthur's time that a great change was made in
small thing. A law was passed that instead of asking thre
cents for a letter stamp, the government should charge bu

SUGAR-CANE two. This law applies to all land owned by the Unite

Two-cent postage States, and that is why we can send a letter to the Philippine
for two cents, while it costs five cents to send one to England.

After Garfield was shot and all knew that there was littl
hope of his recovery, the Vice-President also became seriously il

Succession to the presidency There was nothing in our Constitution to decide who shoul
become president if both died; but under Grover Cleveland, th
next President, a law was made that if both the President an
Vice-President should die, the Secretary of State should rule, an
if he died, the Secretary of the Treasury should take his plac
and so on through the cabinet. As the cabinet is made up c
men chosen by the President, they would be likely to carry ou
his ideas and the wishes of the people who had elected him.

While Cleveland was in office the Chinese were forbidden to enter the United States. Our country is so large that for many years it did not occur to Americans to shut out any one who wished to come in, but after a while it was found that some of the European states were sending paupers across the ocean, because it was cheaper to pay their fare than to support them at home. This was forbidden, and the government began to look a little more closely at the kinds of people who were landing on our shores. It was found that the Chinese differed from other immigrants in two respects. One was that they were willing to work for very small wages ; and the workingmen of the Pacific coast said, "There are so many Chinese, and they work so cheap, that employers are refusing to pay us the wages that we have been receiving." The other difference was that while most men from other nations would stay in the United States and become citizens, the Chinese would stay only until they had made a certain amount of money and would then go home, carrying their money with them. A law was passed forbidding the Chinese to come into the land. Many persons thought that this law ought not to be made, because we had a treaty with China allowing the Chinese the same rights as other nations, but the Supreme Court decided that Congress had a right to say who should be allowed to enter the land.

The Chinese are shut out

France had not forgotten her old friendship of a century earlier, and in token of this and of her respect for the United States, she presented the country with a colossal statue of Liberty. It stands on an island in New York harbor. It is so large that a room in the head of the figure will hold forty persons. In one hand is a torch which may be lighted by electricity.

The statue of Liberty

Cleveland's term of office expired in 1889, and he was succeeded by Benjamin Harrison, the third man by the name of Harrison who has been famous in our country's history. One

The McKin-ley tariff

signed the Declaration of Independence; his grandson, nicknamed "Tippecanoe," was elected president in 1841; and in 1889 the grandson of "Tippecanoe" became president. In 1841 there was much discussion about the tariff. One party said, "The duty on imported goods ought to be just high enough to pay the expenses of the government, and then prices will be low." The other said, "If imported goods are too cheap, our manu facturers will either go out of business or else they wil pay our workmen no higher wages than the workmen in Europe receive." When Benjamin Harrison became presi dent, people were discussing this same question. William McKinley, of Ohio, proposed in Congress a bill whose aim was to impose a high duty upon imported goods that could be manufactured in this country. This bill became a law.

The right was also given to the President to change the duty on certain articles, if the country sending those articles should impose unfair duties upon our products This principle was called reciprocity, and by this means we could be sure of fair treatment, for we had become so large and so rich a nation that other nations were eager to win the privilege of selling their goods in this country.

STATUE OF LIBERTY
Designed by Bartholdi and pre-sented by France to the United States. It was completed in 1886)

Millions of people from Europe had come to make their homes in America. Instead of thirteen little colonies clinging to the Atlantic coast, our nation spread from the Atlantic to the Pacific, and grea

Indian troubles

cities had sprung into life where half a century earlier there had been only a wilderness. In the movement of population to the westward there had sometimes been trouble with the Indians They were here first, but most people have come to feel that roaming over a land does not give a claim to it, and that civilized nations have a right to take possession of "wild land." The Indians were gathered into tracts called reservations, in places where it was thought no white men would wish to live; and then as these tracts became valuable, the Indians were moved, not once, but many times. It is no wonder that they tried to resist, and that there were bloody massacres.

In the year that Benjamin Harrison became president, the Indians were moved from Oklahoma, and one April day there was a strange scene acted on the border of the new territory. Thousands of men had gathered together from all parts of the country. Just at noon a bugle sounded; men ran, horses galloped, wagons swayed wildly to and fro. Everybody was frantically struggling to get possession of a bit of land, for the government had agreed that whoever was first on a lot might have it for his own on payment of a small sum, much less than the land was worth. This was so unfair a way to grant property that when the time came to open another territory to settlers, the plan was tried of allowing them to draw lots for the pieces of land.

The opening of Oklahoma

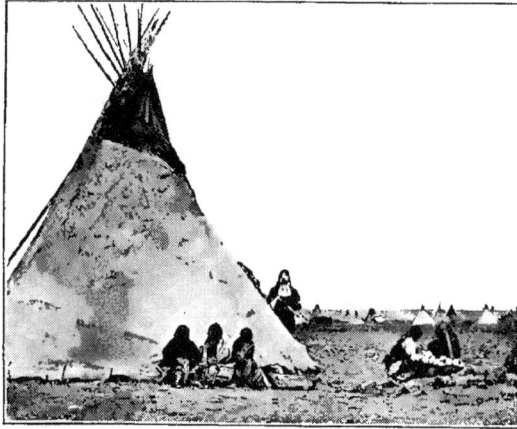

ARAPAHOE CAMP, INDIAN TERRITORY

After Harrison's term of office was over, Cleveland was again elected. In his first term he had done all that he could to help on Civil Service Reform, and during this second term he succeeded in putting many more offices under the merit system.

Civil Service Reform

Before Cleveland's second election there was much discussion

about the best way to celebrate the four hundredth anniversar
of the landing of Columbus. In 1876 the Centennial had cele
brated the one hundredth anniversary of the Declaration c
Independence, and it was now decided to hold an exposition i
Chicago. The buildings of the exposition were exceedingly beau
tiful. So many of them were white that they were known a
the "White City." In Chicago there were more than a mi
lion inhabitants, but many a man went to the Columbian E
position, as it was called, who could remember when the cit
consisted of a fort and a few little huts. The celebration shoul
have been held just four hundred years after the coming c

Columbus, but th
plan was not mad
early enough, an
the doors coul
not be opened u
til 1893.

When peopl
were calling Co
lumbus the "craz
man," how su
prised he woul
have been if som
one had whi
pered, "Four hun
dred years henc

THE PERISTYLE AND FRENCH'S STATUE OF LIBERTY
AT THE COLUMBIAN EXPOSITION

the greatest celebration that the world has known will be hel
in your honor on a continent of which you know nothing." An
when Franklin was flying his kite and finding out that electricit
and lightning were the same thing, how it would have please
him if he had been told that the knowledge which he was gainin
would help to give to the celebration its greatest beauty an

charm, for the thousands of electric lights made the "White City" a fairyland by night.

The next president was William McKinley, the Ohio congress- <accent type="margin">A hopeful outlook</accent> man whose plans for the tariff had been adopted seven years before. Forty-five states had been admitted to the Union, business was flourishing, the crops were large, and throughout the country there

A CUBAN HOMESTEAD [1]
(This was later burned by the Spaniards)

seemed to be good reason to expect a peaceful, prosperous time.

One hundred miles off our coast, however, there was trouble, and it was soon plain that this trouble would affect the United States. Cuba belonged to Spain, and the island had been ruled so harshly that the Cubans had tried many times to free themselves from Spanish control. Soon after McKinley became president, they tried again and fought more desperately than ever. Spain could not suppress the revolt, and her commanders treated the Cubans so savagely that the United States believed it was time to interfere. Another reason for interference was that the Cubans and their friends were trying to fit out vessels in the United States to carry arms and supplies to the island. The only way to prevent this was for our government to keep ships sailing up and down our long coast, and the expense of such patrolling was very great. A third reason was that many Americans owned property on the island, and this war was breaking up their business

GENERAL GOMEZ [1]
(Leader of the Cuban patriots)

[1] From *Marching with Gomez*, by Grover Flint.

and causing them much loss. To protect them if need should come, the United States battleship Maine was anchored in the

Copyright, 1899, by J. C. Hemment
THE MAINE ENTERING HAVANA HARBOR
(Morro Castle appears on the right)

harbor of Havana. It was blown up. There was suspicion that Spaniards had caused the disaster. Spain had shown herself unfit to rule over Cuba, and war was declared.

Spain was supposed to have a formidable navy, but if this could be destroyed, she would be powerless. One of her fleets was in the Pacific, in the harbor of Manila, the chief city of her Philippine colonies. Commodore Dewey was off the coast of China in command of an American fleet of six warships. The order came to him, "Capture [Spanish] vessels or destroy." Mines that would explode at a touch were scattered about Manila harbor, but Dewey steamed in one night, and destroyed ten Spanish warships and one transport without losing a man. The power of Spain in the Pacific vanished in a day.

The Spanish fleet in the East destroyed

THE PHILIPPINE ISLANDS

Spain then sent a fleet across the Atlantic. The United States vessels kept close watch, and it was learned that the Spaniards had gone into Santiago de Cuba for Fighting at Santiago de Cuba coal. An American fleet guarded the mouth of the harbor where the Spanish ships were "bottled up," and American soldiers were

THE WEST INDIES

sent to capture the town. There were white troops and negro troops. There were men who had fought for the Union, and there were men who had fought against the Union. One interesting regi- The Rough Riders ment commanded by Colonel Leonard Wood had been raised by Lieutenant-colonel Theo-

dore Roosevelt. He had graduated at Harvard, had lived on a western ranch and in New York city. He was an enthusiastic student and had written many books. He had also tamed vicious broncos, pursued thieves, been at the head of the New York police commission, and was, at the begin-

ning of the war, Assistant Secretary of the Navy. His regiment was made up of "cowboys" from the West, policemen, millionaires, men who had fought more than one wild battle with the Indians, and men who knew far more about dan-cing than fighting. In one respect they were all alike, for every one of them was a brave man, and was ready to follow "Teddy," as they nicknamed their leader, into danger or death. Some one called them the "Rough Riders," and they were rarely spoken of by any other title. All these men were in Cuba. An attack was

A ROUGH RIDER
(From a photograph of Captain Kane)

made upon Santiago, and the Spaniards saw that it must sur render. Orders were sent for the Spanish fleet to sail out of "th bottle" and attack the American ves- sels. This was done, but the fleet was completely de- stroyed. The rest of the Spanish navy had to stay at home to defend the coast, and soon Spain asked for peace.

Copyright, 1898, by J. C. Hemment
WRECK OF THE SPANISH FLAGSHIP REINA MERCEDES
(Morro Castle, Santiago, is seen in the background)

She agreed to give freedom to Cuba and to surrender Port Rico to the United States as well as Guam, a small island in th Ladrones. The Philippines she was to sell to the United State

WILLIAM McKINLEY
(Died September 14, 1901)

for twenty million dollars. The treaty wa signed in December, 1898, and Spain no longe owned a foot of land in the western hemi sphere. What were supposed to be th remains of Christopher Columbus were re moved to Spain from the cathedral of Ha vana. While the war was going on, th Hawaiian Islands asked to be annexed t the United States, and the request wa granted.

The war with Spain soon ended, but th natives of the Philippines for a time resistec our rule. A degree of self-government was early granted th Filipinos. In 1900 we had trouble with China. A Chinese societ called the "Boxers," feeling sure that the empress of China sharec their hatred of all foreigners, set out to massacre them. An army was formed of English, Americans, Japanese, and others to rescue their missionaries and protect their citizens and business interests. Two of the principal cities in China, Pekin and Tientsin, were captured, and the Chinese yielded.

In 1901 McKinley was again elected. Six months later, the message was telegraphed over the world for the third time within forty years, "Our President has been assassinated." A great wave of sorrow swept over the land. The hatred aroused by civil war had caused the death of Lincoln; the "spoils system" had taken the life of Garfield; McKinley, however, fell by the hand of an anarchist, one who declares that no country should have a government, but that every man should do as

THEODORE ROOSEVELT

The assassination of McKinley

he chooses. The sympathy of the whole world was with the United States. Only a few months earlier, America had shared the grief of Great Britain at the death of Queen Victoria, and now England shared our sorrow. Her flags were put at half-mast, badges of mourning were worn, and memorial services were held, not only in the great English cathedrals, but even in the little country churches.

A few hours after the death of William McKinley, the Vice-President, Theodore Roosevelt, repeated gravely the presidential oath: —

Theodore Roosevelt becomes president

"I do solemnly swear that I will faithfully execute the office of President of the United States ; and will, to the best of my ability, preserve, protect, and defend the Constitution of the United States."

In 1905 President Roosevelt was elected. A few months late
he succeeded in persuading Japan and Russia to end the fierc

warfare that had been raging between them and to agree upoi
terms of peace. Their commissioners met at Portsmouth, Nev
Hampshire, and in August a treaty was signed. Cuba had beer
made free, but her government was not strong enough to main
tain order, and she now appealed to our country for help. In th
autumn of 1906 the United States took temporary control of th
island and appointed a governor. At about the same time ou
Secretary of State paid friendly visits to the South Americar
republics.

Since the Spanish war all sorts of manufactures have pros

pered. Prices have been high, work plenty, and wages in mos
kinds of employment have risen. Enormous fortunes have bee
made, and people have come to feel that they are not comfortabl
unless they have more luxuries than ever before. When a coun
try is growing and changing as rapidly as the United State:
new questions are constantly arising, and the greatest wisdom i
needed to settle them in such a way that all will be treated witl
fairness. One of the most difficult problems of the present da;
is how to divide the profits of any undertaking between capita
and labor. The capitalist furnishes the money for buildings, ma
chinery, and materials, and also the brain for managing, advertis
ing, and enlarging the business; the wage-earner furnishes th
hands for the actual work. Neither party can succeed withou
the other; but what share of the gain each ought to receive is n
easy matter to decide. There is a general belief that a tremendou
fortune cannot be made unless the rights of the people have bee
violated in some way. One of the most important acts of Presi

dent Roosevelt's administration has been the inquiry by the Gov
ernment into the methods by which some of the great corporation
have become so wealthy. One charge was, for instance, that rail

roads had been induced to carry the goods of the large producers at much lower rates than those of the small producers, and that the great companies were thus "killing out" rival concerns and preventing a fair competition. The rights of the people have also been guarded by an examination of the way in which some of the large insurance companies were managing the vast sums of money intrusted to their care. The President himself has been at the front in these movements. He has also used his personal influence as well as that of his position to bring to an end the serious industrial strikes that have arisen, and to forward the work of the Panama Canal.

The power and influence of the United States in the affairs of the world has become much more apparent during the last few years. Fortunately for all concerned, the relations of this country to others were guided by John Hay, Secretary of State until his John Hay death in 1905, who established what was almost a new principle, namely, that dealings between nations should be as frank and honorable as those between individuals.

So it is that with many problems yet to solve, but with a national determination to maintain honesty and justice at home and in our relations to foreign countries, the United States prepares to enter upon the second decade of the twentieth century.

SUMMARY.

President Johnson thought that the seceded states should be allowed to send representatives to Congress, but Congress demanded the "iron-clad oath." Slavery was forbidden, and the right to vote was given to the negroes; but the whites often prevented them from voting. The Confederates were soon pardoned and allowed to hold office.

Between the Civil War and the Centennial of 1876, which marked the nation's progress during its first century, the Atlantic cable was laid, Alaska was purchased, England paid for the damage done by the Alabama, and the Union Pacific Railroad was built.

Between the Centennial and the Columbian Exposition of 1893, our "green backs" became as good as gold, much was done to further Civil Service Reform, the South became more prosperous, the succession to the presidency was assured, the Chinese were excluded, a tariff for protection as well as revenue, and the doctrine of reciprocity won the vote of the majority, and much land in the West was thrown open to settlers.

The inability of Spain to govern Cuba properly brought this country into a war with Spain which resulted in our acquiring Porto Rico, Guam, and the Philippines. During the war the Hawaiian Islands became, at their own request, part of the territory of the United States.

President McKinley was assassinated by an anarchist. During President Roosevelt's administration, the war between Japan and Russia came to an end, the United States took temporary control of Cuba, all kinds of manufactures prospered, the methods of great corporations were investigated, and the power of the United States in the affairs of the world became more apparent.

SUGGESTIONS FOR WRITTEN WORK.

One of the unsuccessful men describes the opening of Oklahoma.

Why should the landing of Columbus be celebrated?

Is it desirable for us to own the Philippines?

Why should the Declaration of Independence be celebrated?

SUPPLEMENTARY CHAPTER

VIRGINIA

Not long after the settlement of Jamestown the colonists learned that the best way to make money from their land was Why Virginia had no villages to plant as much of it as possible with tobacco. It was not easy for a man to care for these great farms, or plantations, if his home was far away, therefore each planter built his house on his plantation. That is why, even when Virginia was a century old, there was hardly a village in the country.

Whether large or small, this house was always known as the "great house," to distinguish it from the smaller houses, or cabins, in which the workmen lived. In later times these workmen were negro slaves, but in the

LOWER BRANDON. AN OLD PLANTATION HOME

earlier days of the colony white men sent over from England were employed. Most of them were "redemptioners," that is, The "redemptioners" poor men who wished to try their fortune in a new land. When they reached Virginia, some planter was always ready to pay the cost of their passage on condition that they should work for him till the value of their labor had "redeemed" the amount. Some of these redemptioners were well-educated, enterprising men; and in that case they had a good opportunity to become tenants or even to gain estates of their own.

Guests were always welcome on the plantations, and a visit in those times was not an afternoon call, but a stay of several days or a week or a month. This hospitality was offered as freely to strangers as to friends. A traveler had only to stop his horse a any door, and he was sure of a welcome and a night's entertain ment. It was so customary to entertain travelers free of cos that the law forbade even innkeepers to make any charge for foo and lodging unless they had told the guest in advance that h would be expected to pay. If a planter was going away from home, he would tell his agent to see that any stranger who migh ask for hospitality should be welcomed and given every comfor that the plantation afforded. If we may trust the old stories, i was not always necessary even to ask, for it is said that some times a sociable planter would station a servant where he woul be likely to meet travelers and give him orders to invite them t stop and pay a visit.

Such a visit must have been well worth making, for on th larger plantations there was much to see that would interest stranger. After the earliest days the houses grew larger to sui the hospitable notions of the colonists, and many of them con tained expensive furnishings that had been brought across th Atlantic. There was always a hall that was used as a dining room and general living-room. The walls were sometimes hun with tapestry or built up with oaken panels. There was a lon dining-table of course, and a cupboard well filled with china There was pewter, too, and silver; spoons, forks, saltcellars, can dlesticks, and snuffers. There was sure to be at least one grea chest, sometimes plain, sometimes carved, full of snowy linen nap kins and tablecloths. On one side of the room was a great fire place in which enormous logs cheerily blazed and roared up th chimney. A sitting-room and parlor usually opened off the hall but the hall was the heart of the home, and it was of the hall an the family gathered about the open fire that the homesick Virginian thought when he was on the other side of the ocean.

The kitchen was a little way from the house. There was always a great fireplace, sometimes ten or twelve feet long, with crane **The kitchen** and pothooks and all sorts of arrangements for roasting and baking and frying. There was room enough in such a fireplace to cook for even the large gatherings of friends that so often came together in this land of visits. Virginia had a most generous supply of food. Oysters, fish, chickens, beef, and venison were exceedingly cheap. Cream and butter and milk were plentiful, and all sorts of fruit and vegetables grew most luxuriantly.

There was much to see outside of the house. A plantation was like a little town, for whatever was needed must either be made on the spot or ordered from England. Most of the large plantations had among the servants carpenters, blacksmiths, tanners, weavers, shoemakers, and coopers. A planter's own men could build sheds and barns and keep them in repair. Hides and

IN COLONIAL DAYS

wool were raised on the place. The tanners and shoemakers and **On the** weavers made shoes and clothes for the negroes, and much of the **plantation** cloth that was used for common purposes at the "great house." When finer articles were needed, an order went to England. With whole forests of wood at hand, even chairs, tables, boxes, bowls, and wheels came across the ocean, for the time and strength ne-

cessary to make these articles would cultivate much more than enough tobacco to pay for importing them.

Colonial dress

A very important part of the things ordered from England were articles of dress. These Virginians, colonists though they were, did not propose to give up the London fashions, and they sent for gowns of brocaded silk or satin or velvet, or calico lined with silk — for calico was expensive in those days. They had petticoats of silk, often shot with threads of silver. They had laces of silk and of gold, scarfs of all colors, silk stockings, scarlet sleeves, and crimson mantles. This gorgeousness was not limited to the women, for the men were just as desirous of fine clothes. The coat was of broadcloth, often olive or some other color, and dazzling with buttons of polished silver. Ruffles fell over the hand. The waistcoat was of any color that struck the fancy of the wearer. The breeches were of plush or fine broadcloth. Silver buckles were worn on the shoes. If the day was cool, a handsome mantle of blue or scarlet was thrown over this array. Such was the gala dress of the colonists. Imagine a ballroom glowing with all this brilliancy in the clear, soft light of dozens of myrtle wax candles!

Education

How were children educated on the plantations? There were a few free schools supported, not by the colony, but by individuals. The houses, however, were too far apart for district schools to flourish, but frequently the children on adjoining plantations were taught by some educated man of the neighborhood, perhaps the minister of the parish, or perhaps a redemptioner. Often a tutor was engaged to come from England to live in a planter's family and teach his children. When the sons grew older, they were sometimes sent to Cambridge or to Oxford. Virginia had plans only fourteen years after the founding of Jamestown for establishing not only a free school but a university. Indians as well as whites were to become pupils. Money was raised and a president was chosen. An Indian massacre and the overthrow of the London Company prevented these plans from being carried out immediately; but even then, the college of William and Mary, founded

EARLY VIEW OF WILLIAM AND MARY COLLEGE

in 1692, was, save for Harvard, the first college in America. A place was chosen for its home which was also to be the capital of the colony. It was named Williamsburg, and the original plan was to lay its streets out in the shape of a W and an M, in honor of the sovereigns of England. The students were always few, but three presidents of the United States have been among them, and governors, judges, and other public officials without number.

So it was that life went on in Virginia in "good old colony The planter times." The planter's wife, with the large house to superintend, was a busy woman. The planter was like a monarch, for on his own plantation his word was law. In one way he had a very easy life, for he was never obliged to do anything for himself that a servant could do for him. On the other hand, there was constant need of the master's watchful eye to prevent the waste and neglect that would soon ruin the wealthiest planter. Mrs. Washington once said that she wished "George" would stay at home and attend to his plantation instead of going off to fight Indians. The planter had to learn how to attend to many things at once, how to decide questions quickly and independently, in short, how to command; and this ability was of the utmost value to the country.

Virginia in the Revolution

The record of Virginia in history is a noble one. When the Stamp Act was passed, the eloquence of Patrick Henry moved the House of Burgesses to vote that the General Assembly of Virginia alone had the right to tax Virginians. This was open rebellion, and it ushered in the Revolution. Richard Henry Lee moved in Congress "that these united colonies are and of right ought to be, free and independent states." Thomas Jefferson wrote the Declaration of Independence, and George Washington became commander-in-chief of the American forces.

JEFFERSON'S HOME AT MONTICELLO

Virginia since the Revolution

The services of Virginia to the United States did not end with the Revolution. George Rogers Clark saved the Northwestern Territory. Virginia generously gave up her claim to it; and to win a share in this vast amount of land was a motive that had much to do with holding some of the states in the Union. Four of our first five presidents were from Virginia, and three of them had pews in the little church in Bruton Parish. John Marshall, our first chief justice, was a Virginian. Thomas Jefferson planned in almost every detail the University of Virginia at Charlottesville. This was the first American college to introduce the elective system of studies, student government, and the honor system in examinations. From the beginning it has stood for a simple, dignified, scholarly student life. When the days of the Civil War drew near, it was not easy for Virginia to leave the Union that she had done so much to found and to strengthen. For months she hesitated. General Lee said, "If I owned the four million slaves in the South, I would sacrifice them all to the Union, but how can I draw my sword on Virginia, my native State?" The Convention finally voted to secede, but the western part of the State refused to accept the decision, and became West Virginia.

Since the war, the commercial growth of Virginia has been surprising. Many manufactories have been built, and new ones are constantly being erected. A great shipbuilding company employs more than six thousand workmen. The old quiet and leisure of the State are departed, but a new State is arising. The old traditions are not dead, and we may confidently expect Virginia to have as noble a history in the future as she has had in the past.

LIBRARY OF THE UNIVERSITY OF VIRGINIA

SUMMARY.

Because of the plantation life Virginia had few villages.

The workmen on the plantation were at first " redemptioners;" later, negro slaves.

Guests were always welcome, and a visit to a plantation was most interesting.

Most of the articles of dress were ordered from England.

Children were generally taught by tutors.   William and Mary College was founded in 1692.

The planter's wife had much to do.   The planter had to learn to command.

Virginia has a noble record in history and has given generous service to the country.   Since the Civil War, her growth in manufactures has been surprising.

SUGGESTIONS FOR WRITTEN WORK.

Write an account of a visit to a plantation.

A redemptioner's letter to England.

One day in the life of a planter's wife.

INDEX

AND PRONOUNCING VOCABULARY

KEY TO PRONUNCIATION. — Marked vowels are pronounced like the same vowels similarly marked in the following words: fāte, făt, fäther, fạll, câre; thēme, yĕt, hêr; pīne, pĭn; bōne, nŏt, ôrb; mōōn, fŏŏt; tūne, bŭt, bûrr. The obscure vowels are pronounced like à in Durhàm, ė in Jerusalėm, ȯ in Burtȯn, and occur ȯnly in unaccented syllables. ḡ is like ḡ in ḡo.

Panama (păn-à-mä'), Isthmus of, 203.

Papoose (păp-ōōs'), treatment of, 36 ; picture of, 37.

Patroon (pä-troōn') system, introduced along the Hudson River, 91.

Pemaquid (pĕm'à-kwĭd), location, 62 *map;* settled, 72.

Penn (pĕn), Admiral, disappointed in his son, 99, 100.

Penn, William, early years, 99 ; portrait of, at twenty-two, 99 ; turns Quaker, 100 ; conduct toward the king, 100 ; obtains Pennsylvania, 101 ; decides to pay the Indians for the land, 101, 102 ; founds Philadelphia, 102 ; makes friends of the Indians, 102, 103 ; autograph and seal, picture, 103 ; returns to England, 103 ; his house, picture, 104.

Pennsylvania (pĕn-sĭl-vā'nĭ-à) granted to Penn, 101 ; settled by Quakers, 102 ; bought from the Indians, 102, 103 ; education in, 103, 104.

Pequots (pē'kwŏtz), make war on the English, 80 ; defeated, 81.

Perry, Commodore O. H., builds a fleet on Lake Erie, 177 ; captures the British fleet, 178, 179 ; his flag, picture, 179 ; his message, 179.

Petersburg, location, 216 *map;* Grant at, 223.

Philadelphia (fĭl-à-dĕl'fĭ-à), founded, 102 ; becomes the largest city in the colonies 104 ; French Neutrals in, 126 ; first Continental Congress meets in, 139 ; British forces take, 160.

Philip, king, makes war on the English, 68 ; killed, 69 ; picture of, 69.

Philippine (fĭl'ĭ-pēn) canoe, picture of, 19.

Philippine Islands, discovered by Magellan, 19 ; map of, 242 ; sold to the United States, 244 ; location of, 247 *map*.

Pierce (pērs *or* pŭrs), Franklin, president, 203.

Pilgrim cradle, picture of, 56.

Pilgrim dress, picture of, 52.

Pilgrims, who they were, 52 ; escape to Holland, 53 ; plan to come to America, 53 ; their departure from Holland, picture, 54 ; their voyage in the Mayflower, 54 ; search for a home, 55 ; sufferings of, 56 ; relations with the Indians, 57, 58 ; going to church, picture, 58 ; their religious feeling, 60.

Pillory, the, picture, 68.

Pinckney (pĭnk'nĭ), Charles, his defiance of France, 174.

Pinta (*Spanish*, pēn'tä), one of Columbus's ships, 7.

Pipe, an Indian, picture of, 40.

Piscataqua (pĭs-kăt'à-kwą) River divides Maine and New Hampshire, 73.

Pistol, of Ponce de Leon's time, picture, 16 ; Dutch flintlock, picture, 94 ; flintlock given by Lafayette to Washington, 156.

Pitt, William, objects to the Stamp Act, 135.

Plymouth (plĭm'ŏth), Mass., reason for the colony begun at, 52 ; named by John Smith, 55 ; landing of Pilgrims at, 56 ; first winter at, 56 ; first Thanksgiving at, 58 ; town meeting begun at, 59 ; location, 62 *map;* people of, establish a post at Windsor, Conn., 78.

Plymouth Company, grant to, 42 ; map of grant, 43 ; sells Massachusetts to the Massachusetts Bay Company, 61.

Plymouth Rock, picture of, 56.

Pocahontas (pō-kà-hŏn'tàs), saves John Smith, 46 ; marries John Rolfe and goes to England, 48.

Polk (pōk), James K., events of his presidency, 201-203.

Ponce de Leon (*Spanish*, pōn'thä dā lā-ōn'), explores Florida, 16.

"Pony Express, The," 233 ; picture of, 233.

"Poor Richard's Almanac," 131.

Population of America in the eighteenth century, 129.

Port Hudson, La., location, 211 *map;* captured, 221.

Port Royal, N. S., location, 119 *map*.

Porto Rico (pōr'tō rē'kō), location, 243 *map,* 247 *map;* ceded to the United States, 244.

INDEX

265

HISTORY FOR GRAMMAR SCHOOLS

TEXT BOOKS

OUR COUNTRY'S STORY

BY

EVA MARCH TAPPAN, PH. D.

*Head of the English Department, English High School
Worcester, Mass.*

A HISTORY OF THE UNITED STATES
FOR INTERMEDIATE GRAMMAR GRADES

Illustrated with more than 200 reproductions of famous paintings, copies of old cuts, portraits, maps, etc. Equipped with summaries and suggestions for written work.

Square 12mo, cloth, 270 pages, 65 cents, net.

A HISTORY OF THE UNITED STATES FOR SCHOOLS

BY

JOHN FISKE, LITT. D., LL. D.

WITH TOPICAL ANALYSIS, SUGGESTIVE QUESTIONS
AND DIRECTIONS FOR TEACHERS

By FRANK ALPINE HILL, Litt. D., formerly Head Master of the English High School, Cambridge, and later of the Mechanic Arts High School, Boston.

FOR UPPER GRAMMAR GRADES

Containing 235 Illustrations (including Maps in black and white), and 6 full-page and 2 double-page Maps in colors.

Crown 8vo, half leather, xxi + 573 pages, $1.00, net.

ENGLAND'S STORY

BY

EVA MARCH TAPPAN, PH. D.

Author of "Our Country's Story."

A HISTORY OF ENGLAND FOR UPPER GRAMMAR GRADES

Containing 142 Illustrations (including Maps in black and white), and 3 full-page and 2 double-page Maps in colors. Also Summaries and Genealogies.

Crown 8vo, cloth, xx + 370 pages, 85 cents, net.

HOUGHTON, MIFFLIN AND COMPANY

HISTORY FOR GRAMMAR SCHOOLS

Hawthorne's Grandfather's Chair : True Stories from New England History (1620–1803). In Riverside Literature Series, Nos. 7, 8, 9, with Portrait of Hawthorne, Biographical Sketch, Notes, and Illustrations. Each part, paper, 15 cents, *net;* the three parts bound in one volume, linen, 50 cents, *net.*

Franklin's Autobiography, with a chapter completing his "Life" (1706–1790). In Riverside Literature Series, Nos. 19, 20. With Notes, a Chronological Table, and Illustrations. Each part, paper, 15 cts., *net;* the two parts in one vol., linen, 40 cents, *net.*

Scudder's George Washington, An Historical Biography (1732–1799). With Portrait and Maps. In Riverside Literature Series, Double No. 75. Paper, 30 cents, *net;* linen, 40 cents, *net.*

Washington's Rules of Conduct, Diary of Adventure, and Farewell Addresses (1753–1796). With Introduction and Notes. In Riverside Literature Series, No. 24. Paper, 15 cents, *net;* linen, 25 cents, *net.*

Longfellow's Paul Revere's Ride, the Cumberland, and Other Poems (1775–1862). With Notes. In Riverside Literature Series, No. 63, paper, 15 cents, *net.*

Fiske's War of Independence (1775–1789). With Biographical Sketch and Maps. In Riverside Literature Series, Double No. 62. Paper, 30 cents, *net;* linen, 40 cents, *net.*

Webster's First Bunker Hill Oration, and Oration on Adams and Jefferson (1825, 1826). In Riverside Literature Series No. 56. Paper, 15 cents, *net;* linen, 25 cents, *net.*

Lincoln's Gettysburg Speech, Inaugural Addresses, and Other Papers, with Lowell's Essay on Lincoln (1861–1865). In Riverside Literature Series No. 32. Paper, 15 cents, *net.*

Dodge's A Bird's-Eye View of our Civil War (1861–1865). With Maps and Illustrations. Revised *Students' Edition.* Crown 8vo, 348 pages, $1.00, *net.*

HOUGHTON, MIFFLIN AND COMPANY

CPSIA information can be obtained
at www.ICGtesting.com
Printed in the USA
BVHW042325140921
616750BV00007B/241

9 781376 626179